JAPAN

Enemy or Ally?

THE INSTITUTE OF PACIFIC RELATIONS

The Institute of Pacific Relations is an unofficial and non-partisan organization, founded in 1925 to facilitate the scientific study of the peoples of the Pacific area. It is composed of autonomous National Councils in the principal countries having important interests in the Pacific area, together with an International Secretariat. It is privately financed by contributions from National Councils, corporations and foundations. It is governed by a Pacific Council composed of members appointed by each of the National Councils. The Institute organizes private international conferences every two or three years. It conducts an extensive program of research on the political, economic and social problems of the Pacific area and the Far East. It also publishes the proceedings of its conferences, a quarterly journal, Pacific Affairs, *and a large number of scholarly books embodying the results of its studies.*

Neither the International Secretariat nor the National Councils of the Institute advocate policies or express opinions on national or international affairs. Responsibility for statements of fact or opinion in Institute publications rests solely with the authors.

INTERNATIONAL SECRETARIAT AND PUBLICATIONS OFFICE
1 East 54th St., New York 22, N. Y.

JAPAN
Enemy or Ally?

by W. Macmahon Ball

An ASIA Book

PUBLISHED UNDER THE JOINT AUSPICES OF THE INTERNA-
TIONAL SECRETARIAT, INSTITUTE OF PACIFIC RELATIONS, AND
THE AUSTRALIAN INSTITUTE OF INTERNATIONAL AFFAIRS.

New York 1949

THE JOHN DAY COMPANY

FIRST PRINTED IN AUSTRALIA, 1948
REVISED AND ENLARGED EDITION, NEW YORK, 1949

Printed in the United States of America by
American Book–Stratford Press, New York

INTRODUCTION

BY NATHANIEL PEFFER

~~~~~~

MODERN JAPAN IS A VARIANT FROM NATIONAL type. It is in politics the equivalent of a biological sport. It conforms to nothing in the history of modern nations, whether European or Western, industrial or agrarian. Certainly in Eastern Asia its development has been unique, especially in the last hundred years. Alone it quickly perceived what the impact of the West signified, perceived that the power of the West derived, not from superior weapons but from the economic and social system, mainly the technological development, that made it possible to produce superior weapons. Therefore, alone in Eastern Asia, so far from resisting Westernism, it deliberately resolved to adopt Westernism and set itself determinedly to making itself over on the Western model—production by machinery, communication and transportation by the telegraph and telephone, railway and steamship, and universal education, military conscription and scientific research. Alone in Eastern Asia in recent centuries, it became a great political and military power and, just before its mad adventure in conquest, was competing on equal terms with the economically most advanced countries of the West.

The adventure in conquest was suicidal as well as mad. For one thing, while Japan had performed almost miraculous feats of transformation, it had not yet arrived at the point where it could challenge the most powerful countries of the West with any hope of success. Its development was unbalanced, mainly top-heavy. It had renounced its earlier wisdom and spent its strength and substance in acquiring modern weapons before it had the social and economic structure that could support them, as was proved in the last two years of the war, when Japan became progressively more helpless, having the men with whom to fight but not the materials or the productive capacity or the technological capacity to provide the means with which to fight. The superstructure was Western and twentieth century; the foundation was still Eastern and eighteenth century. Furthermore, the same insensate ambition that drove it to conquest had aroused fear, suspicion and antagonism in the neighboring countries that otherwise might have been its natural allies. In its final hour of trial it stood helpless, friendless and alone. And thus it went down to defeat for the first time in its history, a defeat that carried humiliation, almost ignominy.

Since then Japan has been not only a variant from type, not only unique; there is an unreality in its conduct, something outside normal political psychology and political experience. It was a people of fierce warrior tradition, as recently as the battle for Okinawa faithful to the warrior rule: victory or death. It was a people of frenetic chauvinism, conceiving its soil and its spirit not only with patriotism but in exaltation. No other people had so vivid a consciousness of uniqueness, of separatism, if not actual xenophobia, however tacit. Then it is conquered and is occupied by the alien army that had crushed it, and its government taken over by the conquering country as completely as if it had been made a colony. The Emperor, till but the day before not only infallible but untouchable, immanent rather than mortally existing, calls on the enemy commander to pay his respects. A new constitution is written by the conqueror, a new polity instituted. The highest in the land are subject to supervision; they report for orders, receive them with submissiveness and depart to execute them. So far from being goaded by their traditional pride of blood, their frenetic chauvinism, to berserk outbursts for revenge, to shed the blood by which alone outraged honor can be assuaged, they revel in self-abasement. They receive their conquerors with cordiality, almost with affection, certainly with all the appearances of deference. They embrace democracy as their own. To the enemy commander they show a respect once reserved for the Emperor. To all appearances it is abandonment in masochism.

But is it? What does it mean? How explain it? Is it genuine? Does it signify a real and lasting change in the people—in their attitude, spirit, values, beliefs? Is Japan now really adopting Westernism, as it only seemed to be in the nineteenth century? Is it now taking the essence as it once took only the externals? Is this all just the effect of a psychic shock from the unprecedented experience of defeat—or is it a genuine conversion—or is it a web of deceit, a shrewd and subtle stratagem to lull the conqueror's fears and dull his aim and thus to speed his departure? Which? Or is it a little of all?

These are questions the answers to which will determine the political configuration of Eastern Asia for the next generation and by so much the political configuration of the whole world: it should not be forgotten how great was the interplay of Far Eastern international relations after 1935 with the making of the European war and, still more, with the conduct of the European war after 1941. They are the questions on which Mr. Ball's analysis bears. Mr. Ball has been in an extraordinarily favorable position to get evidence throwing light on the questions, to weigh the evidence and to come to judgment, if only provisional judgment. Since

1945 Japan has been governed by an Allied occupation authority, which is a pleasant euphemism for American occupation, which is a pleasant euphemism for General MacArthur. But officially there has been joint Allied supervision, its organ being the Allied Council for Japan, functioning in Tokyo for a larger Far Eastern Commission. On that Council Mr. Ball served in 1946 and 1947 as representative of the United Kingdom, Australia, New Zealand and India, the other members of the Council being representatives of the Soviet Union, China and the United States. He was thus in a position to acquire evidence at first hand, and, more important, being neutral in the acrimonious Russian-American differences over Japan, to be objective and to examine the evidence on its intrinsic merits. He has, too, the qualifications of a well-nurtured and disciplined mind, with no little political experience.

The American authority has weighed the new, reborn and repentant Japan and found it not wanting. It has pronounced the new Japan democratic and therefore good. The Russians have looked upon Japan and seen it, as they see everything in which there is a touch of American influence, as a victim and a tool of sinister American designs. Mr. Ball is less glowing than the American authority and less jaundiced than the Russians. Probably his findings are closer to the truth. It would be miraculous if Japan, given the two thousand years of its past and, more particularly, the last thirty years of its past, could have contrived a second incarnation in four years, whether as a result of its defeat or at the evangelical appeals of the American army which had just destroyed many of its cities. The democratic spirit comes neither by invocation nor on the persuasion of the bludgeon. Similarly, it would be miraculous, a satanic *tour de force,* for any country to contrive as much evil as the Russians impute to America everywhere. Both on theoretical reasoning and on objective examination of the evidence,

Mr. Ball's conclusion seems warranted: ". . . there has been no fundamental change in Japan's social structure or in the political outlook of her leaders."

This conclusion, if indeed it be sound, is of immeasurable importance to America, to Eastern Asia, to the world—in the first instance, to America above all, by reason of Mr. Ball's second general observation: ". . . since 1945 there has been a far-reaching change in the attitude of the United States toward Japan." For according to whether the conclusion is validated by the event will it be determined not only whether the United States has been self-cuckolded but whether it has laid fresh destruction for Eastern Asia, renewed conflict for the world. The soundness of Mr. Ball's second general observation will hardly be disputed, nor will there be denial of the reason he imputes for it: "But the root motive is political. It is fear of Russia and communism. America desires a strong and prosperous Japan as a backing against the extension of Russian influence in the Far East and the growth of Japanese communism." Much turns therefore on whether the official American judgment on Japan's reformation is sound, whether Japan really has become democratic. If Japan has and America then takes Japan to its bosom as ally and comrade-in-arms, one set of consequences will follow, consequences neither politically nor socially injurious. But if America is wrong and Japan is unchanged and America then takes Japan as ally and comrade-in-arms and Japan's strength is restored for putative use against Russia, then another set of consequences will follow, consequences politically and socially catastrophic. They will be serious enough for America. The Japanese militarist, now sick, a democratic monk would be; but when recovered, thanks to American illusions, he would be as before. America itself will suffer, for the postwar deference to America would change to lust for revenge against America; American suffering, however, will be at one remove. But the suffering of those closer to Japan will be beyond measure and perhaps fatal. And their wrath will in time be visited on America and justly visited.

The question, Japan: Enemy or Ally?, is still open to examination and revised answers and a different policy and program. For that examination, now imperative, Mr. Ball's calm, fair, cool analysis is of invaluable assistance.

Columbia University
New York
February 14, 1949

AUTHOR'S PREFACE

IN THE PRACTICE OF POLITICS ALMOST EVERY
judgment is a guess, and the best you can hope is that your
guesses will be intelligent and reasonably well-informed.
It is very easy for the Westerner in Japan to guess wrong.
The Japanese language and the traditional Japanese reti-
cence with foreigners make it especially hard to reach confident judgments. Yet judgments about Japan are being
made, and they must be made. In the following chapters I
try to record my personal judgments, or my guesses, about
what has been happening in Japan under the Occupation,
and to draw some inferences about the policy that the
Allies should now follow.

I left Australia for Tokyo in March 1946 to represent
jointly the United Kingdom, Australia, New Zealand and
India on the Allied Council for Japan. I held that post
until September 1947. From April to September 1947, I
was concurrently head of the Australian Mission in Japan.
I had not been to Japan before, had no specialist knowledge of the country, and had a good enough sense of my
linguistic limitations not to attempt to learn the Japanese
language. Yet the positions I held there gave me some special opportunities to observe closely the Japanese reaction
to the defeat and the Occupation, and the American atti-

tude towards the Japanese. Since leaving Japan, I have tried to keep in touch with the main developments there. In June and July of 1948 I led a mission for the Australian Government to East and South East Asia. On this journey I was able to gain impressions of the way the leaders of these countries regard Japan's position and prospects. My short stay in China confirmed the view I have expressed in this book that what happens there will have an immense influence on what happens in Japan.

The Australian edition of the book was published a few months ago in Melbourne. The present edition contains a new chapter on major developments in 1948. For purposes of reference the text of the "Johnston Committee" report on Japan's economic problems and the text of the recent American statement to the Far Eastern Commission on the industrial deconcentration program have also been added as new appendices.

All opinions in this book are my own, but I wish to acknowledge my debt to my Australian staff through whom I learnt most of what I learned wisely about Japan. The recommendations I made to the Allied Council on Land Reform and on Prices and Wages were the work of my economic adviser, Mr. Eric Ward.

W. M. B.

Melbourne
December 1948

CONTENTS

1. ENEMY OR ALLY?

THE TIME HAS COME FOR A PEACE SETTLE-
ment in the Pacific. We want a settlement that will give
military security to those Pacific countries which have during these last years been the victims of aggression; a settlement that will provide for the economic stability of East
Asia and a rising standard of living for Asiatic peoples; a
settlement which, if possible, will lay the basis for cooperation between the United States and the Soviet Union.

Allied postwar aims in the Pacific were declared in their
essential outlines in 1945, first in the Potsdam Declaration
of July 26, and later in the Initial Post-Surrender Policy,
which the United States Government transmitted to General MacArthur on September 6. Although this policy statement was authorized only by the U. S. Government, it was
tacitly accepted by all the Allies, and the basic policy decision of the Far Eastern Commission, published in 1947,
was in agreement with the American Post-Surrender Policy
in all essentials. We were reasonably clear what we wanted
to do in 1945. We were determined that Japan should be
completely demilitarized. We were to foster by every means
in our power the establishment of a responsible and democratic government. We were determined that the Japanese
people should enjoy the same civil and political rights that

3

are possessed by the peoples of Western democracies. We decided to initiate economic reforms that would ultimately replace a feudal economy by a welfare economy. We recognized that fulfillment of these aims would involve revolutionary changes in Japan's social and economic system.

The question which now confronts us is whether we still want to pursue with full earnestness the aims we pursued in 1945. Have changes in the world situation and in the balance of power changed our views about what we want to do with Japan? In 1945 Japan was a still-hated enemy. Russia was an ally. But much has happened since then. Do we still believe that Japan should be completely demilitarized, or do we feel that in the changed circumstances of 1948 we should rather consider her as a potential ally in an area of vast strategic importance? And do we still feel the same enthusiasm about fostering revolutionary changes in Japan's social and economic system? If our primary interest in Japan is military and strategic, then it may well be that any deep disturbance of Japan's social hierarchy might weaken her capacity for effective military organization.

Our answer to these questions will depend on our view of the whole world situation, and much more on what we think about Russia than on what we think about Japan. The problem of Japan will become a fragment of a world problem. If we believe that the differences between Russia and the Western democracies make war between them a real danger, then our military interests in Japan will override everything else. Efforts to bring about economic and political reforms will be subordinated to military aims.

And if we need to re-examine carefully the aims we proclaimed in 1945, it is equally important that we carefully reconsider the most effective methods to make the peace settlement effective. To what extent shall we be prepared to use force to ensure that Japan faithfully carries out her treaty obligations? What kind of sanctions do we propose to establish? What type of control machinery is likely to be most effective?

I believe that the answers to both sorts of question, the formulation of the right aims and agreement on the best methods, must be found in large part in our experience and knowledge of Japan under the Occupation. There can be no doubt that a political observer, both in selecting his facts and in drawing inferences, is influenced by his own political outlook. It may, therefore, be useful for me to begin by explaining the political outlook with which I have approached Japanese problems.

My primary concern in the problems set by Japan has been to protect and promote the best interests of the British nations, and particularly of my own country, Australia. I feel no need of self-consciousness in stating such an aim, lest it may seem narrow and nationalistic. It is right and necessary that the ultimate aim in international politics should be to produce a good life "for all the men in all the lands" without distinction of race and nation. Yet, when faced with immediate and specific tasks, it is necessary to have more immediate and specific goals than the welfare of mankind as a whole. A nationalism which recognizes the interdependence of all nations, which is directed towards peace and welfare and culture, which renounces every impulse to dominate or exploit other peoples, is the friend and not the enemy of internationalism.

To Australia, where we escaped invasion and occupation so narrowly in 1942, whose soldiers went through long years of fighting or captivity in the Pacific, the first interest in Japan is undoubtedly a negative one: to assure by every possible means that she shall not regain the power to become an aggressor in the foreseeable future. This is not revenge, not even retribution. It is an unavoidable impulse of self-preservation. I was often told in Tokyo, not only by Japanese, but by Americans and others, that Australians seemed more bitter and revengeful towards the Japanese people than any other of the Allied peoples. I once had the disagreeable distinction of being described in part of the United States press as the "leader of the revenge school" in Japan. Surely it needs little reflection to recognize that a nation of seven million people in the Southwest Pacific is likely to hold more acute memories of the danger to their own homes in 1942 than either the people of Great Britain, preoccupied as they were with much nearer and greater dangers, or the people of the United States, which must be the least insecure nation in the world.

To place the security of our country first is not to cling to a lasting hatred of the Japanese. In Japan, as in any country, you will find numberless people who are honest, kind and generous, and you will make good personal friends. Yet it is a mistake to argue from the kindness and charm of the individual Japanese to the peacefulness and friendliness of the Japanese nation as politically organized. I was one of those people who nearly fell into that kind of error in Germany after World War I. When I was in Germany in 1930 and 1931, I was deeply impressed with the honesty and intelligence of individual Germans I met. This made me very receptive to propaganda about the injustice of the "dictate" of Versailles, the Allied strangulation of German industries, and the dread of encirclement with which Germans so sincerely plied their foreign guests. This is a very close parallel with what is taking place in Japan today. Sometimes with deliberate political intent, and usually with sincere conviction, the Japanese are sedulous in efforts to impress their Allied visitors with the pains and penalties of life in their overcrowded islands. They point to the need for Japan to get access abroad to raw materials and markets if economic collapse is to be avoided, and the "Red Fascists" on the north are not to overrun and destroy their country.

It seems to me right and natural that Allied people in Japan should meet and make friends with individual Japanese and listen patiently to these views. The danger is that we will be lulled by these new friendships, or the renewal of old friendships, into forgetting that often the most dangerous political organizations are made up of people who as individuals are generous, honest and kind. We can be fully alive to what is good and attractive in ordinary Japanese people without that leading us to false political conclusions. In my view, the people who, within the limits of the Occupation, rule Japan today, belong to the same groups and retain the same outlook as those who ruled Japan before 1941. I hope to give some evidence for this in later chapters.

Our first task, then, as I see it, is to resolve at all costs to prevent the resurgence of an expansionist Japan. If we can agree on that, we should then do all in our power to foster the welfare of the Japanese people. We should do this not merely from goodwill, but in our own interests. There can be no stability or peace in East Asia if there is poverty and turmoil inside Japan. Moreover, it may well be that in working out practicable methods for raising the standard of living of the Japanese people we shall have to revise very radically some of our earlier ideas about the kind of economic penalties we would impose after the defeat. We need to be very careful that in determining the level of Japanese industry and the kind of industries which the Japanese shall be permitted to develop, we make our decisions in terms of military security and not from motives of nationalist commercial jealousies.

Moreover, if we are genuinely concerned with the future welfare of the Japanese people we will recognize that there can be no future for them but disaster if we regard Japan, not as a sick society to be nursed to social and economic health, but as a strategic pawn in the rivalry of the Soviet

Union and the United States, the two great world powers. We must always think of the peace settlement not merely for what it will do for Japan, but for what it will do for China and the countries of Southeast Asia. The Japanese settlement must, in a word, be part of a general Pacific settlement, and there can be no satisfactory settlement in the Pacific without the cooperation of the United States and the Soviet Union.

There is a good deal to astonish the Allied observer in occupied Japan. He will find smooth order everywhere. He can go through the cities and the countryside with the same or a greater sense of security than he would at home. He will be met with the eager greetings of smiling children, the gentleness of women and, with some exceptions, the polite cooperation of men. If he goes to see the Imperial Palace in Tokyo he will find that, like the chief buildings of the Allied forces, it is provided with American or British guards. Until late in 1947 the two greatest shrines in Tokyo, the Meiji, glorifying the Emperor system, and the Yasakuni, honoring the souls of those who have died for Japan in battle, were also guarded by American or British soldiers and out of bounds to Allied visitors. He will read daily in the Japanese press effusive expressions of gratitude to General MacArthur for his benevolence and of reverence for his greatness. Conversely, he will find many Allies tireless in expressing their enthusiasm for the Japanese. Only twelve months after the surrender it was common to read incidents like the following. The *Nippon Times* of August 19, 1946, carried a letter from the captain of S.S. *Henry S. Foote,* which brought wheat from America to Japan. The letter was addressed to the Japanese people, and ran:

The officers and crew of the *Henry S. Foote* would like to express their appreciation for the wonderful time that has been shown to them during their only too short stay in Shimizu. They would like to thank the Governor and the Chiefs of Police for going far beyond the points of duty in making their stay a happy and pleasant one, and they will leave Shimizu with a warm feeling in their hearts towards the Japanese people. . . . There comes a time when all good things must end. So we leave with the impression of a brave people making a brave comeback. However, the sooner we leave the sooner we hope to come back to Shimizu, and if we do not leave soon we are afraid the people of this Prefecture will sink the ship in this beautiful harbor with fine and beautiful presents.

The general tone of the relationship between Americans and Japanese is, of course, set by General Headquarters, which is completely controlled by the authority and dominated by the personality of the Supreme Commander. The attitude of the representatives of other Allied powers in Japan does not always coincide with the American attitude. These divergencies are not very important, since Allied policy in Japan is in practice American policy. The Occupation is in all essentials an American occupation. The GHQ of SCAP (Supreme Commander Allied Powers) is an American organization and employs only a handful of non-Americans in comparatively subordinate posts. The British Commonwealth Occupation Force has been an important addition to the American military forces, but has not been able to play any distinctive or independent part in the work of the Occupation. Its Commander-in-Chief serves under the Commanding General of the U.S. Eighth Army, and, even in the area of Southern Honshu, which British forces occupy, the Military Government's teams, the only link between GHQ, SCAP, and the Japanese authorities, are exclusively American. It is easy to understand why this has come about. It was American material, American transport, and in the main American man power that defeated Japan. Only America had the resources to carry the main burden of the occupation of Japan. Nevertheless, this means that a study of Japan under Occupation must be mainly a study of the American attitude to the Japanese and of the Japanese reaction.

If Allied policy in Japan is American policy, American policy is expressed through General MacArthur. General MacArthur's attitude seems to have been determined by three basic convictions.

First, he believes that defeat, demilitarization and disarmament, together with the loss of her Empire, make it impossible for Japan, in any foreseeable future, to be again a military danger to her neighbors. General MacArthur has said that Japan is destroyed as a military threat "for at least 100 years."

Second, General MacArthur believes that the defeat and the Occupation have completely changed the hearts and minds of the Japanese people. They have become genuine converts to democracy and peace.

Third, General MacArthur believes that, since Japanese democracy can only be overthrown by the "extreme Right" or the "extreme Left," and, since the "extreme Right" has been destroyed or converted, the only actual danger is the "extreme Left." Hence the danger of Soviet influence. It is, therefore, urgent, in General MacArthur's view, to help and strengthen a "democratized" Japan against the menace of Communism and the Soviet Union. It is a key strategic area in this world struggle.

General MacArthur has often expressed these views, but perhaps never so clearly and confidently as in his statement on September 2, 1946, the first anniversary of the surrender in Tokyo Bay.

They [the Japanese] suddenly felt the concentrated shock of total defeat. Their whole world crumbled. It was not merely an overthrow of their military might—not merely a great defeat for their nation—it was the collapse of a faith—it was the dis-

integration of everything they had believed in and lived by
and thought for. It left a complete vacuum morally, mentally
and physically. And into this vacuum flowed the democratic
way of life. The American combat soldier came, with his fine
sense of self-respect, self-confidence and self-control. They saw
and felt his spiritual quality—a spiritual quality which truly
reflected the highest training of the American home. The
falseness of their former teachings, the failure of their former
leadership, and the tragedy of their past faith were infallibly
demonstrated in actuality and realism. A spiritual revolution
ensued almost overnight, tore asunder a theory and practice
of life built upon 2000 years of history and tradition and
legend. Idolatry for their feudalistic masters and the warrior
caste was transformed into hatred and contempt, and the
hatred and contempt once felt for their foe gave way to honor
and respect.

This revolution of the spirit among the Japanese people
represents no thin veneer to serve the purposes of the present.
It represents an unparalleled convulsion in the social history
of the world. The measure of its strength and durability lies
in the fact that it represents a sound idea. . . . Its underlying
concept, new to Japan, but fashioned from the enlightened
knowledge and experience of the free men of the world, will
remain the cornerstone to Japanese freedom unless uprooted
and suppressed by the inroads of some conflicting ideology
which might negative individual freedom, destroy individual
initiative and mock individual dignity. . . .

Should such a clash of ideologies impinge more directly
upon the reorientation of Japanese life and thought, it would
be no slight disadvantage to those who seek, as intended at
Potsdam, the great middle course of moderate democracy,
that a people, so long regimented under the philosophy of an
extreme conservative Right, might prove easy prey to those
seeking to impose a doctrine leading again to regimentation,
under the philosophy of an extreme radical Left.

If we would, in the furtherance of this task, guide the Japanese people the more firmly to reshape their lives and institutions in conformity with those social precepts and political
standards best calculated to raise the well-being of the individual and to foster and preserve a peaceful society, we must

adhere unerringly to the course now charted. . . . *The goal is great—for the strategic position of these Japanese Islands renders them either a powerful bulwark for peace or a dangerous springboard for war.*[1]

On March 17, 1947, General MacArthur developed this theme in a talk to the Allied press. He propounded what became known to visitors to Japan in 1947 as the "doctrine of the three phases." The first phase of the Occupation was military. The task was to demobilize the Japanese fighting forces and destroy all armaments. That phase had been completed with brilliant success. Not only had Japan been demilitarized, but her people understood, perhaps better than any other country in the world, that war did not pay. The second phase was political. The task was the democratization of Japan. While complete democracy had not yet been achieved, the political results already accomplished had been extremely successful. The people had abandoned their feudal outlook. The new constitution and its implementing legislation well and truly laid the foundations of democracy. It was now up to the Japanese people to live up to their new institutions. The third phase was economic. Whether this phase should be carried through with the same success as the earlier two phases would depend not on the efforts of the Occupation forces, but on the readiness of Allied Governments to recognize Japan's plight and take prompt and effective steps to remedy it. General MacArthur claimed that war was still being waged as bitterly against Japan as when the guns were being fired. Indeed, the punishment was now even more bitter. Not even the atom bomb was as deadly as economic strangulation, for the atom bomb kills by thousands, but economic strangulation by millions. And then General MacArthur appealed to the conscience of the Allied world to abandon

[1] My italics.—W. M. B.

its economic warfare against Japan and grant her the aid she needed.[2]

The question now facing the Allies is to what extent it is desirable or possible to build the peace settlement with Japan on the convictions and attitudes that have been expressed by the Supreme Commander during the Occupation. The peacemakers cannot avoid these issues.

[2] No official transcript of General MacArthur's talk to the Press Club was made available, and most of the correspondents present were caught by surprise when he told them that he would be willing to answer questions on the record. The above summary of his statement is based on the reports of the main news agencies, though, since these were not wholly consistent in the quotations they ascribed to the Supreme Commander, nothing in the above statement must be regarded as a direct quotation.

SCAP

ON OCTOBER 2, 1945, GENERAL MACARTHUR set up GHQ, SCAP (General Headquarters, Supreme Commander Allied Powers). This organization was divided into two main parts: the General Staff, to deal with purely military matters, and a number of Special Staff Sections, to deal with non-military matters. For example, the Government Section dealt with political and constitutional reform. Economic affairs were dealt with by three related sections. Economic and Scientific, Natural Resources, and Statistical and Reports. By April 1946, when the Diplomatic Section was established, there were fourteen sections in all.

GHQ, SCAP, issued directives to the Japanese Government through the Central Liaison Office, a channel established for this specific purpose. Most of the members of the Central Liaison Office were former officials of the Japanese Foreign Office. Both the American and Japanese organizations were in Tokyo. On the lower levels of administration, the prefectures, cities, towns and villages, supervision was carried out on behalf of SCAP by the military government teams of the Eighth Army, stationed throughout Japan. It was the task of these teams to ensure that the directives issued by SCAP to the central government would be faithfully administered by the local government bodies.

It may be worth while to remark on certain significant characteristics of the GHQ organization, particularly since there is some controversy on the kind of control machinery that should be established in Japan after the treaty. While General MacArthur has said that he believes all military forces should be withdrawn when the treaty is signed, there are some who believe it desirable to maintain some measure of military control.

Firstly, GHQ, SCAP, was essentially a military set-up, although its most difficult and important tasks were of a non-military kind. The destruction of ammunition and armaments, the supervision of demobilization, the return to Japan of surrendered personnel were primarily military undertakings, and for these tasks a military organization controlled by men with military training was well adapted. Yet the more difficult and constructive work was in the fields of economics, politics and education. Soldiers do not usually receive a professional training in these fields. For this reason GHQ employed throughout its political and educational sections a number of civilians in uniform. Indeed, after the first year of Occupation many of these officers were encouraged to resume their civilian status. Yet the experts in political and economic questions were few in number and generally in subordinate positions. Mr. John R. Stewart, who was formerly with SCAP in Tokyo, has pointed out that four months after the Occupation began, only one officer was working on the problem of the Zaibatsu. The organization of the Zaibatsu industries in Japan is exceedingly complicated, and the project for their dissolution raised the nicest problems of organization, finance and administration. Only one officer was available to handle Japan's huge chemical industry. The textile industry, which had been the most important peacetime in-

dustry, was being handled by only two officers.[1] Many civilian experts in SCAP were men of great professional distinction, but, because the tasks imposed on them were in
most cases far too heavy, and because their findings and
recommendations had to be "channeled" in accordance
with the rules of a military organization, it was not easy for
them to exercise the influence which their ability warranted. It was not easy, for example, for an economist who
held a subordinate status in the military hierarchy, whatever his personal distinction, to get his views passed up to
the Chief of Staff, still less to the Supreme Commander.
And the senior officers were soldiers, who did not always
appreciate the significance of the advice submitted to them
on nonmilitary questions.

The senior officers of GHQ had not only the soldier's
training, but the soldier's outlook. They tended to think
of the Occupation of Japan as the final operation in a military campaign. Surprised by the suddenness and completeness of the Japanese surrender, pleased with the nearly universal compliance of the Japanese with their orders, they
tended to feel that once the actual military power of Japan
had been destroyed their task was done. They thought in
terms of military conflict and of strategic areas and had
little sense of the economic and political issues. They had,
however, retained from their wartime experience a full
sense of the value of propaganda and tended to maintain
throughout the Occupation the propaganda technique
which they had adopted in the face of the enemy during
the war. In the face of the enemy it was generally considered sound policy to play down difficulties and failures, if
they could not be completely concealed, and to anticipate
and exaggerate successes.

One of the most highly organized and efficient sections

[1] John R. Stewart, *Notes on the Economic Aspects of the Allied Occupation of Japan.* Institute of Pacific Relations, New York, April 1947.

of SCAP was the Public Relations Section. This section was insatiable in its desire to publish endless praise of the Occupation's achievements, however fulsome in tone and however dubious in source. The Public Relations Section took pains to arrange that visitors to Japan, particularly if they were publicists, should be properly "orientated." Every precaution was taken to protect these visitors from coming into contact with any of the unpleasant facts of life. Conversely, the SCAP censorship organization attempted to prevent publication in Japan of any facts or comments which might conceivably be considered a reflection on the success of any aspect of the Occupation. At times the censorship seemed to overreach itself. An interesting example of this occurred in October 1946. The *Jiji Shimpo,* an evening newspaper which seemed to take a relatively independent line, published an editorial on October 11 on the fact that the Japanese-language publication, *The Life of General MacArthur,* had been a best-seller in Japan since the surrender. It warned its readers that there were some misguided Japanese people who expressed an adoration of General MacArthur which verged on idolatry. It pointed out that the existence of such an uncritical reverence created the danger that, once General MacArthur had withdrawn from the country, another living god might be searched out to take his place. And the next time it might be a Japanese Hitler. The article concluded:

Among the Japanese people at large there are not lacking those who at one time or other called Hitler greater than Napoleon. Whatever the reasons, there must be still more people in this country who hoped for a Japanese Hitler. The writer who said that the Japanese should quit discussing the Emperor institution and let General MacArthur run the country directly, probably represented quite a large number of the Japanese. Nevertheless, unless this servile attitude is overcome, the opportunity afforded us of standing on our own feet and of establishing democracy would be shamefully wasted.

It is only the nation that has the independence of spirit to resolve upon mastering its own fate that can really establish democracy and work it. To break up the 2,000-year-old hero-worshipping mentality must be the first step toward democratization. On the other hand, it is precisely by such an establishment of democracy that the security of the Imperial lineage would be assured. Whereas, if the respect for the throne depended merely on the traditional spirit of hero-worship, it would be easy for another hero to replace the Emperor, there can be no such change of heart among those who do not idolize the Imperial family. Under a democratic government, the real power is in the hands of the people. An Imperial family divorced from this political power becomes the object of popular love and respect.

The way to express the gratitude of the Japanese people to General MacArthur for the wisdom with which he is managing postwar Japan and for his efforts to democratize the nation is not to worship him as a god or as a hero, but to cast away that very servile spirit and to gain self-respect that would bow the head to no one, and to take hold of the power of government themselves. Only thus would General MacArthur rest content that the aims of the Occupation have been achieved.

This article had been passed by the American censor in the ordinary way. On the following Saturday *Nippon Times,* the Tokyo English-language newspaper, reprinted it. When the first edition appeared, SCAP censorship officers ordered the burning of the 50,000 copies containing the reprinted article and its removal from later editions.

One of the greatest difficulties I found in my own efforts to understand the situation in Japan, and I know that this difficulty was shared by other Allied observers, was the extraordinary sensitiveness of senior SCAP officers to any inquiries which seemed to demand a precise and objective reply. The senior officers seemed always to be nervous lest the information they provided might in some way be used to reflect on the achievements of GHQ. Brigadier-General Courtney Whitney, the Head of the Government Section, exhibited this reaction very clearly when, in reply to the first question asked by a member of the Allied Council, he reminded Council members that they had not been brought to Japan to pry into the Supreme Commander's armor.

Moreover, a military organization is perforce a hierarchy. In structure and in atmosphere it does not seem to be well suited to foster democratic procedures. A military set-up, by its very nature, seeks to eliminate the individualism, the independence, the freedom of discussion and the atmosphere of equality which make the fabric of democracy. I am well aware that it was not possible to establish in Japan the kind of well-trained and experienced civil administration that would have been best adapted for the work of political reform and economic restoration. My comments are in no way a reflection on the military qualifications or achievements of the senior officers in SCAP. Still less are they a reflection on the notable work done by certain of the technical and scientific sections. This work has often been of a very high order, and it seems a pity that it could not have been publicized in a more sober and objective way. The Public Relations Section of SCAP seemed to place little confidence in the art of understatement.

The Allied Council for Japan

The United States Initial Post-Surrender Policy of September 6, 1945, provided that, in the event of differences among the Allies, "the policy of the United States shall govern." This was a clear indication that the United States was prepared in the last analysis to accept full responsibility for the occupation of Japan. Nevertheless, in the last quarter of 1945 other powers which had played a part in the Pacific War made it clear through diplomatic channels that they wished to play an active, if subordinate, part in framing Occupation policy, and even to share in the work of carrying it out. Mr. Molotov urged the creation of a Four Power Control Council. This was not acceptable to the United States, and, although an effort was made to enable all belligerents to have some say in Occupation policy by the creation of the Far Eastern Advisory Commission, it was emphasized that the work of this Commission was purely advisory. These provisional arrangements did not satisfy the Soviet Union and some other countries. Australia, in particular, was anxious to share responsibilities in a more active way. After some months of negotiation, the machinery for Allied control of Japan during the Occupation was decided at the Moscow Conference. In the Moscow Agreement of December 27, 1945, provision was made to set up an Eleven Power Far Eastern Commission, with its headquarters at Washington, and a Four Power Allied Council, with headquarters in Tokyo. It was to be the responsibility of the Far Eastern Commission to formulate the main lines of policy. The Allied Council was to be the eyes and ears of the Far Eastern Commission in Japan. The following were the terms of reference of the Allied Council:

1. There shall be established an Allied Council, with its seat in Tokyo, under the chairmanship of the Supreme Commander for the Allied Powers (or his Deputy), for the purpose of consulting with and advising the Supreme Commander in regard to the implementation of the Terms of Surrender, the Occupation and Control of Japan and of Directives supplementary thereto, and for the purpose of exercising the control authority herein granted.

2. The membership of the Allied Council shall consist of the Supreme Commander (or his Deputy), who shall be Chairman and United States member, a Union of Soviet Republics member, a Chinese member, and a member representing jointly the United Kingdom, Australia, New Zealand and India.

3. Each member shall be entitled to have an appropriate Staff, consisting of military and civilian advisers.

4. The Allied Council shall meet not less often than once every two weeks.

5. The Supreme Commander shall issue all orders for the implementation of the Terms of Surrender, the Occupation and Control of Japan, and Directives supplementary thereto. In all cases, action will be carried out under and through the Supreme Commander, who is the sole executive authority for the Allied Powers in Japan. He will consult and advise with the Council in advance of the issuance of orders on matters of substance, the exigencies of the situation permitting. His decisions upon these matters shall be controlling.

6. If, regarding the implementation of policy, decisions of the Far Eastern Commission on questions concerning a change in the régime of control, fundamental changes in the Japanese constitution structure, and a change in the Japanese Government as a whole, a member of the Council disagrees with the Supreme Commander (or his Deputy), the Supreme Commander shall withhold the issuance of orders on these questions pending agreement thereon in the Far Eastern Commission.

7. In cases of necessity the Supreme Commander may make decisions concerning the change of individual Ministers of the Japanese Government or concerning the filling of vacancies created by the resignation of individual Cabinet members after preliminary consultation with the representatives of the other Allied Powers on the Allied Council.

The circumstances in which I myself was appointed to represent jointly the United Kingdom, Australia, New Zealand and India on the Allied Council showed a new and interesting development in British Commonwealth relations. Australia had originally hoped that the Allied Council would be made up of representatives of each of the eleven belligerent powers. The Soviet Union, however, held out for a Four Power Council. Then the United Kingdom Government, recognizing Australia's primary interests in the Pacific, agreed that the Australian Government should nominate a representative who would speak not only for Australia, but for the United Kingdom itself. New Zealand and India both supported this arrangement.

In accepting this appointment, I went to Japan with high hopes that the Allied Council might be able to do useful work. I fully recognized the leadership of the United States. Moreover, as an Australian, I was deeply conscious that General MacArthur and his forces had, between 1942 and 1945, created in Australia an eternal reservoir of admiration and gratitude. I recognized that, while Australia's interest lay primarily in the Pacific, the United States, Soviet Union and United Kingdom had vital interests in Europe and the Middle East, and that it would consequently be unreasonable to expect the Australian view to be adopted without modification. It was clear that the problems of Japan were only one segment of a world-wide problem. Nevertheless, the countries I represented had carried heavy burdens, made great sacrifices and faced real dangers throughout the Pacific campaign. In India, Burma, Malaya and New Guinea, in the air and on the sea, British Commonwealth forces had made notable contributions to the final victory. For these reasons, I felt that the countries I represented had both the right and the obligation to express a distinctive and independent point of view on the control of Japan after the surrender. Respect for the achievements and recognition of the power of the United States did not, to my mind, involve the obligation to give in all circumstances uncritical support to United States policy.

The atmosphere at the opening meeting of the Council in April 1946 revealed in a sudden and unexpected way the immense difficulties to be overcome if the Council was to be of any constructive service. The atmosphere was heavy with mistrust and hostility between American Headquarters and the representative of the U.S.S.R., Lieutenant-General Kuzma Derevyanko. It was no secret that General

MacArthur had strongly opposed the establishment of the Allied Council. He believed that Mr. Byrnes had made this concession to Russia at Moscow in a spirit of appeasement, without properly considering its mischievous implications in the administration of Japan. The Soviet Union had not accepted the United States invitation to contribute to the Occupation forces, but had instead established a large military mission in Tokyo. The purpose and activities of this mission were mistrusted and feared by American GHQ. Senior officers in SCAP believed that its primary purpose was to organize a secret service in Japan, to support and strengthen the Japanese Communist Party, and to sabotage American Occupation objectives. General Derevyanko was the Head of the Russian Military Mission, as well as the Russian member on the Allied Council. It was, therefore, hardly to be expected that the United States Chairman of the Council, or the officers of GHQ, who attended the Council as expert witnesses, would take General Derevyanko into close and friendly confidence. The strained relations between the American and Russian members of the Council set the tone of every meeting.

In his speech of welcome to the members of the Council at the opening meeting on April 3, 1946, General Mac-Arthur made it clear that he held the Council's powers to be exclusively consultative and advisory. He pointed out that all major directives to the Japanese Government had already been issued, and that these would set the lines of future Occupation policy. He insisted, moreover, that the Council should not concern itself with his past actions. He asked that the Council should meet in public. He said:

The suspicion, the distrust and the hatred so often engendered by the veil of secrecy will thus be avoided, and in the undimmed light of public scrutiny we will, therefore, invite full confidence in the sincerity, the high purpose and the rectitude of our aims. As Supreme Commander, I can assure you that I entertain no fears that such an opportunity for public discussion will have the slightest adverse effect upon the discharge of my responsibilities.

Nevertheless, General MacArthur went on to warn the Council against "sharp and ill-conceived criticism of our Occupation policies," and reminded it that there were evil forces in the world which, for various reasons, sought to sabotage the success of the Occupation. General MacArthur explained that he would normally be too busy with his administrative duties to act himself as chairman, and announced that he had appointed Major-General W. F. Marquat, the Head of the Economic and Scientific Section of SCAP as his deputy.

On finishing his address, the Supreme Commander withdrew, and General Marquat, as chairman, called the meeting to order for the consideration of procedural questions, it having been agreed that no questions of substance would be raised at the first meeting.

It was of some interest that General MacArthur, in describing the functions and powers of the Council, made no reference to the existence of the Far Eastern Commission, and that he should have insisted that the Council's powers were purely advisory. It seemed to me that paragraph 6 of the Terms of Reference provided that the "control authority" of the Council mentioned in Article I would, in certain circumstances, be not only advisory but permissive. In other words, if any member of the Council disagreed with the Supreme Commander in the way he was carrying out policy decisions of the Far Eastern Commission on questions concerning "a change in the régime of control, fundamental changes in the Japanese constitutional structure, and a change in the Japanese Government as a whole," this dissent would have the effect of invalidating the Supreme Commander's action until the question had been considered by the Far Eastern Commission. It seemed to me that it was this provision in Article 6 which gave the Council its main authority. I, therefore, thought it remarkable that General MacArthur should have omitted all reference to it.

It was not, however, until the second meeting of the Council, at which questions of substance were first discussed, that SCAP's attitude towards the Council was revealed with unmistakable clarity and force. The first question on the agenda had been proposed by General Derevyanko. The question was:

According to the available information, undesirable persons, falling under the directive, dated January 4, 1946, in many cases have not yet been removed from the leading positions they hold. Since this fact endangers normal progress of democratization of Japan and may negatively affect loyal realization by the Japanese authorities of all directive instructions of the Supreme Commander for the Allied Powers in general, it is desirable that the Allied Council be informed on this matter as fully as possible by the appropriate representatives of the General Headquarters, Supreme Commander for the Allied Powers.

The Chairman introduced Brigadier-General Courtney Whitney, Head of the Government Section, SCAP, to reply to the Russian question. General Whitney behaved in an unusual way. On mounting the rostrum he clearly indicated by his manner the anger and indignation he felt that this question should have been asked, or at least asked in this particular form. He said that, since, nevertheless, the question had been asked, he would give a comprehensive reply, "even though it took all summer." He then delivered an address lasting for about three hours, although the relevant answer to the Russian's question could have been given in five or ten minutes. General Whitney spent the greater part of the three hours in reading slowly long

lists of political organizations that had been banned by
SCAP. This was the kind of information which could not
in any sense be regarded as a genuine answer to the question, and it was anyway available to all members in published form. The published text of General Whitney's
address gives an incomplete picture of the reactions which
it created, partly because it gives no indication of the sar-
castic and contemptuous tone in which he spoke, and
partly because it omits his asides. For example, after reading a seemingly endless list of banned organizations, he
said in an aside: "There are 30,000 members of these organizations, and I must apologize to the Council for not
having the names with me. That was an oversight of mine.
If I only had them with me I should read them to you with
the greatest pleasure."

General Whitney's performance was a gross and ill-
mannered affront to every member of the Council. Before
any member had been given the opportunity to express
any question of substance, General Whitney had come to
the Council as the representative of General MacArthur,
and he took control of the meeting out of the hands of the
Chairman, General Marquat. The Chairman was in a very
unhappy position. He had already shown himself anxious
to be friendly and cooperative. There was no doubt of his
desire to do all in his power to enable the Council to work
in harmony, but the circumstances were too difficult for
any chairman. General Marquat seemed to feel that he was
bound to support General Whitney, but was obviously un-
comfortable in doing so. It was inevitable that his chairmanship was at times confused and inconsistent.

This second meeting of the Council was very important,
since it really decided the Council's fate. It showed that it
would henceforth be hardly possible for the Council to
cooperate in any serious work if an inquiry from the
Soviet member were always to evoke a frivolous, hostile

and contemptuous reaction from the representative of the Supreme Commander. General Derevyanko behaved throughout this meeting with dignity, courtesy and restraint. It might be argued that the form in which he put his question about the carrying out of the political purge was provocative, and implied the suggestion that SCAP had not been efficient or wholehearted in carrying out this program. It will be noticed, however, that the English of the Soviet member's question is clumsy, like many statements that are obviously translations from another language. I think it highly probable that if either the Secretary-General or the Chairman had invited General Derevyanko to rephrase his question he would certainly have been prepared to do so. During the Council's discussion he declared with some feeling that in framing the question he had no intention of making any criticism of what had been done by General MacArthur, but simply pointed out that any undue delay in carrying out the purge would impede the progress of democratization. It was notable, moreover, that the Chairman did not follow the usual committee practice of asking General Derevyanko, the proposer of the question, to open the discussion. He was not invited to explain his reasons for asking it, or to elaborate it in any way. He, with other Council members, was instead compelled to submit to listening without interruption to General Whitney's outburst.

This second meeting was important not only in that it revealed very clearly SCAP's general attitude towards the Council, and exacerbated so unfortunately the relations between the American and Soviet members, but more specifically because it made clear that SCAP would tend to regard any question, however pertinent and important, as an effort to secure information which might reflect on the accomplishments of the Supreme Commander. General Whitney, speaking on behalf of General MacArthur, in-

insisted that "the Council is not set up for the purpose of prying into SCAP affairs, attempting to find some weak point in SCAP armor, probing for something by which to create national sensationalism." This placed Council members in a dilemma. It was hardly possible to give "constructive advice" on any question without information. It was only possible to get information by asking questions. But it would not be possible to ask for information which might supplement or correct the picture of the Occupation being regularly provided by the Public Relations Section.

The effort to get information continued throughout my eighteen months in Japan to be a major difficulty for the non-American members of the Council. These difficulties were increased in April 1946 by the issuance of a GHQ order that all requests for information by Council members should be made in writing to the Secretary-General, who would then send them to Diplomatic Section and to G2 before they passed to the particular Section possessing the requested information. The reply, as drafted by this Section, was to be sent back through the same devious channels. In my own experience this procedure usually took three or four weeks to complete, even when the information asked appeared comparatively simple and uncontentious. In many instances it should have been practicable to get information by personal interview with the officer who possessed it in a ten minutes' talk. Such direct contacts were, however, sternly disfavored.

During the early days of the Council there was a great deal of discussion on the number of days which it would be reasonable to allow the Council to consider directives before their issuance. General MacArthur had offered in the normal course to send every directive to Council members at least forty-eight hours before its issue.

The Russian member persisted in his request that these

directives should be made available at least five days before they were sent to the Japanese Government. That, in his view, was the minimum period necessary for their proper study and consideration. As time went on it became clear that this debate had been largely unreal, since, after April 1946, SCAP normally controlled the work of the Japanese Government without issuing any important directive. The offices of GHQ gave two reasons for this. They claimed that all important aspects of the Occupation had already been covered by a series of major directives issued between September 1945 and January 1946. And they pointed out that, after the free elections in April, it was important, if the Japanese were to learn respect for the institution of free government, to avoid giving the impression that the Government and the Diet were merely the instruments of SCAP, instead of the expression of the people's will. Consequently, General MacArthur decided that it was wiser to give guidance and direction to the Japanese Government privately and informally rather than by directives.

The formation of the Yoshida Government, the drafting of the new Constitution, and its debate by the Diet, the passing of the laws implementing the Constitution, the efforts for land reform and for the liquidation of the Zaibatsu—all these events were of fundamental importance, and involved continuous guidance of the Japanese authorities by SCAP. They generally took place without the issue of fresh directives. Since GHQ did not inform Council members of the progress of its private dealings with the Japanese authorities, it was hard for Council members to know what was going on, or to make any informed contribution to the discussion of these questions. Moreover, when the Council was consulted by SCAP about some aspect of Occupation policy, its members would usually receive first news of this when the agenda was issued on the Friday before the Wednesday meeting. This would

leave only three working days for the study and consideration of what were sometimes highly complex and technical
questions.

Land reform was the only question among those I have
just mentioned on which SCAP consulted the Council.
This unwillingness to consult the Council placed its members in a peculiar position and gave them the feeling that
they were very remote from the source of executive
authority. They were aware that each week SCAP was
making major decisions in the direction and guidance
of the Japanese authorities. A number of expert missions
came from the United States to Japan to advise GHQ on
various political and economic questions, on the Constitution, on food, on trade unions and labor relations and
on the dissolution of the Zaibatsu. Council members, however, would generally only learn of efforts towards the
solution of these problems through the columns of the
press, or in discreet official reports, which were usually
published some time after the critical decisions had been
taken. In a word, General MacArthur steadfastly declined
to take the Allied Council into his confidence or to provide
the means by which Council members or their staffs could
have direct, informal day-to-day contact with officers of
GHQ.

An examination of the agenda of Council meetings
makes it hard to understand what determined SCAP's
choice of those subjects which he submitted for advice.
Apart from asking advice on certain highly technical questions which the Council was not the proper or competent
body to deal with—for example, the most effective method
of inoculating repatriates against specific contagious dis-
eases—the Supreme Commander did invite Council opinion on certain major questions, on land reform, on methods
for increasing coal production, and on the stabilization of
prices and wages. Yet, when these important questions

were introduced, the American Chairman, Mr. George Atcheson,[2] invariably tried to prevent any effective discussion, and sought instead to extract individual statements from each of the other three Council members, and then close the debate.

In these circumstances it was difficult to develop the kind of free discussion which might have enabled members to maximize agreement. The Chairman sought only the advice of Council members, not the advice of the Council. It seemed that GHQ often worked on the assumption that the Council was non-existent. I cannot recall any reference to the Council's existence or work in the *Monthly Summation of Non-Military Activities,* produced by GHQ, nor in any other SCAP publication. The effort to avoid any reference to the Council's place in the Occupation set-up sometimes appeared trivial and a little ludicrous. For example, in May 1946 the Far Eastern Commission published a policy decision setting out the principles that should be followed in estimating Japan's need for food imports. This decision provided, *inter alia,* that the Supreme Commander should act "with the advice of the Allied Council." The wire agencies transmitted this policy

[2] It is not possible to write this record without many references to Ambassador George Atcheson, Jr., Head of the Diplomatic Section GHQ, SCAP. Mr. Atcheson replaced General Marquat as Chairman of the Allied Council and Deputy of the Supreme Commander in April 1946. He lost his life in an accident on August 15, 1947, when the aircraft on which he was traveling from Tokyo to Washington came down off Hawaii. On several occasions in Japan I was under instructions to take a line which diverged from official American policy, as put forward by Mr. Atcheson. Moreover, the personal opinions I express in this book will sometimes show sharp disagreement with Mr. Atcheson's statements and policy. These political differences in no way affected our personal relations. During a close association over eighteen months, I formed for Mr. Atcheson a strong affection and very deep personal regard. He always acted in accordance with the highest standards of professional and public service. The driving power of his immense industry was a disinterested loyalty to his chief, to the United States, and to liberal and humanitarian ideals. In private life he was one of the most thoughtful and generous men I have ever known.

decision in full to Japan. After it had been submitted to GHQ censorship, it was published verbatim in the Japanese press, except for the omission of the phrase referring to the Allied Council.

On those rare occasions when the Council was asked to advise on important questions, and when members made considerable efforts to formulate careful and helpful recommendations, it was difficult to escape the feeling that GHQ treated these recommendations in a light-hearted fashion. At a meeting in August 1946, the Chairman was asked whether it might not be possible for General MacArthur to tell the Council of his reaction to some of its previous recommendations, and indicate the extent to which he had found this advice acceptable, and how far he had felt able to act on it. In reply, Mr. Atcheson made it clear that Council members should be content with the privilege of offering advice, and then rest assured that the Supreme Commander would give it the consideration it merited. It would be improper and impracticable for members to follow up their advice by inquiries whether it had been acceptable. Normally members would be able to discover, by watching the course of events, the extent to which their advice had been incorporated in the Supreme Commander's decisions. Mr. Atcheson said:

If the Supreme Commander consults and advises with the Council in accordance with the Terms of Reference, it doesn't seem to me that there is any particular question whether he considers the advice of the Council or not, or any reason that I can see, after action is taken, to prolong the discussion.

And, if Members of the Council are dissatisfied, their recourse would be to make representations to their own Governments and to take the question up on governmental level, with a view to having the basic policy decision altered.[3]

To sum up SCAP's attitude towards the Allied Council:

[3] Minutes of the Allied Council.

At its inception, General MacArthur's representative treated it with frivolous derision. General MacArthur omitted to consult it on many major questions. The procedure prescribed for providing members with information severely limited their opportunities to give informed advice. The representatives of SCAP showed exceptional sensitiveness to any question or comment which might be construed as a criticism of any aspect of the Occupation. In these circumstances, it was inevitable that the Council should have been on balance a failure, and at times a fiasco. It provided periodical opportunities for the American and Russian members to give public expression to their mutual distrust. To that extent, Council meetings aggravated a relationship that was already unhappy enough. Yet I believe the Council was able to make some useful contributions to the Occupation. Statements and questions by members sometimes seemed to stimulate GHQ to activity in desirable directions. Indeed, I believe that on several important issues, *e.g.*, land reform, coal mining, prices and wages, members of the Council were able to contribute useful and constructive advice, and that this advice affected the subsequent actions of both SCAP and the Japanese Government.

Since the establishment of the Allied Council was a serious, if largely unsuccessful, effort for Allied cooperation in Japan, and since, presumably, these efforts to cooperate will continue after the peace treaty, it may be worth while to try to state the main reasons for the Council's failures.

It was the custom in GHQ circles to ascribe all, or nearly all, of the Council's failures to the attitude of General Derevyanko, the member for the U.S.S.R. For my part, I formed the following impressions of General Derevyanko's work on the Council. I thought that he behaved consistently in a friendly and dignified way. I felt that on most occasions when he asked for information, which

GHQ seemed reluctant to provide, his inquiries were fully justified, although he often presented his requests in a way that would have made it impracticable to meet them in precisely the way that he desired. For example, at the opening meeting the Russian member asked GHQ to provide the Council with copies of a large number and variety of documents, including every single regulation and decree that had been issued by the Japanese since the beginning of the Occupation. Neither the Chinese member nor I was able to support General Derevyanko in the form in which he put his request, since it would have involved GHQ in the gigantic and impracticable task of making copies of tens of thousands of documents. General Mac-Arthur, in his reply to this request, pointed out that the physical volume of work involved would be so great that it was impossible for him to agree to it. This did not, however, always deter General Derevyanko from making similar requests later.

When General Derevyanko suggested at Council meetings that the aims of the Occupation were not being satisfactorily carried out in some particular field, he tended to make charges of default and failure without producing reliable evidence to support them. He was often pressed by the American Chairman for the evidence on which he based his criticisms, but was generally shy of producing the specific information which might have given weight to his charges. This tendency to make general and imprecise criticisms produced continuous irritation among the officers of GHQ. Moreover, General Derevyanko, like all official representatives of the U.S.S.R., was clearly compelled to work under close instructions, which allowed him the minimum of individual discretion. There was, consequently, a certain rigidity and lack of adaptability about the lines he pursued at Council meetings. Basically, however, the reason for American hostility towards General

Derevyanko was the conviction that Russia's primary interest in Japan was to discredit the achievements of SCAP and to sabotage American objectives. I believe there were good grounds for this conviction. Whether American objectives, as pursued by SCAP, always completely conformed to Allied objectives, as expressed in the policy decisions of the Far Eastern Commission, was another question. There were reasons to suspect, as I shall try to show in later chapters, that General MacArthur's policy on economic questions, for example, placed an emphasis on the value of free competition and the dangers of socialist organization which would not faithfully express the view of the United Kingdom Government or those of some other Allied Government.

The basic mistrust between the American and Russian members cast its shadow over every moment of the Council's work. It meant that it was hardly possible to examine any question on its merits. There were no problems of Japan: every problem of Japan came to be considered for its effects on Russian-American relations.

A second important reason for the difficulties and failures of the Council was that its deliberations were always open to the press. General MacArthur had been particularly anxious that the Council should work in open session. At the opening meeting, I had put forward a modification of this proposal. I had urged that there should be two kinds of Council meeting. Normal discussions, which might often involve detailed and technical proposals, would be held in private. This would enable members to talk more freely and modify in the light of discussion their initial attitudes in an effort to reach agreement. To provide the press with a ball-to-ball description of these debates might be dangerous, since a newspaper reporter, in order to meet his deadline, might often report the statement which a member made early in the discussion, when this would not accurately express that member's final viewpoint. I agreed that it was desirable for the press to be admitted to meetings at regular intervals. My idea was that at these public meetings members would be able to state their definite views on agenda questions and give their reasons for them. This proposal that we should have both private and public meetings was supported by the Council. Unfortunately, however, this scheme came to grief after only one private meeting had been held, in April 1946. The Chairman felt that certain confidential material discussed at this meeting had been improperly disclosed to the press, and, therefore, declined to hold any more private meetings.

The presence of the press at all Council meetings produced a number of unfortunate consequences. The press corps in Tokyo included a number of able and objective journalists. Yet the atmosphere in which it worked seemed to be hostile to the writing, or, at least, the publication of balanced and objective reports.[4] The reporters tended to fall into two sharply divided groups, the supporters and the critics of General MacArthur. General MacArthur's journalist supporters tended to show that undivided and uncritical loyalty which is so desirable in the attitude of a soldier to his commanding officer in wartime. This group maintained intimate relations with the Public Relations Section of GHQ, and Public Relations officers went to great pains to provide them with the sort of background information that supported their convictions. The second

[4] I had personal knowledge of several cases in which GHQ went to extraordinary lengths, by threats or inducements, to suppress news reports that were critical of certain aspects of the Occupation. GHQ was satisfied with nothing less than unqualified praise of SCAP policy and achievements. Every effort was made to remove offending correspondents if the pressures applied in Tokyo failed to bring them into line. GHQ did not seem to recognize any inconsistency between these practices and its frequent exhortations to the Japanese to emulate the democracies in establishing a free and independent press.

group contained some who felt an emotional antipathy to General MacArthur, and some who, on Left-wing ideological grounds, were anxious to expose what they considered to be the undesirable conservative tendencies in SCAP's political and economic outlook. The prevailing tension between the U.S. and Russia unhappily provided both groups with excellent opportunities to pursue their different missions. It did not foster the detached and objective view. It meant that any differences of viewpoint between Council members, however minor in substance, or however quiet in tone, tended to be reported as a dramatic clash between the American and Russian members. This feature of reporting in Japan was described by Mr. Lauterbach in the October 1946 issue of *Front Page*—the journal of the American Newspaper Guild. Some of his comments may be worth reporting:

Many correspondents must still depend on the graces of the Army—even for living necessities. For ethical or other reasons, they believe they owe General MacArthur's administration the same uncritical loyalty which they owed him as a wartime commander. . . .

Sources are more unreliable than usual. In Japan nearly all journalists, politicians and intellectuals are anxious to show how pro-American they are by tipping U.S. correspondents to stories or supplying factual information.

Home Office cables reiterate that the U.S. versus Russia stories make the headlines. It would be superhuman of the men assigned to the Orient if they did not dig around for a good Russian-American squabble or an angle that slammed the Soviets.[5]

[5] From the standpoint of the British member of the Allied Council, it was unfortunate that the reporting of the Occupation to the outside world was left almost wholly to American journalists. The United Kingdom and British Dominions were, of course, themselves entirely responsible for this failure to send their own representatives to cover Japan. In May 1946 there were 70 Allied correspondents in Japan. This included the representatives of news agencies, newspapers, and radio organizations. Fifty-six were Americans, seven from all parts of the British Commonwealth and Empire, and the remaining seven came from other Allied countries. The

I have myself from time to time become unwittingly involved in what sections of the press presented as serious conflict with the American member. On one particular occasion at the seventeenth meeting, on October 16, 1946, a number of newspapers gave great prominence to what was described as a "clash" between Mr. Atcheson and me, and headlined the "outburst" by me which had precipitated the clash. It may be of interest to give, as well as I am able, an objective account of what actually occurred at this meeting.

The meeting had proceeded for nearly two hours when Mr. Atcheson took exception to General Derevyanko's references to the election of April 10. He claimed that the general election "demonstrated to the people of the world a free, honest and orderly election, such as few, if any, of the Western democracies could boast to a more complete degree." Mr. Atcheson said:

I may say that I often wonder at the continued allegations and charges against the Japanese authorities in connection with their efforts under the Occupation. They seem never in this Council to receive credit for the good work they do.

Developing this theme, he went on to say:

In fact, the time has come when Japanese aims have become virtually identical with Allied aims.

B.B.C., the London *Times*, the *Daily Telegraph* and the *Manchester Guardian* all relied for their news on American wire agencies and newspapers, or on American journalists in Japan who sometimes sent them supplementary material. There were then two Australian journalists in Japan, but the Australian Broadcasting Commission had no representatives. When the new arrangement between Reuters and A.A.P. came into effect at the end of 1946, the situation was considerably improved. An Australian was appointed to represent both associations. I am not wanting to suggest that American reporting is in any way inferior to British reporting. Yet the British Commonwealth has its own distinctive interests in Japan, and it seemed to me unfortunate that British newspaper readers should have had to rely mainly on the picture of Japan presented by Americans for American consumption.

He ended his statement with an invitation to other members to make comments. I now quote the following exchanges from the verbatim minutes:

Mr. Ball: Mr. Chairman, I should just like to say that I agree wholly with you that the Members of this Council should try to be just and objective in their assessment of developments here. I would also like to go on record as saying that I would not, without very careful further consideration, be able to identify myself with your expressions of cordiality and confidence towards the present Japanese Government.

The Chairman: I am sorry, I didn't hear your last words.

Mr. Ball: I should not like to identify myself with your expressions of cordiality and confidence towards the present Japanese Government.

The Chairman: I do not think, Mr. Ball, that you will find in the record that I have made any expressions of cordiality or confidence in the present Government. I made a plea for recognition of merit where merit exists.

Mr. Ball: I should only be very glad, indeed, to join with you, Mr. Chairman, in any recognition of merit where merit exists.

The Chairman: Does the spokesman for the British Commonwealth imply that no merit exists in connection with the conduct of the elections or other activities of the Japanese Government?

Mr. Ball: I think that the Member for the United States has expressed the view that the Members of this Council are reluctant to express appreciation of the good work of the Japanese Government where it does good work. And I think I have noticed in the last few months, when any Member of this Council has raised questions which might possibly be construed as a criticism of the Japanese Government, that the United States Member has been very quick and eager to defend the work of the Japanese. All I am wanting to say, today, Mr. Chairman, is that I should not wish to identify myself with the attitude that you have expressed until, or unless, I have received much fuller evidence, much more complete information, about the actual course of affairs in Japan today.

In making my comments, I had several things in mind.

First and foremost, I did not believe it to be true that the aims and ideals of the Japanese Government were virtually identical with Allied aims. If such a statement by the representative of the Supreme Commander of the Allied Powers had been accepted in silence by other members of the Council, it might have been inferred that this silence implied agreement. Moreover, if it were true that Japanese aims had become virtually identical with Allied aims, it would be difficult to justify continued Allied occupation and control.

In referring to the cordiality and confidence which Mr. Atcheson had expressed in his references to the Japanese Government and people, I had in mind not only statements made by Mr. Atcheson in the Council, but other statements made by General MacArthur and his senior officers during the preceding few months which, in my view, gave the Japanese people and the world a greatly exaggerated impression of the progress made in the development of democracy in Japan. The most notable statement was that made by General MacArthur on September 2, the first anniversary of the surrender.

Nevertheless, Mr. Atcheson had himself, on several occasions in the Council, expressed a sympathy and support for the Japanese Government which appeared to me not wholly warranted.

I first noticed this tendency at the seventh meeting (June 17) when Mr. Atcheson, after pointing out that the land reform program submitted by the Japanese Government on March 15 was "inadequate," went on to say that he believed that the Government had, nevertheless, presented this program "in a sincere spirit." In my view, this particular program was evasive and insincere, and indicated that the Japanese Government was anxious to frustrate rather than to fulfill the purposes of the SCAP directive on land reform. It, therefore, seemed to me surprising that Mr. Atcheson should have felt it desirable to commend the Japanese Government for its "sincere spirit."

When, at the eleventh meeting (August 7), I had asked Mr. Atcheson whether he considered the Japanese Government a suitable body to be entrusted with the carrying out of the purge directive, he had shown some impatience at my question and had remarked that it was easy enough to criticize the Japanese Government when it was "not in much of a position to defend itself."

At the thirteenth meeting (August 21), while explaining the reasons for advocating the "unofficial" extension of the Council membership, Mr. Atcheson had said that the Japanese people were "in the spirit of a team," "seeking the same goal" as the Allies.

At the sixteenth meeting (September 2), Mr. Atcheson had referred to the dissolution of the Commission for the Investigation of the Causes of the War and the Defeat. He showed regret that this Commission had been dissolved. He said the Japanese Government had dissolved it on its own initiative, as a result of the criticism directed against it by the Soviet member and me, and "in order to avoid further misrepresentation of its purposes."

Since the early days of the Council, the Chinese member and I had been reluctant to place items on the agenda, even in the form of questions, since it was clear that GHQ was extremely sensitive and resentful about any question or comment which might be construed as a criticism of General MacArthur or his officers. For my part, I felt that on many occasions it was highly desirable to ask certain questions on the Council about the progress of the Occupation, but I avoided doing so for fear that in presenting these questions I might become involved in the charge of aiming criticism at General MacArthur. The situation had now developed that Mr. Atcheson seemed to feel nearly, if not quite, as sensitive about criticism of the Japanese Government as he would have felt about criticism of SCAP. This made it difficult, if not impossible, for Council members to take part in any objective examination of Occupation policy without becoming involved in a clash with Mr. Atcheson.

These, then, were the three main reasons why the American and other members found it difficult to make the Council a cooperative and constructive body: the hostility between the United States and Russian members, the attendance of the press at all meetings, and the extraordinary sensibility to criticism shown by GHQ.

3. JAPANESE INSTRUMENTS OF CONTROL

The Emperor

IN THE CLOSING STAGES OF THE WAR WITH Japan there was much debate and considerable disagreement in Allied circles about what should be done with the Emperor after defeat. One school of thought, pointing out the dangerous fusion in the Emperor's person of Japanese tribal idolatry and aggressive militarism, claimed that the Emperor system must be forthwith abolished if the danger of Japanese imperialism was to be removed. Some went further and urged that Hirohito be tried as a war criminal. The second school of thought claimed that if the Allies retained the Emperor it would be possible to exploit his prestige with the Japanese people to our advantage. Some members of this school claimed that the Emperor had, in any case, always been a mere figurehead and that it would be unrealistic to saddle him with responsibility for Japan's aggression or for the conduct of the Japanese fighting forces during the campaigns.

The second school of thought won the day. I believe that, looking back, the conclusion is ineluctable that the retention of the Emperor was fully justified. The promptitude and completeness of the Japanese surrender in every theater of war undoubtedly saved the lives of tens of thousands of Allied soldiers. Since the surrender, the compliance of the Japanese Government and people with the orders of their conquerors must be attributed at bottom to the Emperor's authority. After due credit has been given to General MacArthur's firm benevolence, and the generally high standard of behavior of the Occupation troops, the extraordinary smoothness of the Occupation stems ultimately from the Emperor's will.

I believe, therefore, that the decision to retain the Emperor was wise, and I think that General MacArthur's attitude towards the Emperor has shown just the right mixture of tact and firmness. Yet it is important to remember that our tacit support of the Emperor system and of Hirohito means a price to be paid and risks to be run. Without vigilance to minimize that price and guard against these risks, the consequences of our policy may seriously threaten the aims of the Occupation.

Memories are short, and it is worth while to recall that the issue of the Emperor system was the pivot of the surrender negotiations. In these negotiations it became clear that the Japanese Government was prepared to sacrifice almost everything but the Emperor. In the Potsdam Declaration, issued July 26, 1945, it was laid down in Article 6 that "there must be eliminated for all time the authority and influence of those who have deceived and misled the people of Japan into embarking on world conquest." This is apparently the one provision that the Japanese Government was prepared seriously to contest. In its qualified reply to the Potsdam Declaration of August 10, the Japanese Government declared that it was ready to accept the terms of the joint declaration "with the understanding that the said declaration does not comprise any demand which prejudices the prerogative of His Majesty as a sovereign ruler." Mr. Byrnes, on behalf of the Governments of the United States, United Kingdom, U.S.S.R. and China, sent a reply on August 11, which in effect accepted the Japanese Government's condition, since this reply specifically referred to the Emperor as the authority that would be required to ensure that the Government of Japan and the Japanese Imperial General Headquarters should carry out the provisions of the Potsdam Declaration. It is true that Mr. Byrnes's reply insisted that from the moment of surrender the authority of the Emperor should be subject to the Supreme Commander of the Allied Powers, and that the ultimate form of government in Japan should be established by the freely-expressed will of the Japanese people. There is little doubt, however, that the Japanese Government and people regarded Mr. Byrnes's reply as an expression of Allied willingness to retain the Emperor system in Japan.

Some weeks later, when the Premier, Prince Higashi-Kuni, described to the Japanese people the circumstances in which the final decision to end the war had been taken, he said: "It was decided to accept the terms of the Potsdam Declaration, with the understanding that this did not comprise any demand that would prejudice the prerogatives of His Majesty as sovereign. The war of Greater East Asia has thus been brought to an end."

The Imperial Rescript, in which Hirohito broke the news to his subjects that the war had ended, was a remarkable document:

To our good and loyal subjects:

After pondering deeply the general trends of the world and the actual conditions obtaining in our Empire today, we have decided to effect a settlement of the present situation by resorting to an extraordinary measure.

We have ordered our Government to communicate to the Governments of the United States, Great Britain, China and the Soviet Union that our Empire accepts the provisions of their Joint Declaration.

To strive for the common prosperity and happiness of all nations, as well as the security and well-being of our subjects, is the solemn obligation which has been handed down by our Imperial Ancestors, and which we lay close to heart. Indeed, we declared war on America and Britain out of our sincere desire to ensure Japan's self-preservation and the stabilization of East Asia, it being far from our thought either to infringe upon the sovereignty of other nations or to embark upon territorial aggrandizement. But now the war has lasted for nearly four years. Despite the best that has been done by everyone—the gallant fighting of military and naval forces, the diligence and assiduity of our servants of the State, and the devoted service of our one hundred million people, the war situation has developed not necessarily to Japan's advantage, while the general trends of the world have all turned against her interest. Moreover, the enemy has begun to employ a new and most cruel bomb, the power of which to do damage is indeed incalculable, taking the toll of many innocent lives. Should we continue to fight, it would not only result in an ultimate collapse and obliteration of the Japanese nation, but, also, it would lead to the total extinction of human civilization. Such being the case, how are we to save the millions of our subjects, or to atone ourselves before the hallowed spirits of our Imperial Ancestors? This is the reason why we have ordered the acceptance of the provisions of the Joint Declaration of the Powers.

We cannot but express the deepest sense of regret to our Allied nations of East Asia, who have consistently cooperated with the Empire towards the emancipation of East Asia. The thought of those officers and men, as well as others who have fallen in the fields of battle, those who died at their post of duty, or those who met with untimely death, and all their bereaved families, pains our heart night and day. The welfare of the wounded and the war sufferers, and of those who have lost their homes and livelihood are the objects of our profound solicitude. The hardships and sufferings to which our nation is to be subjected hereafter will be certainly great. We are keenly aware of the innermost feelings of all ye, our subjects. However, it is according to the dictate of time and fate that we have resolved to pave the way for a grand peace for all the generations to come by enduring the unendurable and suffering what is insufferable.

Having been able to safeguard and maintain the structure of the Imperial State, we are always with ye, our good and loyal subjects, relying upon your sincerity and integrity. Beware most strictly of any outbursts of emotion which may engender needless complications, or any fraternal contention and strife which may create confusion, lead ye astray and cause ye to lose the confidence of the world. Let the entire nation continue as one family from generation to generation, ever firm in its faith of the imperishableness of its sacred land, and mindful of its heavy burden of responsibilities, and the long road before it. Unite your total strength to be devoted to the construction for the future. Cultivate the ways of rectitude; foster nobility of spirit; and work with resolution, so as ye may enhance the innate glory of the Imperial State and keep pace with the progress of the world.

This is perhaps the most significant statement of the real attitude of the Emperor and the Japanese Government after the defeat of Japan became certain. It was made before the American forces landed in Japan, and when the Emperor consequently retained some degree of freedom. In my own view, the weeks between the day when the Japanese Government decided to surrender and the day on which the Occupation forces landed were of incalculable historical importance. It is my firm belief, though I cannot produce documentary evidence to support it, that during this brief breathing space the rulers of Japan quietly agreed upon the strategy and tactics they would follow during the Occupation period. There were to be two keynotes of this strategy: complete outward compliance with the orders of the conquerors, combined with lasting spiritual resistance to the conqueror's will.

Whether or not this version of happenings at the time of the surrender is accepted, the Rescript contains within itself considerable interest. It will be noticed that it makes no reference to surrender. The Emperor has merely decided to "effect a settlement of the present situation." In conducting this course, the Emperor is striving for "the common prosperity and happiness of all nations." There follows a strangely brazen attempt to justify Japan's aggression. The Emperor declared war from his "sincere desire to ensure Japan's self-preservation and the stabilization of East Asia." There is no suggestion that Japan has been forced to the point of unconditional surrender. Rather the "war situation has developed not necessarily to Japan's advantage." The Emperor expressed his deep sense of regret to the nations of East Asia that were forced to ally themselves with Japan, since they had "consistently cooperated with the Empire towards the emancipation of East Asia." And, lastly, there is the statement that the acceptance of the Potsdam Declaration enables Japan "to safeguard and maintain the structure of the Imperial State."

In my view, the Emperor expressed in this Rescript more of his real mind than it has been opportune for him to express since the arrival of the Occupation forces. The Rescript gives no hint of any change of heart or mind.

The public debate continues on whether Hirohito can justly be regarded as guilty of the kind of crimes for which Japan's political and military leaders were tried by the International Military Tribunal for the Far East. This question hinges on whether we believe that before and during the war the Emperor's political position in Japan prevented him from exercising any effective influence over his advisers. It seems to me clear that he did exercise some real influence, though it seems nearly impossible for the foreign observer to know what degree of influence he was able to exercise on particular occasions. I think it is significant that the wartime rulers of Japan should be so insistent that the Emperor was free of all responsibility for aggression. Yet a careful reading of the diaries of Prince Konoye and of the Marquis Kido, and of the evidence in defense of General Tojo, seems to me to provide clear evidence that the Emperor was a party, though sometimes a reluctant and subordinate party, to actions which are now considered as war crimes. It may be true that at the critical meetings in the last quarter of 1941 the Emperor always sought to break the deadlock with the United States by diplomatic negotiation rather than by resort to arms. Yet he allowed himself to be swayed by his advisers, and thereafter contributed to the efforts of the Government to work the Japanese people up into a fighting mood. While there may be little evidence that he played a positive role in the decision to make war, failure to act is sometimes as culpable as positive action.

If Allied public opinion today accepts the thesis that the Emperor was a helpless pawn in 1941, I think it is difficult to give him credit for the part he played in bringing about Japan's surrender. There is a tendency among some people to insist that the Allies should feel great gratitude to the Emperor for having brought the war to an end at a time which saved the lives of numberless Allied soldiers. Undoubtedly this is the response which the Emperor and his friends wish to produce. It seems to me quite inconsistent with the available facts.[1]

[1] I believe that the real part played by the Emperor before and during the war has been accurately described by Mr. T. A. Bisson in the following passages: "As to the Emperor's influence with respect to aggression and territorial aggrandizement, no elaboration need be made. He supplies the tribal ideology which knits the coalition together, with its unrivaled motivation of the 'sacred mission' of a 'master race.' The aggressive instincts of Japan's dominant groups are buttressed by a divine imperative: to extend the 'benevolent sway' of the Emperor over previously unfavored regions. Under these conditions, with an Imperial influence tending invariably in a given direction, the effort sometimes made to pass off the Emperor as a puppet without political responsibility of any kind, or as an institution which can be directed towards good ends, hardly merits serious consideration. To regard the Emperor system as something which is by nature politically neutral and can be used for good or ill, as if it were some inanimate object like a pistol, in which inhere no social values, but which takes on such significance only when it is used, is a gross misunderstanding of its history. In the complexities of Japanese social development the institution of the Emperor has inevitably given the Japanese State structure a certain bias which has predisposed it to the side of reaction." *Pacific Affairs*, December, 1944, p. 399.

The Emperor system in Japan has been a dynamic fusion of patriotism and religion or, to put it more bluntly, of tribal ideology and superstition. The task of the Allies was to purge this system of militarism and feudalism, and, so far as possible, of superstition. If the Emperor were to be retained it was essential that he be humanized. The god was to become a man, the sovereign a symbol, the warrior a man of peace. This was an ambitious project, yet there was some historical evidence to suggest that it might be feasible. Sir George Sansom has pointed out that, despite the halo of sanctity that is supposed to have surrounded the Emperor from earliest times, no nation has treated its titular rulers so cavalierly as the Japanese. The history of Japan is strewn with emperors forced to abdicate, emperors exiled and emperors slain. Between the eighth and the nineteenth centuries even the religious functions of the emperors made little impact on the life of the nation.

The kind of emperor worship we have witnessed in Japan during the last decades is a modern product. After the restoration of 1868 the rulers of Japan made tireless efforts to inculcate in the Japanese people the belief in imperial divinity as the first article of faith. During the life of the Emperor Meiji his rescripts were treated as holy writ. In schools and public offices there was compulsory worship of his portrait. In moments of national crisis the leading statesmen and generals did obeisance to the imperial ancestors at the Shrine of Ise. This elaborate build-up of the Son of Heaven, with his divine mission to rule the world, was greatly aided by Japan's victories in war and by the spectacular development of her industries and increase in her wealth. The defeat of China in 1895, with the annexation of Formosa; the defeat of Russia in 1905, with the annexation of Korea, fostered the myth of imperial invincibility. Yet these were all very recent developments in the long history of Japan. It was hoped that the overwhelming defeat of Japan in 1945 would, in destroying the myth of invincibility, make it possible to destroy the associated myths.

It was, therefore, natural that observers in Allied countries should have attached great importance to Hirohito's message to the people on New Year's Day, 1946, when he "voluntarily" renounced divinity. The Emperor said:

The ties between us and the people have always stood upon mutual trust and affection. They do not depend upon mere religion and myths. They are not predicated on the false assumption that the Emperor is divine, and that the Japanese people are superior to other races and fated to rule the world.

The new Constitution provides that the Emperor's powers shall be reduced to those of a constitutional monarch. This is, undoubtedly, a revolutionary change in Japan's constitutional structure. The Meiji Constitution was the gift of the Emperor to his people. Under the Meiji Constitution the Emperor was the absolute sovereign. It was only possible to amend it at the Emperor's initiative, and it was perhaps, therefore, not surprising that it was never amended. The following articles illustrate the place this Constitution gave the Emperor. "The Emperor is sacred and inviolable" (Article 3). "The Emperor is Head of the Empire, combining in himself the rights of sovereignty and exercising them according to the provisions of the present Constitution" (Article 4). "The Emperor gives sanction to the laws and orders . . . to be promulgated and executed" (Article 6). The prerogatives of the Emperor as the Supreme Commander of the Army and Navy were defined in Articles 11 and 12. Although no mention was made there of the way in which that prerogative was to be exercised, the general burden of the Constitution and the authoritative commentaries on it showed that there was no intention to place the control of the armed forces under the civilian government. This was one of the most dangerous features of this Constitution of 1889.

The new Constitution makes a complete change in the Emperor's status and powers. It provides that he can act only on the advice of the Cabinet, which is, in turn, responsible to a Diet elected by universal suffrage. "The Emperor shall be symbol of the state and of the unity of the people, deriving his position from the sovereign will of the people" (Article 1). "The Emperor shall perform only such acts in matters of state as are provided for in this Constitution, and he shall not have powers related to government" (Article 4). The few functions left to the Emperor by the new Constitution are formal and ceremonial. This is the purpose of the distinction between "acts in matters of state" and "powers related to the government"; he may perform such "acts in matters of state" as the Constitution provides, but "all powers related to the government are denied him."

The nature of the debate on the draft Constitution, in both the House of Representatives and the House of Peers, indicated that many Diet Members were deeply perturbed at the way in which the draft sought to undermine the Emperor system. There was no feature of the new Constitution which aroused anything like the same interest or concern. Tokujiro Kanamori, the Minister of State in charge of the Constitutional debate, found himself in constant difficulties. His last line of defense in the face of conservative critics was the curious argument that, because the Emperor and the people were really one and always had been, sovereignty continued to reside in the Emperor, as well as the people, for the two were one and inseparable.

Whether the new Constitution brings about a real, and not merely a temporary, legal change in the Emperor's position depends at bottom upon the seriousness with which the Japanese people regard this document. The draft which the Japanese Government presented to the Diet bore all the marks of Western political ideas and a very strong American influence. There was no doubt that most educated Japanese regarded it as alien to the Japanese spirit. Premier Yoshida repeatedly warned the Diet that it was essential to adopt the Government's draft "in the exigencies of the present international situation" and "because of the feelings of the Allied countries." He begged the Diet to remember that "the Japanese Government, because of its present position, is subject to restrictions on its policies." He insisted that the new Constitution did not, despite appearances, mean a sharp break with the past. It was not to be assumed that it brought democracy to Japan for the first time. The charter oaths of the Emperor Meiji fully expressed the spirit of democracy. The new Constitution simply expressed it in a new form. Above all, it did not mean any change in the "national character," and the national character meant that the Emperor, who comes of the imperial line, "unbroken for ages eternal," still forms the center of the unity of the people.

I think it was significant that the day the Japanese Government chose for inaugurating the Constitution, which was to strip the Emperor of all political power and separate religion from the state, was Meiji Day, and that the Emperor's first act that day was to report on this strange event to his ancestors at the three main shrines in the Palace precincts. Later a great rally of citizens was organized on the Imperial Plaza. After the crowd had listened below the Palace to speeches by political leaders explaining the significance of the new Constitution, the national anthem was sung. Suddenly the imperial carriage was seen crossing the bridge over the moat. The Emperor was arriving. The crowd shouted itself hoarse in a fever of devotion. Allied newspapermen present told me they had never heard such banzais since the death charges of the war. When, after two minutes, the Emperor withdrew, the crowd surged after him, treading many underfoot in their excitement. Priests beat their drums to ward off evil spirits. For hours afterwards the crowd filed over the dais for the honor of treading where the Emperor had trod.

Since early 1946, the Emperor has visited a number of prefectures outside Tokyo. He usually appears in slightly threadbare civilian clothes, and moves about in a shy way, as though he were perpetually startled. The reports of his exchanges with the common people seem to the Westerner to be strangely drab and meaningless. Yet these appearances have aroused turbulent and overwhelming popular enthusiasm. It is often necessary for the Occupation forces to come to the aid of the Japanese police to protect the Emperor from the consequences of his subjects' reverence. In whatever way open to him, Hirohito seems anxious to foster and maintain a sense of national unity and tradition amongst the Japanese people. It is the custom each year for him to prescribe a subject for a poem for the Imperial New Year Poetry Competition. For the New Year of 1946 the subject selected was "Snow on the Pine." The people were thereby invited to contemplate the tree they loved so much, the tree which bends under the winter's burden of snow, but never breaks. The Emperor himself wrote a verse appealing to the people to emulate the pine tree.

It is difficult for the foreign observer to assess the impact of these changes in the position and habits of the Emperor on the minds of the Japanese people. So far as I could discover, when the Emperor disclaimed divinity, this created an immense impression in Allied countries but hardly any impression in Japan. Experts on Japan have pointed out that divinity means something quite different to the Japanese from what it means to Westerners. Moreover, the educated Japanese never took the doctrine of imperial divinity with literal seriousness. It is well to remember that in Japan it is considered good form for a public speaker to end his address, no matter how eloquent and able it may have been, with an apology to his audience for having wearied it with so many stupid ideas, presented in such halting and stumbling words. It is, therefore, possible that many Japanese regarded the Emperor's disclaimer as a superlative example of the self-deprecatory statement that is part of good manners in Japan.

It is my strong impression, despite all efforts at democratization, that the Emperor is still the political sovereign and still the Son of Heaven in the hearts and minds of the overwhelming majority of the Japanese people. I think it probable that his real political power is even stronger than before the war. He is all the Japanese people have to hold on to. They have lost their empire and their fighting forces. The wartime political leaders are discredited by failure. The Emperor alone remains. He is the divine ruler, who preserves their national unity and who will restore that leadership among nations that has been temporarily lost through the blundering of their generals and the overwhelming material resources of the United States.

The Japanese are an adaptable people, with a great facility for compromise. It may be that they will come to think of the Emperor in much the same way as the British people have come to think about the King. But an attempt to graft a Western concept on an Eastern mind is a ticklish operation. I think it useful to remember the circumstances in which the Emperor was restored to dignity and power in 1868. The Satsumo and Choshu clans engineered the restoration and set out to persuade the people that the Emperor was divine and infallible, because they felt that this was the most likely means by which they could assert and maintain supremacy over other rival clans. The Emperor system was to be the facade behind which they ruled Japan. We need to be wary today lest those conservative groups that are so anxious to protect the Emperor system are not merely hoping to exploit the Emperor's new human and democratic attributes in the same way that the Satsumo and Choshu clans tried to exploit the Emperor Meiji's divine attributes. A feudal system could hardly have a more acceptable front than a human and democratic Emperor.

Cabinet and Parliament

If the new Constitution strips the Emperor of all political authority, it is in order to give to a Cabinet responsible to a freely elected Diet supreme executive power. It is through the Japanese Government that General MacArthur has ruled Japan, and it is likely to remain an indispensable instrument of Allied control after the peace settlement. A great deal will, therefore, depend on the political outlook and capacity for leadership and organization possessed by Japan's leaders.

In this chapter I shall discuss only the Yoshida and Katayama Governments. They have been the product of free Parliamentary elections. The earlier post-surrender Governments had been too obviously tainted by their wartime inheritance to be adaptable to political life under the Occupation.

The election of April 10, 1946, was a notable event. SCAP had already produced striking changes in the political scene. The Great Japan Political Association, which claimed 377 out of 466 Members of the House of Representatives at the time of the surrender, had been dissolved in August 1945. The "Purge Directive" of January 4, 1946, had ordered the abolition of all ultra-nationalist societies, and had debarred about 200,000 persons from public life. Consequently, only about 50 Members of the former House of Representatives were able to stand in the election of April 1946. The more conservative parties were particularly hard hit by the purge. Meanwhile the Communists had been freed from prison and the Communist Party was given full freedom to organize and campaign. Women had been given the vote and the right to stand for Parliament. The voting age had been reduced from 25 to 20. In all these circumstances, it was natural that the election should have aroused world-wide interest. Yet polling day was remarkably free from excitement or drama. The impression I formed in the polling booths I visited in Tokyo was of quietness and order. Men and women moved through the booths in endless lines and seemed to be performing a drab routine according to instructions. The Emperor and General MacArthur wanted them to vote, and so, of course, they voted. I saw no faces shining with a sense of exhilaration at this new freedom. Yet the conditions of polling were undoubtedly quite new. There were no police or officials to exercise open intimidation. No charges of improper pressure on the voters were brought to SCAP's notice by any parties or defeated candidates. It would be unrealistic to suppose that there were no such pressures. But this was, nevertheless, certainly the freest election in Japan's history.

Voting was not compulsory, yet polling was heavy by American or British standards—78.5 per cent of the men, 67.1 per cent of the women enrolled. The election produced a House of Representatives with the following distribution of parties: Liberals, 140; Progressives, 93; Social Democrats, 92; Cooperatives, 14; Communists, 5; Minor Parties, 38; Independents, 82. The Liberals and Progressives, despite their names, were the most conservative parties in Japan. Neither party was either liberal or progressive by British or American standards. The differences between these Right-wing parties were mainly due to group and personal rivalries. The Social Democrats avow socialist objectives. The party is sharply divided into Right and Left wing. About three-quarters of the Social Democrat members of Parliament belong to the Right wing, and seemingly regard socialism as part of the theory, rather than the practice, of politics. Nearly all the Independents, and most of the members of the minor parties, could be safely classed as conservative. Hence, despite the increase in the number of Social Democrats from 17 to 92, free elections produced a Diet that was fundamentally conservative. This was recognized by SCAP, which summarized the election results as follows:

In general terms the basic issue may be discerned between the older political forces, chiefly represented by the Progressive and Liberal parties, and the new element, represented by the Socialists and Communists. All parties recognized the need for change. The Progressives and Liberals would limit the scope and temper, while the Socialists and Communists would move more rapidly towards fundamental reforms. Seen in this light, the election represents a victory, possibly temporary, for the more conservative forces in Japanese civilian life.[2]

After six weeks of party maneuvering, the Yoshida Cabinet was installed on May 22, based on a coalition of Liberals and Progressives. Mr. Shiguru Yoshida was an outstanding member of the Japanese group of intellectuals commonly described before the war as "liberals." There was a widespread absence of enthusiasm for the new Cabinet. Most of its members were aging and weary men (their average age was 61), retrieved from obscurity because more able and vivid figures were either unwilling to accept responsibility at this time or had been debarred from office by the purge directive. It soon became apparent that this Government could hardly provide the united leadership,

[2] *Summary of Non-Military Activities,* April 1946.

initiative and vitality so badly needed to remake Japan. Yet nothing in the election appeals of the Liberal or Progressive parties had foreshadowed quite how nerveless and hesitant, nor quite how conservative the Yoshida Cabinet would prove to be.

The basic weakness in the Yoshida Government's policy was that it was unwilling or unable to impose direct controls over productive resources. At the end of the war Japanese industry was in a run-down condition. Capital equipment had deteriorated through lack of maintenance and some had been destroyed in air raids. Production of key raw materials had been falling for two years. It was essential that capital equipment should be reconstructed and repaired and the output of basic raw materials revived, as the necessary basis for any permanent recovery. This was particularly so in the coal industry, where mines and plant had been badly overworked. Transport equipment, such as railway rolling stock, was also in a poor state. Industrial efficiency generally was at a low ebb.

Such a program required the mobilization of all available resources, and would only have been possible with the strictest control over the distribution of raw materials, the rationing of major consumption goods and the prohibition of unessential production. On the financial side, balanced budget, high taxation and control over wages and prices would have been necessary. It was a case of husbanding Japan's scarce resources for the rebuilding of its industrial machine. Individual initiative was weak. There was, therefore, a strong case for the Government's taking over the control of certain basic industries, not necessarily permanently, to mobilize resources for their reconstruction where ordinary commercial incentives might have been too weak and uncertain a motive.

For the first two or three months after the surrender the Government's authority was weak, and little in the way of firm control could have been expected. Early in 1946, however, especially after the general election, conditions were more favorable, and an attempt might have been made to exert firm control to avert the dissipation of valuable resources in production which would not contribute to permanent recovery, and to provide a basis for effective financial controls.

The Yoshida Government, however, did not take this opportunity, but placed its faith in the operation of ordinary commercial incentives within a framework of limited and weakly-applied controls and in its own financial policy. The effect of this policy was to provoke inflation and to delay industrial reconstruction by allowing resources to be drawn away from the basic and essential consumption goods industries to unessential production.

The Yoshida Government's policy mainly expressed the economic philosophy of Mr. Tanzan Ishibashi, the Finance Minister, who was a firm believer in free enterprise, and appeared to put complete trust in the adequacy of the profit motive in all circumstances.

Meanwhile, the American economists in GHQ were in private becoming increasingly alarmed at the Japanese Government's incapacity to control the worsening economic situation. Yet in public the representatives of GHQ continued to compliment the Yoshida Government on its aspirations and achievements. However, by March 1947, after the Yoshida Cabinet had for ten months been showing that it had neither the will nor capacity to do what was necessary, General MacArthur staged a personal intervention of a surprising and significant kind. On March 22 he wrote to Mr. Yoshida; at the Allied Council meeting of April 2 he not only asked for advice on the best way to stabilize wages and prices, his Chief of Staff, Major-General Paul Mueller, sent a Minute to the Council, which elaborated the thesis of the MacArthur letter, and Dr. Sherwood Fine, the senior economist in GHQ, gave the Council his views of the economic situation and what the Government should do to meet it.

General MacArthur's letter was courteous and restrained, but made it quite clear that GHQ was deeply dissatisfied with the Japanese Government's failure to take essential steps to protect and restore the economy. After discussing food as an example of the need for more effective Government action, the letter went on:

At this time I wish to call to your attention Directive No. 3, which I issued to the Imperial Japanese Government on September 22, 1945. This directive made it the responsibility of the Japanese Government to maintain a firm control over wages and prices, and to initiate and maintain a strict rationing program for essential commodities in short supply, as well as to ensure that such commodities are equally distributed. It is imperative that the Japanese Government carry out this responsibility to the Japanese people. The Allied Powers, of course, are under no obligation to maintain, or to have maintained, any particular standard of living in Japan, nor is there any responsibility to import foodstuffs to meet deficits arising from the failure of Japan to assure the just and efficient distribution of its own food supplies.

The food problem, though basic to the peaceful reconstruction of Japan, is not an isolated phenomenon, but is on the contrary only one part of the over-all problem of economic stabilization which includes the additional factors of increased production of raw materials and industrial products, stabilized wages and prices, maximum exports, and sound public finance. By the same token, black marketing of food and failure to realize full collections are only two manifestations of general maldistribution. These problems are so inextricably interwoven that it is not practical to think in terms of a solution for one independent of the others. *What is required is an integrated approach across the entire economic front. Accordingly, it is essential that the Japanese Government, through the Economic Stabilization Board, which was created for this purpose, take early and vigorous steps to develop and implement the inte-*

grated series of economic and financial controls which the current situation demands.[3] These economic objectives are national in scope, transcending the special interests of any group, and, therefore, should be non-partisan. Unless determined measures are undertaken at once by the Japanese Government, the inflationary condition of the economy, together with its attendant maldistribution of food and other necessities, will become increasingly serious, industrial recovery will be further retarded, and the achievement of the social and political objectives, toward which the Japanese people have made such an encouraging start, will be endangered.

The social and economic welfare of Japan will depend largely on Japan's own efforts in the redirection of its human and natural resources to peaceful living, and upon competent public administration of democratic and effective economic controls. Aid to Japan cannot be expected upon a scale sufficiently great to overcome maldistribution and inflation within Japan. Outside assistance is contingent upon full utilization of indigenous resources, which is entirely a responsibility of the Japanese Government.

In explaining the situation to the Allied Council, Dr. Fine expressed more bluntly GHQ's dissatisfaction. He said, *inter alia:*

As indicated in our partial staff study, we are not without experience in trying to effectuate economic controls with the Japanese Government responsible for implementation. However, we are forthright in admitting that we are quite dissatisfied with the results realized.[4]

The overt intervention by General MacArthur and senior officers of GHQ was significant for two reasons: it was a public statement of SCAP's dissatisfaction with its main

[3] My Italics.—W. M. B.

[4] *Minutes of Allied Council for Japan,* 29th Meeting, p. 15. It was at this meeting of the Allied Council that, after giving my fullest support to the line taken in General MacArthur's letter, I said that the Chief of Staff's Minute was "a most disquieting record of continuous failure." The context should have made it quite clear that I was referring to the continuous failure of the Japanese Government, not the continuous failure of General MacArthur, as reported in a section of the press.

and indispensable instrument for pursuing the aim of the Occupation—the Japanese Government; and it was an unequivocal statement of SCAP's belief that in the existing situation it was essential that "free enterprise" should be replaced by a directed economy.

It may be worth while to speculate why SCAP delayed so long in rebuking the Yoshida Government for its inactivity and instructing it to take firm and comprehensive control measures. One reason may have been the tendency, which I repeatedly noticed, of the senior soldiers in GHQ to try to shield the Supreme Commander from gaining official knowledge of what was unpleasant. Being untrained themselves in economics or public administration, these officers may have failed to appreciate the seriousness of the economic trends, and, therefore, failed to give due weight to the warnings of those civilian subordinates who were well aware of what was going on. It may have been, too, that General MacArthur was reluctant to instruct the Japanese authorities to carry out the sort of policy that would be difficult to harmonize with his own "individualist" outlook on economic questions, even though the controls he directed were only to meet a temporary emergency. Finally, it was normally the considered policy of SCAP to avoid publicity in putting pressure on the Japanese Government.

To make a sound appraisal of the Allies' chosen instrument—the Japanese Government—it is very important to remember SCAP's deliberate decision, after the issue of the basic directives in the first months of the Occupation, normally to guide and control the Japanese authorities behind closed doors. To forget this may mislead us seriously, for we may assume that a number of liberal and reform measures sprang from Japanese initiative, not from the advice or direction of GHQ. And this would often give us a false picture of the outlook and aspirations of Japan's political leaders. We should appreciate the solid and disinterested reason that made General MacArthur decide to do good by stealth. One of his primary tasks was to educate the Japanese in the habits of responsible government. That meant they must respect the authority of their freely-elected Parliament and the Cabinet responsible to it. The Government would almost certainly lose face if the people came to regard it merely as a body set up to take orders from SCAP. Moreover, if the Government's policies were ostensibly the expression of its own will it might be expected to make greater efforts to administer them efficiently than if they were publicly recognized as SCAP decisions. Lastly, some future Japanese Government might find it easier to repudiate the reforms during the Occupation if they could be stigmatized as the mere imposition of the conquerors' will. For all these reasons, SCAP's direction of the Japanese has normally been carried out secretly. GHQ officers have tried to persuade and induce, rather than compel. Yet the Japanese have recognized that General MacArthur has force in reserve, and they have, therefore, shown sensible compliance. Explicit disagreement or overt opposition have been excluded from the tactics of resistance.

When all has been said in favor of private pressure against public compulsion, it is a technique possessing certain disadvantages and dangers. SCAP's hand is never completely concealed. The Japanese political leaders know what happens and they tend to discuss freely in private, sometimes with resigned good humor, sometimes with bitterness, their subservience to "requests" of GHQ. The sense of responsibility which General MacArthur has been trying hard to inculcate does not seem to develop. Instead the Japanese attitude is, "Well, let's leave it to SCAP. SCAP will decide anyhow, so let us not worry too much about it at present."

During the course of a Diet session the officers of GHQ would industriously work out drafts of desirable legislation in many fields. As the session wrangled along its course, it would be observed that the tempo of legislation was slow. There would be insistent prodding by GHQ. And in response the Diet would "process" at breakneck speed a series of measures which sometimes bore in every line the mark of American authorship. Once these measures had been made law, the Japanese Government tended to feel that it could relax again. Perhaps it realized that it is not legislation, but administration, that gives life to a law.

The chief danger of the policy of concealing SCAP pressure is that it may seriously mislead some Allied peace makers in their decisions on the sort of controls that should be established after the settlement. Anyone who relied exclusively on the official reports of the activities of the Japanese Government and Diet under the Occupation would have immense difficulty in reaching a true view of the outlook of these bodies. In conformity with the policy of concealed pressure, these reports record a number of liberal and reform measures in a way that implies they were spontaneous. "After a free and comprehensive debate the House of Representatives, by almost unanimous vote, adopted the following amendment to the Bill." Or, "Despite its previous disagreements, the Cabinet at yesterday's meeting reached complete agreement on the measures it should take."

It is perhaps not desirable to give prominence to specific instances, but anyone officially associated with the Occupation knows that on many important occasions the "unanimity" in the Diet or the "final agreement" in the Cabinet was the simple result of a firm instruction issued privately by SCAP, sometimes on his own initiative and sometimes in carrying out an explicit directive from Washington.

It may be thought that, in emphasizing the difficulties that have faced SCAP, and that are likely to face the future Allied control body, in working through a Japanese Government, I am failing to give due credit to Japanese cooperation or to recognize the liberal-mindedness of some of Japan's postwar leaders. I try to avoid that error of judgment. I met and had very happy social relations with Mr. Yoshida and some of his senior colleagues. Mr. Yoshida himself has a fine record of resistance to the "militarists." I am sure that he and his close associates sincerely desire good relations with the United States and British Commonwealth. I can express my feelings towards the significance of men like Mr. Yoshida and Mr. Ashida and Mr. Katayama and their "liberal" trend by quoting three passages from a chapter entitled "Japanese Liberals" from *Japan in Defeat:* [5]

(1) Perhaps in every country motives of patriotism come first. It is probably wrong to speak of, say, a French statesman as a friend of England; he is, first and foremost, a French statesman, but one who is susceptible to the argument that good relations with Britain are conducive to the interests of France. This is true in a far higher degree in Japan, since patriotism is for the Japanese a religion in itself. A European statesman is aware of the brotherhood of man, of the principles of right and wrong, universal in their application, and has an abstract sense of justice, before which all men are alike. He may not always act upon these principles. He may turn them to the patriotic end in view, but he is aware of them and influenced by them the whole time. The Japanese, on the other hand, have little conception of right and wrong as standards by which the conduct of all mankind is judged; to them whatever conduces to the greater glory of Japan is right. The Japanese statesman is, therefore, unencumbered by the scruples which

[5] *Japan in Defeat.* Report by a Chatham House Study Group. Oxford University Press, N. Y. and London, 1945.

beset European statesmen. He comes direct to the point and means to achieve the end are justified, provided they show some probability of success.

(2) The decade following the last war, therefore, saw the emergence in Japan of democratically-minded statesmen. Such statesmen were picked for their sincere advocacy of democracy by the committees behind the scenes, and, in particular, by the Genro, in order to try out this experiment. The scene to be presented to the world was to be in conformity with the prevailing democratic lines. The facade was to be democratic; the interior was, at the same time, to remain true to Japanese traditional conceptions. The politicians themselves were probably sincere, but they were manipulated and never did they sink the aims of Japan in visions of the brotherhood of man or the comity of nations. They attempted to see how democracy would work; they attempted to probe the possibilities of peaceful penetration, as opposed to military aggression.

(3) It is highly probable that the Japanese will dress their window at least partially in democratic fashion. Liberal elements will be of use; they will be used. Their influence will not be as individuals, but as instruments. Once again this will not necessarily imply a change of heart, but only a change of dress. The frock coat will replace the military tunic, but the body will remain the same.

It would be a mistake to assume that all, or most, Japanese postwar political leaders are liberals. Indeed, the election of April 1946 and the formation of the Yoshida Cabinet both revealed how men who were previously associated with the militarists still held powerful places in Japan's politics. In these free elections, Ichiro Hatoyama, the President of the Liberal Party, received a greater plurality of votes than any other candidate, and his party became the leading party in the new Diet. Shidehara, the retiring Prime Minister, decided to recommend Hatoyama as the new Prime Minister, and Hatoyama accordingly had a preliminary audience with the Emperor. But already some pertinacious Allied newspapermen had been investigating Hatoyama's antecedents. Their reports prompted

GHQ to make enquiries and then to disqualify Hatoyama from public life. [6]

It was surely interesting that a man with Hatoyama's record should have been the most successful candidate and most successful party leader at the first free elections in Japan.

After his disqualification, Hatoyama continued to take

[6] The directive barring Hatoyama, dated May 3, gave the reason for his removal as follows:

"1. Under the memorandum of January 4, 1946, 'Removal and Exclusion of Undesirable Personnel from Public Office' (SCAPIN 550), the Japanese Government was directed to disqualify any candidate for the Diet who had deceived and misled the people of Japan within the spirit and letter of that directive.

"2. After the election on April 10, 1946, the Central Liaison Office was informed that the eligibility of one Ichiro Hatoyama (member-elect of the House of Representatives from the First Electoral District, Tokyo), to hold any public office being open to doubt in the light of evidence published subsequent to his screening by the Japanese Government, it was expected that his eligibility would be re-examined by the Government forthwith.

"3. The Japanese Government, having failed to act on its own responsibility, the Supreme Commander for the Allied Powers has determined the facts relative to Hatoyama's eligibility and finds that he is an undesirable person within the meaning of paragraphs 1 and 3 of Category 'G,' Appendix 'A,' SCAPIN 550, in that:

"a. As Chief Secretary of the Tanaka Cabinet from 1927 to 1929, he necessarily shares responsibility for the formulation and promulgation without Diet approval of amendments to the so-called Peace Preservation Law, which made that law the Government's chief legal instrument for the suppression of freedom of speech and freedom of assembly, and made possible the denunciation, terrorization, seizure and imprisonment of tens of thousands of adherents to minority doctrines advocating political, economic and social reform, thereby preventing the development of effective opposition to the Japanese militaristic regime.

"b. As Minister of Education from December 1931 to March 1934, he was responsible for stifling freedom of speech in the schools by means of mass dismissals and arrests of teachers suspected of 'Leftist' leanings or 'dangerous thoughts.' The dismissal, in May 1933, of Professor Takigawa from the faculty of Kyoto University on Hatoyama's personal order is a flagrant illustration of his contempt for the liberal tradition of academic freedom, and gave momentum to the spiritual mobilization of Japan, which, under the aegis of the military and economic cliques, led the nation eventually into war.

"c. Not only did Hatoyama participate in thus weaving the pattern of ruthless suppression of freedom of speech, freedom of assembly and freedom of thought, but he also participated in the forced dissolution of farmer-labor bodies. In addition, his endorsement of totalitarianism, specifically in its application to the regimentation and control of labor, an active "unofficial" interest in politics and consulted privately with Cabinet Members.

When Mr. Yoshida was forming his Cabinet he asked Chuzo Iwata to be Minister for Justice and Shiroshi Nasu Minister of Agriculture. SCAP barred both men for their past militarist activities. It was not until many months later that several other of Yoshida's Cabinet colleagues were dismissed from office under the Purge Directive,

---

is a matter of record. His recommendation that 'it would be well' to transplant Hitlerite anti-labor devices to Japan reveals his innate antipathy to the democratic principle of the right of labor freely to organize and to bargain collectively through representatives of its own choice. It is a familiar technique of the totalitarian dictatorship, wherever situated, whatever be its formal name, and however be it disguised, first to weaken and then to suppress the freedom of individuals to organize for mutual benefit. Whatever lip service Hatoyama may have rendered to the cause of parliamentarianism, his sponsorship of the doctrine of regimentation of labor identifies him as a tool of the ultranationalistic interest which engineered the reorganization of Japan on a totalitarian economic basis, as a prerequisite to its wars of aggression.

"d. By words and deeds, he has consistently supported Japan's acts of aggression. In July, 1937, he traveled to America and Western Europe as personal emissary of the then Prime Minister Konoye to justify Japan's expansionist program. While abroad, he negotiated economic arrangements for supporting the war against China and the subsequent exploitation of that country after subjugation. With duplicity, Hatoyama told the British Prime Minister in 1937 that 'China cannot survive unless controlled by Japan,' and that the primary motive behind Japan's intervention in China involved the 'happiness of the Chinese people.'

"e. Hatoyama has posed as an anti-militarist. But in a formal address, mailed to his constituents during the 1942 election, in which he set forth his political credo, Hatoyama upheld the doctrine of territorial expansion by means of war, referred to the attack on Pearl Harbor as 'fortunately . . . a great victory,' stated as a fact that the true cause of the Manchuria and China 'incidents' was the anti-Japanese sentiment (in China) instigated by England and America, ridiculed those who in 1928 and 1929 had criticized the Tanaka Cabinet, boasted that that Cabinet had 'liquidated the [previous] weak-kneed diplomacy toward England and America,' and gloated that 'today the world policy drafted by the Tanaka Cabinet is steadily being realized.' This identification of himself with the notorious Tanaka policy of world conquest, whether genuine or merely opportunistic, in and of itself brands Hatoyama as one of those who deceived and misled the people of Japan into militaristic misadventure.

"4. Accordingly, in view of these and other considerations not herein recited, the Imperial Japanese Government is directed to bar Ichiro Hatoyama from membership in the Diet and to exclude him from Government service, pursuant to SCAPIN 550." *G.H.Q. Summation*, May 1946.

including Yoshinara Kawai, Minister for Education; Tanzan Ishibashi, Minister of Finance; Keinosuke Zen, Head of the Economic Stabilization Board; and Tsunesiro Hiratsuka, Minister for Transportation. The Democratic Party, which replaced the Progressive Party in March 1947, and later came into the Katayama Coalition Government, met a serious reverse in the first weeks of its life when several of its most influential leaders were barred under the purge. The new party was formed on March 31, and by the end of April half of its Supreme Committee had been disqualified under the purge for their past activities or associations. The purgees were Yoshinari Kawai, Ken Inukai, Wataru Narahashi, and the Secretary-General, Takeshiga Ishigure. It may well be that the purge has sometimes been used by the Japanese screening committees for party purposes, and that some of the purged politicians have records no worse than those who have escaped disqualification. Some of the purgees may have come to regret their past policies. It is still significant that so many prominent political leaders of the Occupation period should be considered by GHQ or the Japanese Government's Screening Committee disqualified from public office owing to their past ultra-nationalistic or militarist activities. This strongly suggests that the historical continuity of the Japanese political outlook has not been broken. And it must be remembered that these men who have been purged have not been imprisoned or exiled. They usually remain active and influential behind the scenes. In Japan most important political decisions are made behind the scenes.

The Katayama Government

By the end of 1946 it was becoming clear that the authority of the Yoshida Government had become precarious. It was the target for new assaults from three directions: from the political parties in Opposition, from the trade unions, and from the press.

Until December 17, 1946, the Social Democrats, the leading Opposition party, with 99 House seats, maintained a tacit truce with the two Government parties. The Liberals (with 148 seats) and the Progressives (with 111) had an absolute majority in a House of 464 members, but they, nevertheless, seemed to rely greatly on the temporary immunity the Social Democrats had granted them. However, the Social Democrats brought the truce to an abrupt end on December 17, when their leaders in Parliament launched a no-confidence motion that was synchronized with street demonstrations demanding the immediate resignation of the Cabinet. The Social Democrats' attacks on Yoshida have been eagerly supported by the Cooperative Democrats, with 45 House seats.

In a New Year's Day broadcast, Yoshida expressed the view that labor disputes were fomented by lawless and irresponsible union leaders; that Japan could not survive without help; and that the Allies would hardly desire to continue to help an economy disrupted by strikes. This broadcast exacerbated the union resentment against the Premier and his Cabinet, and this resentment was built up into the threat of the "general" strike on February 1.

The more influential newspapers, which appeared to reflect moderate opinion, rapidly became more critical of the Yoshida Government. In a *Nippon Times* editorial it was stated that Yoshida's New Year's Day broadcast was "bound to enrage the labor elements" and that "the trend of the Yoshida Government to wage battle from a decidedly conservative position, therefore, seems unmistakable" (January 9). The *Mainichi*, the *Asahi*, and the Tokyo *Shimbun*, with other papers, had been attacking the Yoshida Cabinet for its impotence and incapacity, its lack of good faith and its conservatism.

Faced with this widespread hostility, Yoshida made repeated attempts to broaden the base of his support. In particular, he attempted, with the persistent private encouragement of GHQ, to form a coalition with the Social Democrats. The last effort to get Social Democrat collaboration failed on January 29. The Social Democrats insisted on the resignation of Ishibashi, the Finance Minister, as the first prerequisite for a coalition. Yoshida refused to sacrifice Ishibashi. The following day, January 30, *Mainichi* made the following comment on this situation:

It is clear that the position of the Finance Minister now is next in importance to that of the Premier, and it is only natural that this post should become an important issue. But the fact that the final key to the political situation should now rest with the question of the Finance Minister cannot fully be explained merely by saying that his post is important. The problem goes deeper than that. Why are the Liberals and Progressives ready to defend a Finance Minister, even at the risk of inviting a political crisis? And why are the Socialists concentrating their attack on that one point?

To put the matter in a nutshell, the struggle now going on is an offensive and resistance between the class that is profiting from the present inflation and the one that is suffering from it. This is the crux of the matter. We see no need of expounding a theory of inflation here, but it should be noticed that inflation is decidedly profitable for capitalists and decidedly damaging to the working class. But it is clear that the main props of the Yoshida Cabinet are the capitalist class. From such a point of view, Finance Minister Ishibashi is the god of the class that is profiting from the inflation.

On January 31 Mr. Yoshida announced a Cabinet reshuffle, which was primarily a shift further to the Right. Meanwhile trade union militance had reached its highest point in the plan for a "general strike" on February 1. It seemed that some four million workers might be involved. This project was killed by General MacArthur's direct order. But nothing could give life or power to the Government. Then, on February 7, General MacArthur wrote to Mr. Yoshida that there should be a fresh general election soon after the close of the Diet session.

April 1947 was a month of elections. The Japanese people went to the polls four times during the month: to elect local governors, mayors and village chiefs; to elect the new national House of Councilors, which was to replace the House of Peers; to elect local legislators, and to elect a new House of Representatives. Naturally most interest centered on this last election.[7]

Its most striking feature was the success of the Social Democratic Party, which increased its members from 98 to 143, and became the first party in the House. Four weeks later Mr. Tetsu Katayama was elected Prime Minister by the Diet, and by June 1—after five weeks of party maneuvering—formed a coalition Cabinet, based on the support of the Democrats and the People's Cooperatives.

General MacArthur made two significant comments on these events. On April 27 he issued a statement on the general result of the elections. He pointed out that they were the last in preparation for the new Constitution, which reflected "one of the great spiritual reformations of mankind." He went on to say:

[7] Election of House of Representatives, April 25, 1947:

		Gain or Loss
Social Democrats	143	+45
Liberals	132	— 8
Democrats (former Progressives)	126	—19
People's Cooperatives	31	—32
Communists	4	— 2
Minor Parties	18	+14
Independents	12	+ 3
Total	466	

The basic issue before the electorate was a selection between political philosophies. That of the totalitarian extreme Right had already been discredited and rejected for its responsibility for war and defeat and long suppression of the rights and liberties of the masses. On the other hand, that of the extreme Left, the Communistic philosophy, was still the issue, with its leaders strongly bidding for the popular support. Since the inception of the Occupation, when thousands of its adherents were freed from the stern suppression of prison cells, this philosophy and its leaders had been given the fullest liberty and freedom of political action in open and fair competition with democratic forces and beliefs. It thus had its full chance, and on the merits has failed. The Japanese people have firmly and decisively rejected its leadership and overwhelmingly have chosen a moderate course, sufficiently centered from either extreme to ensure the preservation of freedom and the enhancement of individual dignity.[8]

On May 24 the Supreme Commander made the following comment on Mr. Katayama's election as Prime Minister:

It is significant, too, from a broad international viewpoint that three great Oriental countries now have men who embrace the Christian faith at the head of their Governments—Chiang Kai-shek, in China, Manuel Roxas, in the Philippines, and Tetsu Katayama, in Japan.

It bespeaks the steady advance of this sacred concept, establishes with clarity and conviction that the peoples of the East and West can find common agreement in the spirituality of the human mind and offers hope for the ultimate erection of an invincible spiritual barrier against the infiltration of ideologies, which seek by suppression the way to power and advancement. This is human progress.[9]

[8] *Summation of Non-Military Activities in Japan,* April 1947. It seems likely that one of the reasons why the Communist Party lost some electoral support was that at this time the Truman doctrine was arousing intense interest in Japan. The opponents of Communism took every opportunity to drive it home that Japan could only expect American aid to the extent that she was a bulwark against the spread of Communism from East Asia.

[9] *Summation of Non-Military Activities in Japan,* May 1947.

The Katayama Government not only had the sympathy and moral support of SCAP, but at the beginning appeared to have a wide support among the people. Yet it was already clear, on its formation, that it would not be able to carry out a socialist policy, and that it was doubtful whether it would be able to set up and enforce the economic control measures so urgently needed.

Despite the electoral success of the Social Democrats, they were heavily outnumbered in the Diet. They held only one-quarter of the seats, and clearly conservative groups outnumbered them two to one. Indeed, the Social Democrats were in a minority of one in the Cabinet itself, in which they had eight members, the Democrats seven, and the Cooperatives two. Moreover, the other elections of April, particularly those for the executive heads of local governing bodies, had generally been conservative victories, though in the local elections conservative candidates often ran as "independents." This meant that any radical control measures which the National Government might launch would be administered throughout the prefectures, cities and villages by officials who, in the majority, were conservatives and bureaucrats.

In any case, the circumstances in which the Katayama Government was formed seemed to preclude it from the outset from effecting the firm and comprehensive controls which SCAP had told Mr. Yoshida were essential. Mr. Katayama was only able to scrape a Cabinet together by publicly jettisoning most of the radical and distinctive planks of his party. The Liberal Party had refused to support him unless he excluded all Left-wing members not merely from the Government, but from the party. Mr. Katayama was not able to agree to that, for, although the Left-wingers were perhaps less than a quarter of the Social Democrats' Diet strength, they gave the party its plurality. He did exclude them from the Cabinet.

On May 12 the Social Democrats had adopted a six-point program to which both wings subscribed. It provided for a "state-controlled economy" and "democratic state control of vital key industries." It was noteworthy that it did not include the suspension of interest on state bonds or the freezing of the new yen, two measures which the party had previously sponsored. The Social Democrats were clearly prepared to compromise in the effort to lead a Government. The Cooperatives responded by urging that key industries should be state-controlled "only when necessary." The Democrats supported the Cooperatives in this. Under pressure, the Social Democrats compromised further. They explained that the key industries to be controlled included only coal, steel, fertilizer, shipping and electric power. They had no intention of nationalizing banking or insurance, or of putting them under state management. At last, in a desperate effort to get leadership in a Coalition Cabinet, the Social Democrats agreed with the Liberals, Democrats and Cooperatives to a ten-point "policy agreement." The Social Democrats agreed that there should be state management of key industries "only when necessary to effect a concentrated industrial policy for increasing production," that there should be financial controls "only when necessary," that the new yen would not be frozen or blocked, and that interest payments on war bonds should not be suspended. It will be seen that the Social Democrats had to water down their policy to an extent that made it hardly distinguishable from the policy of their conservative opponents. It was more like capitulation than compromise.

The subsequent history of the Katayama Government is easily understandable if these circumstances of its origin are borne in mind. The story of its frustrated efforts to control critical materials, the black market and inflation is again a story of how projects, begun in compromise, ended with capitulation. Perhaps the history of the Temporary Coal Mines Control Bill gave the clearest proof that the Katayama Government was powerless to do what it originally set out to do, and what, to many non-political observers, it seemed necessary to do if Japan were not to come near to economic collapse.

During the Occupation the shortage of coal has held up the whole program of industrial recovery. Coal was nearly as important to the Japanese as food. To increase production was a primary and urgent task for the Katayama Government. It realized this, for, on June 1, it announced its intention to put the coal industry immediately under state control as an emergency measure. After long wrangling between the three Government parties, and major concessions by the Social Democrats, the Cabinet reached agreement on a Draft Bill on August 10. But this met with stiff opposition from the mine owners, who succeeded in forcing several amendments protecting their interest. At last, the Bill was brought down on September 25 and at once referred to the House of Representatives Mine Industry Committee, made up of nine Social Democrats, nine Democrats, eight Liberals, two Cooperatives, one member of the Dai Ichi Club, and one of the Farmers' Party. The conservatives had a big majority on this Committee, and it was not surprising that it rejected the whole measure. The Government then attempted to bypass the Committee by referring the Bill back to the House. The debate there produced repeated disturbances, described by the Japanese press as "pandemonium" and "hooliganism." The pandemonium produced further amendments, and the Bill was passed by the House of Representatives on November 25 and the House of Councilors on December 8. But it was not to come into operation for six months, and the Social Democrats had agreed to so many amendments, pressed on them by their conservative colleagues, all directed to weaken the control provisions, that its final passage seemed pointless. A *Nippon Times* leading article seemed to size up the situation accurately:

In name it provides for state control of the coal mines. In fact, however, it has been so watered down as to mean practically nothing. From the very first the Social Democrats, despairing of getting any legislation passed which would establish full Governmental control over the coal industry, drew up a Bill full of compromises designed to win the adhesion of the Democratic Party. But the inability of the Democrats to make up their minds caused the Social Democrats to seek to lure them with more and more concessions, until, as the result of the deals of the last few days, the Bill has reached a form in which virtually nothing remains of its original characteristics.[10]

The struggle over coal control set the general pattern of the Social Democrats' difficulties. The conservative parties always called the last tune. These parties depended for their support on the classes who were profiting by the inflation. The wage and salary earners that had voted for the Social Democrats, in the hope that they would improve their lot, became steadily disillusioned. It was, therefore, not surprising that, by the end of 1947, the Katayama Government found itself in a precarious position. Mr. Katayama's dismissal of Rikizo Hirano from his post of Minister for Agriculture and Forestry widened a split within the party. On January 6, 1947, sixteen Right-wing members of the Diet left the Social Democratic Party. This threatened the party plurality in the Diet. Meanwhile, the Asahi Public Opinion Poll for December showed that the Katayama Government was rapidly losing popular support. Of those polled, only 15.9 per cent supported the Government, while 53.1 per cent opposed it, and 31 per cent were undecided. In its early days the

10 *Nippon Times*, November 15, 1947.

Government had had the support of over 50 per cent of those who took part in these polls.[11]

In this discussion of the Yoshida and Katayama Governments, I have been attempting to show the immense difficulties that faced SCAP, in using them as instruments of social-economic reform. The Yoshida Government was unwilling, and the Katayama Government unable, to take any decisive steps to transform a feudal economy into a welfare economy.

The Diet

Though the Diet has staged some able debates, it has in general been a confused and ineffective body. The initiative has always been in GHQ, SCAP, or in the Cabinet, and Parliament has mainly been a disquieting mirror of party and personal feuds, with feverish bouts of "processing" measures, which it has not seriously examined or debated. Again, to quote from a leading article from the *Nippon Times:* [12]

Barely meeting its midnight deadline Tuesday night with no more than one minute to spare, the first Diet session to be held under the new Constitution has finally brought its long deliberations to a close. For those who are interested in records, this Diet session stands out as a notable historical event. Not only was it the first Diet to be held under the new Constitution, its session was the longest in the Parliamentary history of the nation. It disposed of more than 130 Bills, the largest number of Bills to be acted upon by any Diet in Japanese history. It received more petitions than any previous Diet. It passed the largest budget in the history of the nation. It engaged in more extended debate, necessitating more voluminous records of its proceedings, than any other Diet in the nation's history.

But these records, while interesting, are not the most significant facts about this session of the Diet. To the average citizen,

[11] The Katayama Government resigned on February 10, 1948.
[12] *Nippon Times*, December 11, 1947.

despite all the "firsts" and other records, this Diet has left the impression of unprecedented disorderliness and ineffectiveness. Although the Diet passed a record number of Bills, the overwhelming proportion of the Bills was presented by the Cabinet and did not initiate with the Diet itself. It is true that the Cabinet was slow in presenting many of these Bills, but the Diet was even more dilatory in handling them; and, after seemingly interminable and futile wrangling, they were then hurriedly rammed through at the eleventh hour under Government pressure.

Even more distressing is the fact that for several days virtual pandemonium prevailed in the Diet chambers, when there should have been dignified and enlightening deliberation. Even in the less disorderly meetings, the frequent noisy heckling made it apparent that many of the Diet Members considered the Diet as a place for partisan demonstrations, rather than a place for deliberating on the highest affairs of the nation as a whole. The disorderliness of the Diet session, which received much unfavorable publicity, both at home and abroad, has left the average citizen with the impression that the new Diet, if not an outright failure, is at least nothing to be particularly proud of. Some may even have doubts, judging from this performance, as to whether Japan is really capable of operating democratic political institutions successfully.

The article goes on to list achievements to the Diet's credit, and concludes:

All in all, therefore, the achievements of the first Diet session must be considered as being more than reasonably creditable. There is much that should be improved about the Diet, but the Diet certainly does not present itself as a hopeless problem. It is to be hoped that the Diet, which has now technically gone into its second or regular session, will profitably make use of the past extraordinary session as a point of departure for progress and improvement.

It is doubtful, however, whether the Diet, or the Cabinet, is the repository in fact, and not only in form, of political power. It seems more likely that the real holders of power in Japan today keep behind the scenes as far as possible. In the last quarter of 1947, just after I had left Japan, a great press publicity was given to "revelations" about the existence of a "hidden government," which worked behind a "black curtain." It seemed to me unfortunate that these stories should have been so highly dramatized and taken the form of a "revelation." They can only have been that to superficial observers who had been led to believe that, under the Occupation, the Japanese people had suddenly abandoned habits ingrained for hundreds of years.

In Japan, more than in most countries, the most important deliberations and decisions take place behind the scenes. In Japan, as in all countries suffering from acute shortages and inflation, groups of black marketeers seek to exploit others without scruple. To do this effectively on a national scale considerable organization is necessary. It is also highly desirable, if the black marketeers are to prosper, that every effort be made to corrupt politicians and public servants. Japan is not the only country in which this sort of thing happens; it is simply that the social habits of the Japanese provide an atmosphere that fosters this sort of extralegal or illegal organization. The oyabun-kobun system is a very old and basic feature of Japanese life. It was inevitable that GHQ should find it an obstacle to "democratization." That presumably explains why Colonel Kades, Deputy-Chief of the Government Section of GHQ, decided in October 1947 to try to arouse public opinion against the oyabun-kobun system. Colonel Kades is reported to have said that every Japanese political party received most of its funds from secret organizations. A more detailed description of GHQ's concern with this system was published on November 27, 1947. Mr. Howard Handleman, the Far East Bureau Manager of International News Service, reported, *inter alia:*

SCAP officials' meeting on September 12 reported the following instances of oyabun-kobun activity:

"Industry Division.—Oyabun activity has disrupted production and hampered distribution of critical industrial materials into black-market works. The black market provides much of the funds on which the system exists. Oyabun have sent their men into the coal mines of Kyushu to terrorize miners on the job. Oyabun organize construction companies, obtain contracts for Occupation work and buy construction materials from themselves at inflated black-market prices. The Government pays.

"Anti-Trust and Cartels Division.—Oyabun hold monopolistic control in the field of construction and among stall vendors. In Tokyo alone there are 45,000 street stall vendors, all of whom must pay exorbitant rents, dues, service charges and even official city taxes to the oyabun. Most street stalls are on public sidewalks, owned by the city, but the vendors must pay rent to the oyabun. The division said information has been obtained showing connection between the oyabun in this field and certain of the political parties; that ranking oyabun have run for public office in large numbers of cases; that the oyabun-kobun system extends into all types of construction, transportation and other industries.

"Collect Taxes.—Finance Division: Oyabun collect taxes for the Government. Officially they receive two per cent of their collections. Unofficially they receive much more, as they pay the Government on an estimate basis, which assumes that only half the street stalls, for instance, operate each day.

"Government Section.—'Our investigation indicates extragovernmental controls are exercised by a number of political oyabun upon the National Government, both in the Diet and in the Ministries, and also upon local governments.'

"Labor Division.—In 1946 American authorities found 20,000 enslaved Japanese working coal mines in Hokkaido, under guard day and night. Under American prodding, the slave-labor gangs were broken up. Labor Division said, 'Apart from the slave-labor system, the oyabun control the black-market rice and use it as an economic weapon to force new kobun to join and organize and remain out of any labor union.'

"Eighth Army Procurement.—'The cost of Occupation [to the Japanese Government] has been increased materially, due

to the fact that no inquiry has been made into the cost of procurement of materials by the contractor.' It is clear, it was
repeated, that no inquiry was made, because of the link between
the gangsters, turned contractors, and the political bosses, who
get both economic support and the votes of the kobun by their
work with the contracting oyabun.

"Stevedore Monopoly.—Transportation Section: It was found
that every port in Japan has a stevedore monopoly, organized
by oyabun.

"Natural Resources Section.—Both on land and sea the
oyabun-kobun relationship is the rule. Landlords customarily
were the oyabun, who controlled village politics and the all-
important agricultural society, which controlled fertilizer, rationing and marketing. The land reform law, designed to limit
the area of any farm to the amount the owner and his family
can cultivate, has tended to break the system on the farm, although it is still strong. Oyabun-controlled associations hold
wide fishing rights, forcing individual fishermen into the inferior kobun position.

"Public Safety Division, G-2.—Gangs in the cities are divided
into three groups—gamblers, strong-arm men and street-stall
associations. 'The police are severely hampered by the fact that
the kobun are often well armed, and because political pressure
often prevents effective police action. Furthermore, the police
are involved, being paid off by the system. In many cases, the
only way that the police can arrest a criminal at large in an
area controlled by an oyabun is to ask the oyabun to turn over
the criminal. Detailed investigations indicate the oyabun-kobun
system extends into politics, controls black market activities,
controls the price of every-day commodities, controls the flow
of goods through regular channels, and performs local governmental functions in the issuance of licences and the collection
of taxes.[13]

I think it impossible for Allied officers in Japan to assess
with any accuracy the strength and significance of "underground" organization. There are too few officers with a
mastery of the language to make possible the study of
more than a few small patches of Japanese life. There is

[13] *Nippon Times,* November 27, 1947.

the traditional reluctance of Japanese, however friendly, to take foreigners into their confidence on "purely Japanese" questions.

The military government teams are more closely in touch with what is actually happening in the prefectures and villages of Japan than any other group of Occupation officers. GHQ must rely mainly on their reports for its knowledge of how the directives issued in Tokyo affect the lives of ordinary people. These teams contain many intelligent and enthusiastic people, and in some areas they are doing good and notable work. But in number and in training the military government teams, through no fault of their own, find themselves quite unequal to their task. Military government has a total strength of about 2,500 Americans. That means that each American military government officer or enlisted man is responsible for the surveillance and supervision of over 30,000 Japanese. Few of these officers have more than a nodding acquaintance with the language, and most teams, therefore, rely on local Japanese for all interpretation and translation. This places an extraordinarily heavy strain on the interpreter's loyalty to his American employers. It would not be surprising if patriotism and the ties that bind him to his relatives and local leaders sometimes produced an elastic linguistic conscience. Most members of the military government teams have had little or no previous experience in problems of government, and there is a very high rate of turnover in their ranks. During 1946 the rate of replacement was reported to be about 90 per cent.

In these circumstances, it is clear that "revelations" about the Japanese underground are exceedingly hard to check with any precision. It must, however, be accepted that powerful underground organizations exist, and that their activities enormously complicate Allied efforts to control Japan through the established Japanese Government. For the Government's power is everywhere limited by these "hidden" forces.

The Bureaucracy

In the political life of Japan, from the Restoration of 1868 until the surrender of 1945, power was never the monopoly of a single group or organization. There was nothing, even in the war years, to parallel the one-party rule that existed in Germany under the Nazis or Italy under the Fascists. Final decisions in Japan were the product of the prevailing distribution of power between four groups—the armed forces, loosely called the militarists; the big business interests, the Zaibatsu; the political parties; and the bureaucrats. The Emperor was the fulcrum round which these groups revolved. Changes in policy could be traced to shifts in the continuously changing balance of these four bodies.

The Tojo period was one in which the militarist group enjoyed unusual strength, but, even at the height of his power, Tojo was compelled to make concessions to the other three elements, temporarily subordinate in the national coalition. The place of the bureaucrats in this four-power system was always strong. The Japanese public service has often been likened to a feudal guild for its exclusiveness and for the iron discipline it exercised over its members. Its responsibility to its political heads was generally nominal; it had its own policy, directed to strengthening its own entrenched interests; its senior members usually held key Cabinet posts, where they jostled for position with the other three groups.[14]

General MacArthur was aware that this feudal state machine, if left to itself, could sabotage all reforms. Its old rivals had fallen on evil days. The militarists were

[14] See the excellent article, "Japan as a Political Organism," by T. A. Bisson, *Pacific Affairs*, Vol. XVII, No. 4.

largely discredited and their organizations dissolved. The Zaibatsu was forced to lie low. The political parties were rent with discords. This might be the great opportunity for the bureaucrats to achieve unchallenged predominance. And, in fact, I think, of all the four former groups, the bureaucrats have undoubtedly had most success in retaining their power. It could hardly have been otherwise. It is true that the purge has skimmed off most of those senior public servants who had blatantly and overtly supported Japan's ultra-nationalism and aggression. But the purged officials are only a small percentage of the public service. The whole process of government would have been brought to a standstill if the purge had been applied too drastically.[15]

GHQ has sponsored ambitious and comprehensive measures for the reform of the bureaucratic system; among them is the decision to abolish the Home Ministry and decentralize administration. Some of these measures have already been "processed" by the Diet and are now law. But the Japanese have the gift of postponing, for "regrettable, unavoidable and unforeseen circumstances," the carrying out of these reforms. And they have a gift for "democratizing" an institution by changing its name and reshuffling its personnel without changing its nature. Hence the real reform of the public service is likely to be one of the toughest tasks of the future.

Conclusion

To sum up these reflections on the Japanese instruments of Occupation policy: It was decided that we should

15 On December 10, 1947, the Japanese Government announced that the public service purge could be regarded for all practical purposes as completed by December 7. Central and local screening committees had examined the records of 663,989 officials and "designated 6,965 as falling under the purge directive." (*Nippon Times*, December 11, 1947.)

use the Emperor and the Japanese administrative machinery and, most important, that SCAP should control Japan, not by direct military government, but through the Japanese Cabinet. Since April 1946, the Cabinet has had the majority support of a Diet elected by universal suffrage. But both free elections in April 1946 and April 1947 have produced strong conservative majorities. The conservative parties have won their support from the industrialists and businessmen, from farmers and fishermen, from the black marketeers and from those who have assets to sell. These are the people profiting from the inflation. Such people stubbornly resist the introduction of economic controls which would deprive them of their chance to exploit the present situation. It is easy to say that General MacArthur should force the Japanese Government to adopt the control measures necessary for economic efficiency and social justice. But no Japanese Government has been able or willing to put such measures into effect.

The decision to work through a freely-elected Japanese Government has been the main key to the Occupation. It is likely to be equally important after the peace settlement. It may, therefore, be worth while to examine the implications of this decision more carefully. These implications can be brought out clearly by considering the problem that has faced SCAP, in its efforts to provide food for Japan.

When I arrived in Japan in April 1946, this food question appeared to be the major problem facing GHQ and the Japanese Government. It was repeatedly stated that millions of Japanese were faced with the threat of starvation between April and September. On April 27, 1946, the Economic and Scientific Section of GHQ issued a report in which it estimated that for the five months, May-September, there would be only enough indigenous food to give the rationed population (about 44 million), from both official and unofficial sources, an average of 471 calories a day. Yet it was believed necessary to provide a minimum of 1,550 calories a day to prevent disease and unrest, which would endanger the Occupation forces and frustrate the purposes of the Occupation. On the basis of these estimates, SCAP requested authority to import 2,600,000 tons of food in rice equivalents. The Japanese Government had asked for imports of over three million tons.

In actuality, because of world shortages, only about 600,000 tons of rice equivalents were imported from May through October. This was less than one-quarter of the quantity SCAP had requested. But it seems clear that throughout this period the average consumption by the rationed population was between 1,500 and 1,800 calories a day. The greatest shortage was in August and Tokyo was one of the most poorly supplied areas, yet a SCAP report, "Food Situation During the First Year of the Occupation," estimated that average consumption in Tokyo in August was 1,828 calories a day.

This food question shows clearly the three great difficulties and dangers produced by SCAP's dependence on the Japanese Government. First, GHQ has to rely on the Japanese Government for its information. Japanese official statistics are notoriously inaccurate. This is partly due to inefficiency, but in many cases there are excellent reasons for deliberate concealment or falsehood. There was a strong temptation to farmers to underestimate their production, since whatever stocks they could hold back after delivering their quota to the Government could be eaten by their own families, used for barter, or sold at very high black-market prices. There was a strong temptation for the Government to underestimate home production, in the effort to get large imports. And GHQ was forced to work on the Japanese figures, because, at least in 1946, it did not have the resources to make any effective independent survey of the indigenous food available.

By 1947 the small, but very efficient, Natural Resources Section of GHQ was in a much better position to detect falsities in Japanese reports, but was still dependent on these reports in many ways. The colossal errors in the SCAP estimate of the food situation in 1946 remain an outstanding example of the risks involved in relying on Japanese official information.

Second, the food question shows the frustrations involved in depending on the Japanese Government's administrative machinery. In 1946 there was enough home-produced food in Japan to avert any starvation if the food produced had been properly collected and equitably distributed. It would be foolish to expect full efficiency and justice. Japan is not the only country with a black market, or where farmers try to evade Government controls. Yet this maldistribution of the available food was so gross that it was hard to credit the Japanese Government with even a reasonable minimum of efficiency and earnestness in its food administration.

Thirdly, when SCAP, in its desire to avert disease and unrest, due to food shortages, imported food from the United States for distribution by the Japanese Government, it was unavoidable that it should thereby give political aid to the conservative forces on which the Government relied for its existence. Food shortages—irrespective of the cause—produce political unrest. The mass demonstrations in Tokyo in May 1946 were clamors by city wage-earners for more food. The distribution of imported food helped the Government to avoid some of the political penalties of its own inefficiency. Food is a political weapon. We must have an established authority for the control of Japan. If we decide that this authority shall be a duly-elected Japanese Government, then we must protect that Government's authority. And if, for whatever reasons, the Government depends on conservative forces for its continuance, we cannot support the Government against "lawlessness" without thereby indirectly supporting the conservatives against their political opponents.

4. DEMILITARIZATION

~~~~~~

IN TOKYO IN THE SUMMER OF 1947 I WAS TALK-
ing privately with an American general about Australia
and Japan. He was anxious to know, for one thing, why
Australia seemed to be having difficulty in providing
Japan with the quantities and types of wool she had asked
for. I was trying to explain Australia's difficulties, when
my friend cut in sharply. "When, for Pete's sake, will you
seven million Australians realize the importance of having seventy million allies in this country?" The general's
views were clear-cut and logical. He felt that Australia
was thinking and acting as though it were still 1945, not
1947. He deplored the two years' time lag. In 1945 Japan
was a hated and still-dangerous enemy. In 1947 it was the
general belief that there was only one enemy, the Soviet
Union. He could not quite understand Australia's slow-
ness in adapting herself to the changed situation.

I believe that we must face the question the general put
if we are to be realistic about security in the Pacific. We
must be clear whether we still hold to the objectives we
stated in 1945, or whether, in the light of the changing
situation, we want to amend or abandon them. What precisely do we mean by the demilitarization of Japan, and
what exactly do we want to do about it? This question
has three sides. First, physical or material demilitariza-

tion, which includes the demobilization of the Japanese armed forces and the destruction or removal of arms and ammunition. Second, economic demilitarization, depriving Japan of primary and secondary war industries. It is clear, for example, that during the 1930's the feverish development of the steel and shipbuilding industries was mainly for war purposes, and unnecessary to provide the peaceful needs of the Japanese people. Third, there is the problem of moral or psychological disarmament. Do we want a Japan that is not merely temporarily unable to make war, but also permanently unwilling to make war?

Physical Demilitarization

We seemed to be quite clear about what we wanted in 1945. In the Potsdam Declaration it was agreed in paragraph 9 that "The Japanese military forces, after being completely disarmed, shall be permitted to return to their homes with the opportunity to lead peaceful and productive lives." In the United States Initial Post-Surrender Directive it was provided in Part I (b) that "Japan will be completely disarmed and demilitarized . . ." and in Part III that "Disarmament and demilitarization are the primary tasks of the Military Occupation and shall be carried out promptly and with determination. . . . Japan is not to have an army, navy, air force, secret police organization or any civil aviation. Japan's ground, air and naval forces shall be disarmed and disbanded, and the Japanese Imperial General Headquarters, the General Staff and all secret police organizations shall be dissolved. Military and naval material, military and naval vessels and military and naval installations, and military, naval and civilian aircraft shall be surrendered and shall be disposed of as required by the Supreme Commander." Let me first give my impressions of the progress of this program.

Demobilization

The demobilization of the Japanese fighting forces has on the whole been carried out very smoothly and efficiently by the Japanese High Command. This work was at first entrusted to the First (Army) and Second (Navy) Demilitarization Ministries. Early in 1946 it was seemingly felt that the retention of these Ministries was undesirable, even though their ostensible purpose was now restricted to demobilization. In June 1946 they were replaced by a Demobilization Board, with Mr. Shidehara, a civilian, as head. The Demobilization Board, however, was divided into two bureaus. The first was headed by Yoshio Kamitsuki, the former First Mobilization Vice-Minister, and the second by Vice-Admiral Minoru Maedo. In October 1947 SCAP made a further change in this organization. The Second, or Navy, Bureau was abolished, since the demobilization of sailors had been virtually completed, and the work of the First Bureau was transferred to the Welfare Ministry.

These organizational changes were an interesting example of the way in which it was so readily assumed during the Occupation that a change of name meant a change of nature. It has been pointed out in several meetings of the Allied Council by General Derevyanko that the officers in charge of demobilization were former high-ranking General Staff officers. These officers seemed to carry on their work unperturbed by the changes in the names of their organizations. It was natural and inevitable that SCAP should rely on senior staff officers to demobilize the Japanese fighting forces. I think it highly probable, nevertheless, that the admirals and generals who demobilized their forces so smoothly will have taken every care to ensure that remobilization may be carried out with equal smoothness, if this should become practicable or necessary. Some of the members of these demobilization bureaus were under suspicion for war crimes, and many, if not all, consistently sabotaged the efforts of Allied prosecutors to pick up war crimes suspects. It may have indicated some uneasiness in SCAP about the activities of the demobilization bureaus that, in directing the abolition of the Second Bureau, SCAP ordered the Japanese Government to "undertake a complete and comprehensive study and survey . . . of all boards, bureaus and agencies of the Japanese Government now engaged in, or charged with, responsibility for demobilization, repatriation, investigation or research of matters pertaining to the war or persons serving or connected with Japanese military organizations.

During 1946 it was reported that the destruction of Japanese arms and ammunition had been completed. There can be little doubt that this work was carried out effectively insofar as it was directed to destroying Japan's actual military resources. It has since become clear, however, that the Japanese authorities have astutely evaded SCAP directives on the disposal of large quantities of army stores. It was only in November 1947 that GHQ officers became aware of the secret disposal, through illegal channels, of something like 100 billion yen worth of war goods which had been accumulated during the war in Osaka arsenal, Japan's largest war goods depot. This discovery was given great prominence in the Japanese press, and was described as "the biggest scandal in Japanese history." It is further evidence of the way in which GHQ, through shortage of skilled personnel, was unable to keep itself informed about the actual course of events in Japan.

Demobilization was closely linked with repatriation. At the time of the surrender there were more than three million servicemen, and another three million Japanese civilians, abroad. The repatriation of these people was carried out with great promptitude and efficiency. The United States provided the ships, and they were mainly operated by the Japanese. I would fully concur with the official claim that this repatriation has been one of the most efficient mass migration movements ever organized. There has, however, been one major difficulty. Russia seemed very reluctant to release the Japanese, nearly a million in number, whom they held in custody in North Korea, Manchuria and Eastern Siberia. This provided fuel for bitter exchanges in the Allied Council between the American and Russian members. However, in December 1946, Russia agreed to send these people home at the rate of 50,000 each month. This undertaking seemed to be carried out satisfactorily until December 1947, when Russia announced that it would be necessary to suspend repatriation for about four months, owing to the climatic conditions in the northern ports. The Soviet authorities reminded SCAP of a clause in the agreement of December 1946, by which both parties reserved the right temporarily to suspend repatriation if unforeseen circumstances arose.

It was inevitable that the Soviet announcement should have aroused SCAP's indignation and suspicion. SCAP pointed out that in the winter months of 1946–47 Russia had apparently not experienced the same climatic difficulties in carrying out the program. General MacArthur offered to send ice-breakers to the Soviet's northern ports to make a path for the repatriation ships, and alternatively suggested that the repatriates might be brought to warm-water ports. He pointed out that there were still more than 800,000 Japanese in Soviet-controlled areas, and he undertook to provide the means for bringing them back to Japan in five months. This offer was coldly received by the Soviet representative in Tokyo.

This repatriation question is actively exacerbating

American-Russian relations. SCAP officers claim, and, I believe, on good evidence, that the Soviet authorities are trying to indoctrinate selected groups of Japanese in their custody with militant Communist convictions, in the hope that when they return home they will sow the seeds of Communism throughout Japan. In an effort to meet and control this movement, GHQ has called in the help of former members of the Kempeitai and Japanese secret police to help them in "processing" repatriates. Naturally, the Japanese Government is gratified that American authorities should value the collaboration of their own experts in maintaining a common front against Communist infiltration. The Japanese are well aware that, while American Intelligence Officers concentrated their attention during the early months of the Occupation on the investigation of Japanese suspected of militarism or ultra-nationalism, by 1947 these officers were almost wholly pre-occupied with the investigation of Communist activities.

Economic Demobilization and Reparations

In Paragraph XI of the Potsdam Declaration it was provided that "Japan shall be permitted to maintain such industries as will sustain her economy and permit the exaction of just reparations in kind, but not those which would enable her to rearm for war." In the Initial Post-Surrender Policy the economic demilitarization of Japan was laid down in Part IV:

The existing economic basis of Japanese military strength must be destroyed and not be permitted to revive.

Therefore, a program will be enforced containing the following elements, among others: the immediate cessation and future prohibition of production of all goods designed for the equipment, maintenance or use of any military force or establishment; the imposition of a ban upon any specialized facilities for the production or repair of implements of war, includ-

ing naval vessels and all forms of aircraft; the institution of a
system of inspection and control over selected elements in Japanese economic activity to prevent concealed or disguised military preparations; the elimination in Japan of those selected
industries or branches of production whose chief value to Japan
is in preparing for war; the prohibition of specialized research
and instruction directed to the development of warmaking
powers; and the limitation of the size and character of Japan's
heavy industries to its future peaceful requirements, and restriction of Japanese merchant shipping to the extent required
to accomplish the objectives of demilitarization. The eventual
disposition of those existing production facilities within Japan,
which are to be eliminated in accord with this program, as between conversion to other uses, transfer abroad, and scrapping,
will be determined after inventory. Pending decision, facilities
readily convertible for civilian production should not be destroyed, except in emergency situations.

The Far Eastern Commission's Basic Post-Surrender
Policy, published June 19, 1947, gives substantial support
to the aims of 1945.

This program presented the Allies with several nice
problems. At what level should the Japanese economy be
sustained? What would be a reasonable standard of living
for the Japanese people? How were their needs to be balanced against just claims for reparations? How far was it
possible to separate the industries necessary to provide
peaceful needs from those that were mainly concerned
with the provision of war potential?

The answers we give to these questions will depend
mainly not on judgments of facts, but on judgments of
value. They will be the product of our underlying moral
and political attitudes. Should we try to sustain Japan's
economy at a level that will only allow Japanese to exist,
or at a level that will enable Japan to make important
contributions to the economic development of East and
Southeast Asia? And how are we to balance the needs of
the Japanese against the needs of the Chinese or Siamese?

What the Japanese need will depend on what we want them to do. If they are to staff "the workshop of East Asia" they will need much more than if they are merely to have a subsistence economy. The role we assign to Japan will depend in turn on how we think our own national interests can best be served in the Far East.

Until the end of 1945 Allied thinking about economic disarmament and reparations was greatly influenced by wartime emotions. It seemed just and desirable to transfer a number of Japan's industrial plants, particularly in primary and secondary war industries, to the countries which her armies had devastated. This would serve the double purpose of disarming Japan and helping restore the damaged economies of countries like China and the Philippines. It was in this atmosphere that the Pauley Reparations Commission carried out its work in Japan in November-December, 1945. After a quick survey of Japanese industry, Mr. Pauley recommended a comprehensive program of interim reparations removals, including the following:

(1) Half the capacity for manufacturing machine tools.
(2) All equipment in army and naval arsenals, in the aircraft industry, in ball- and roller-bearing industries and in plants making aircraft engines.
(3) All equipment and accessories in 20 shipyards, if not needed to repair shipping essential to the Occupation.
(4) All steel capacity over 2.5 million tons a year.
(5) Half of coal-burning electric plants.
(6) All contact-process sulphuric acid plants, four large solvay process soda-ash plants, and 20 out of 41 large modern plants for caustic soda.
(7) All capacity for producing magnesium and alumina and for reducing alumina to aluminum (except facilities for processing scrap) and all finishing mills.

These recommendations were carefully studied by the Far Eastern Commission. Its deliberations produced two main sets of policy decisions. First, it reached an agreement on certain questions of principle. It agreed that the peaceful needs of Japan should be defined as the level of production necessary to give the standard of living that was enjoyed by the Japanese people during the years 1930–34. It designated 1950 as the year in which the Japanese might reasonably be expected to recover this standard. The FEC went on to lay down rules for selecting interim reparations. First preference was to be given to primary and secondary war industries. Priority should be given to plants owned by Zaibatsu concerns. In this way, reparations and economic disarmament would help to contribute to SCAP's program for domestic economic reform. Secondly, the FEC prescribed the maximum production levels which the Japanese should be permitted to retain in certain key industries.[1] Its findings were a good deal more generous to Japan than Mr. Pauley's earlier recommendations. Mr. Pauley recommended that Japan's steel production should be limited to 2½ millions tons a year. The FEC would allow 3½ million tons. Mr. Pauley provided for a Japanese merchant fleet of one and a half million tons gross tonnage. The FEC raised this to three million tons. Mr. Pauley would have prohibited the production of aluminum, magnesium and ball and roller bearings. He would have allowed 12,500 tons of nitric acid to be produced each year. The FEC recommended a nitric acid production limit of 30,000 tons a year, and provided for the manufacture of limited quantities of aluminum, magnesium and ball and roller bearings. The FEC has carried on its deliberations under increasing pressure from the United States to scale down reparations.

In 1947 Mr. Clifford S. Strike took over the study of

[1] *Activities of the Far Eastern Commission.* Report by the Secretary-General. U. S. Department of State, Far Eastern Series 24, Washington, D. C.

the reparations question, under the auspices of the United States War Department. It is clear that Mr. Strike decided that the FEC had not gone nearly far enough in its downward revision of Mr. Pauley's recommendations. "We must," he has written, "in my judgment, immediately take steps to repeal those rulings of the Far Eastern Commission which make it impossible for Japan to become a self-supporting nation." [2]

It is not necessary to review reparations discussions in greater detail to recognize that the dominant trend has been to scale them down to the minimum, perhaps to abandon them altogether. The United States has taken the lead in this movement, sometimes in opposition to protracted resistance by other Allies. During the last twelve months authoritative statements about reparations in American official circles in Tokyo and Washington have all pressed the case for their reduction or abolition. It is pointed out that, since the whole world is economically interdependent, the real job of the victors is to restore the economies of the defeated countries, in order that they may be able once again to make their distinctive contributions to the economic welfare of the world. In the case of Japan, it is pointed out that much of the industrial equipment coveted as reparations is obsolescent by Western standards and would hamper rather than help those Allied countries anxious to develop or extend their industries efficiently. It is pointed out that the removal of heavy industries is uneconomic and impracticable, partly because of the physical difficulties in their transfer and partly because they are so closely geared to associated industries that it is impossible to regard them as independent and transferable units. The countries that clamor most insistently for heavy industries are usually those that lack the highly-organized industrial context which gives

[2] *The American Magazine*, September 1947.

these industries their economic value. It is usually con-
ceded that the light industries, such as textiles, are much
easier to transfer. They are not so dependent on associated
industries, and demand less technical experience for their
successful operation. Moreover, they produce with relative
ease and simplicity the kind of consumption goods so
sorely needed by the countries of East Asia. Yet American
official opinion produces powerful arguments against the
transfer of these industries. It is pointed out that only by
an early restoration of the exports of these industries can
Japan earn the foreign exchange necessary to buy food
and raw materials. It is to these industries that the American taxpayer must look first if he is eager that Japan
should repay as soon as possible her heavy bills for American food and commodity goods. To strip Japan of her
light industries would be to deprive her of the chance to
become solvent. Lastly, it is argued that, if we are deeply
concerned with the needs of those East Asian countries
that suffered so much from Japan's aggression, the most
effective way to help them is to enable the Japanese to
provide the things they need. If Manchuria and China
and Korea will send food and raw materials to Japan,
Japan will be able to provide them with the consumption
goods much more rapidly than they could hope to do for
themselves. It is as Asia's workshop that Japan can help
Asia most. On all these counts, then, the case for reparations and for the economic disarmament of Japan should
be reconsidered.

It would be foolish to make too hasty and critical a reaction to this trend in American opinion. It certainly
represents a significant change in American foreign policy.
In 1945 the great emphasis was on reparations and disarmament. Today the trend is to subordinate both to the
restoration of Japan's prosperity.

The first reason for this change is the steady worsening

of Soviet-American relations during the last two years.
The second reason is the changes which have taken place
in America's relations with China during the same period.
In 1945 the Soviet Union was still an ally. Today the
whole world is divided by the clash of interests and policies between America and Russia. America's growing fear
of Russia makes her increasingly anxious to find strong
and faithful allies. In East Asia, as in Europe, the end of
the war produced an immense increase in Russia's stra-
tegical strength. Not only were her frontiers pushed east-
wards in Sakhalin and the Kuriles, but her influence in
Mongolia, Manchuria and North China steadily increased.
In Korea, the Russian and American forces glower at each
other across the 38th parallel. In these circumstances the
United States has never had greater need for a good neighbor in the Far East. In 1945 it was hoped that China
would form this "point of stability," but China has been
a tragic disappointment. Not all of America's direct aid to
China, nor the indirect aid given through such organizations as UNRRA; not all the diplomatic power of General
Marshall, whose vast projects were underwritten by Mr.
Truman; neither warnings nor inducements prevailed to
give China economic stability or political unity. And so
China has been replaced by Japan as the power which,
with American support, is assigned the task of stabilizing
the Far East. Seldom can a defeated nation have had such
an important role allotted to it so soon after its defeat.

These are issues which involve the whole world and not
only the Far East. In relation to Japan they call forth
some important observations.

It should be clearly recognized that Japan's present economic difficulties are mainly the result of the failures of
her own Government. In comparison with other defeated
nations, like Germany, and, indeed, in comparison with
many nations that were nominally victors in World War

II, Japan's economic position since the surrender has been fortunate. Even during 1946 she produced enough food in her home islands to avert starvation. If a small number of Japanese died from starvation in 1946, that was not because there was not enough food in Japan to save them, but because the Japanese Government has been unable or unwilling to prevent it being recklessly consumed in the first few months after harvest by people with unlimited money to spend. The food crisis of the Occupation has been mainly a crisis of distribution, not of production. Other commodities have been equally mismanaged. At the surrender Japan had considerable stores of consumer-foods and industrial materials, but a big proportion of these were illegally transferred by Army and Navy heads into the hands of the Zaibatsu, who proceeded to sell them on the black market.[3] At the same time, industrial production remained at about 30 per cent of the prewar level. This failure to produce is attributed by Japanese industrialists to uncertainty about reparations and the prospects of importing raw materials. But these uncertainties do little to explain the general inertia and the failure to use industrial capacity and unemployed labor in the industries unaffected by reparations. Japan's failure to make a determined attempt to restore her economy cannot be explained in purely economic terms. Comparisons with other countries make that clear.

There is an apparent contrast between the countries of Western Europe (including Italy, also a former enemy, subject to reparations), which came out of World War II with great physical destruction, and in the course of little more than one year restored their industrial production to between two-thirds and four-fifths of the prewar levels, and Japan, whose industries have been operating for months at around 30 per cent of their 1931–33 level, despite their more limited damage. In a

[3] Cf. T. A. Bisson's "Reparations and Reform in Japan," *Far Eastern Survey*, December 17, 1947.

world economy dominated by coal shortages, it is significant to note that—on the basis of prewar levels—a one-half supply of coal in Western European countries is maintaining a two-thirds or four-fifths level of industrial production, whereas Japanese industries operate at less than one-third level, despite a two-thirds or larger supply of coal.[4]

In the face of this hoarding and black-marketing of scarce commodities, and of the hold-up of industrial production, Japan's Governments have persisted with reckless budgetary policies which have greatly aggravated the inflation.

This is the background against which we should try to assess the Japanese complaints about the overwhelming burden of Occupation costs, and the pleas for foreign loans and credits. The Japanese Government has shown a singular unwillingness to undertake the kind of internal reforms which might have added strength to its appeals for external aid.

For my part, I am unable to escape the conclusion that the economic and financial policy of the Japanese Government has been carefully calculated to frustrate the Allied aims of 1945. The facade of cooperation and compliance is part of this policy. The Japanese political leaders had studied carefully the stratagems pursued by Germany after World War I. Overt resistance was ruled out, but short of that they were determined to make it difficult for the Allies to collect more than token reparations, and to make it unpolitic for them to persist with the program of economic disarmament. It was a risky game to play because, although inflation brought great immediate profit to some, it held the risk of producing a total economic disaster. But Japanese leaders have come increasingly to count on the United States to protect them from that disaster. They have come to feel sure that America's fear of Russia would

[4] Frank M. Tamagna, *Politics and Economics in Far Eastern Reconstruction.* Institute of Pacific Relations, Paper No. 5, New York, 1947.

force her to prevent economic collapse in Japan. The Japanese came to feel that they were indispensable to the United States, and could, therefore, put a high price on their indispensability.

It would seem that Japan's leaders have been very successful. General MacArthur's declaration of March 1947, that they must be saved from "economic strangulation" by the Allies, was a sign-board to victory. Mr.Clifford Strike's conclusions and the reported proposal that Congress would be asked in 1948 for a grant of 500 million dollars for Japan's industrial and trade recovery, together with a larger relief appropriation, suggested that General MacArthur's projects for Japan's restoration will be carried out.

It is important to recognize that the Japan now asking so successfully that reparations be reduced to a minimum, that the cost of Occupation should be pruned, that the implications of economic disarmament be re-examined, that foreign loans and credits should be given her, is in all fundamentals the same Japan that we knew between 1931 and 1945. Can we be sure that, in emphasizing the role of industrial leadership for which Japan is equipped, and in helping establish her as the "workshop of East Asia," and as the "point of stability in the Far East," we are not helping her to re-establish that economic imperialism which in the war years we spent so much blood and treasure in an effort to destroy? It would be strange if the Allies, under United States leadership, were now to help Japan achieve those ambitions which she failed to achieve by force of arms.

I am not arguing that Japan should be kept economically weak. It is true that an economically healthy Japan, even a prosperous Japan, is essential to the economic health of East Asia. It is true that access to overseas markets and raw materials is essential to Japan's economic health, and that the restoration of Japan's foreign trade will depend, in its early stages, on substantial foreign credits. All this is agreed.

The crucial question is whether, in existing circumstances, there is any reasonable assurance that Allied economic aid will restore economic health to Japan. Is it not more likely that Allied concessions and credits will be used, not for the welfare of the Japanese people, but that the old guard, which still controls Japan's economy, will use its new resources to do what it formerly did: maintain a semi-feudalism at home and extend an economic imperialism abroad? Unless internal reform is made the condition of external aid, it is likely not only to fail in its avowed economic purpose, but to enable Japan's rulers to frustrate economic and social reforms. If SCAP has not been able to prevent the old and the new Zaibatsu from flagrantly misappropriating available resources for selfish and sectional advantage during the Occupation, what precautions are the Allies taking to prevent continued misappropriation when the Occupation is over? That is why it is dangerous to make economic concessions and grant economic aid unless this policy is tightly geared with an effective program of economic and social reform. Otherwise what purports to be economic aid to the Japanese people may be a disguised subsidy to Japanese reactionaries.

Moral Demilitarization

The psychological atmosphere in Japan everywhere suggests that the armed forces are not dead, but dormant. The Japanese are acutely aware of the hostility between the United States and Russia. This clash of interests between the two Great Powers sets the tone of everything that happens in Japan. The restoration of the Japanese fighting forces in some form or other is sympathetically discussed at Allied social gatherings, and this is well known to the Japanese. It was, therefore, not surprising that early in 1947 the

Japanese Foreign Office informally sounded out Allied representatives on the prospects of being allowed a standing army of 100,000 men and a small air force. It is sometimes said that the Japanese have come to hate war and their war leaders. I think it would be more correct to say that they hate losing a war, and are glad to repudiate the particular military leaders they blame for the defeat. It was an Englishman, Jeremy Bentham, who said that vice was a miscalculation of chances. The Japanese today disown Hideki Tojo and his friends, not for being militarists, but for their blundering miscalculation of chances.

It would probably be false to assume that Japan's present leaders desire another war. They have too fresh a memory of the risks. Yet they are eager to exploit the atmosphere of war, and in particular the American fear and suspicion of Russia and Communism. It is often remarked that Japan, under the Occupation, has become very pro-American. I do not believe that the Japanese at bottom are either pro-American or pro-Russian. They are pro-Japanese. In the present situation it is elementary common sense to play along with the United States. Two years ago the primary political intention was to please General MacArthur, in the hope that Japan might thereby achieve a gentle and short Occupation. In the last two years the emphasis has changed, but not the aim. The primary political purpose today is to qualify for American aid in terms of the Truman doctrine. A senior Japanese diplomat summed up the situation this way: "Well, we Japanese have been fighting Communism in our part of the world since 1931, and it is nice to know that the United States is now awake up to the importance of helping us in the job."

It will be recalled that in the new Constitution Japan renounces forever resort to war and abolishes forever her armed forces.

In its preamble the Japanese Constitution declares:

Desiring peace for all time and fully conscious of the high
ideals controlling human relationships now stirring mankind,
we have determined to rely for our security and survival upon
the justice and good faith of the peace-loving peoples of the
world.

And Article IX of the Constitution reads:

War, as a sovereign right of the nation, and the threat or use
of force, is forever renounced as a means of settling disputes
with other nations.

The maintenance of land, sea and air forces, as well as other
war potential, will never be authorized. The right of belligerency of the state will never be recognized.

There are two interesting questions to ask about these
parts of the Constitution: What do the Japanese feel about
them, and what do Americans, as the representatives of the
Allies, feel about them?

I think there can be no doubt about what the Japanese
feel. They do not take this renunciation of war and of
armed forces with the least seriousness. During my stay in
Japan I noticed three phases of response when, in talking
to influential Japanese, I sought their reactions. In April
or May of 1946 the reaction was usually coy and pious. "We
rely for our safety on the high ideals of the United Nations." Some months later the reaction changed: "Well, it
was made clear to us that we could not have any armed
forces, and that we would win favor by 'voluntarily' re-
nouncing them. That seemed the sensible thing to do." And
the last phase I noticed showed another change of emphasis. "Japan is of such vital strategic importance to the
United States that we can rely on the Americans to defend
us. It is, therefore, unnecessary for us to have our own
armed forces. Of course, if the United States would wish

us to share the burden of defending this area, we should be glad to do so, provided we are granted the means."

From reports I have had since I left Japan it seems that the Japanese attitude towards demilitarization and pacifism has continued to harden. I think the spirit in which Tojo and his fellow prisoners presented their defense before the International Military Tribunal for the Far East, and the Japanese reactions to these defense pleas, strongly suggest that Japanese penitence is not deep or durable. One of the most interesting sidelights on Japanese psychology under the Occupation is the way in which the major war crime suspects have gradually been regaining a place in public esteem. At the opening of the major war trial in mid-1946, the general tendency among the Japanese I met was to disown the accused. The Japanese were still shocked by defeat, and it may have been a natural impulse of self-defense to offer up the Tojo group as scapegoats. But as time went on and relations between America and Russia grew worse, Japanese were not so eager to repudiate their former war leaders. Had not those leaders after all been waging a war against Communism in the Far East since 1931? No doubt, it was wrong and foolish of them to go to war with the United States, but if the United States at that time failed to appreciate the menace of Communism in East Asia, it was hard for Japan's leaders to avoid war. That was the trend of Japanese talk.

It was, therefore, not surprising that Tojo's defense seemed to win a respectful response throughout Japan, however reticent in expression. The *Nippon Times,* which has close, if unofficial, links with the Japanese Foreign Office, gave ten columns of its four-page issue on December 27, 1947, to reporting Tojo's statement. The six leading Japanese-language dailies in Tokyo gave most of the front page to the Tojo story and played up his contention that the war had been one of self-defense forced on Japan. None of these papers brought out the angle emphasized by most Allied reporters: that Tojo's affidavit was reminiscent of Japan's wartime propaganda. Tojo took little trouble to conceal the note of quiet defiance. He said, *inter alia:*

> May I reiterate that the policy of Japan, and certainly the choice of her duly-constituted officials of state, involved neither aggression nor exploitation. Step by step . . . our country finally was brought face to face with stark reality, and to us, who at that period were weighted with the duty of deciding the fate of our nation, a war of self-existence was our only alternative. . . . I believe firmly and will contend to the last that it was a war of self-defense and in no manner a violation of presently-acknowledged international law.

I believe that that faithfully expresses the beliefs still held by at least ninety per cent of the Japanese people.

For some time the Japanese Foreign Office has had senior officers engaged in formulating Japan's aims at the Peace Conference. Towards the end of 1947 a Foreign Office document fell into the hands of the press. This document suggested that the northern Kuriles, which were given to the U.S.S.R. as part of the Yalta Agreement, should be claimed by the United Nations and put under trusteeship. The document did not disclose whether Japan's eagerness to join the United Nations as soon as the Treaty comes into force was partly due to a desire to qualify as the trustee for this area. The document went on to indicate that Japan should resist by all means in her power the setting up of any Allied Supervisory Commission to ensure the fulfillment of the Treaty. If some Allied Commission were unavoidable, Japan was to push for a council of the heads of the diplomatic services of the Big Four, and the functions of this council were, if possible, to be limited to "observation." Japan should ask for a merchant marine of four million tons and some aircraft for "control patrol work." Most significant of all, it was urged that SCAP directives issued during the Occupation should, when the Treaty comes into force, become null and void, and Japanese legislation giving effect to these directives should be subject to repeal in the ordinary way.

It is not possible to know whether the policy set forth in this Foreign Office document had been examined and accepted by the Japanese Government or whether it represented merely a list of proposals prepared by senior officials. Apparently GHQ wished to play down the document. It was reported that General MacArthur had not seen it and did not propose to read it.[5] Nevertheless, it gives an interesting glimpse of how some members of the "purged" bureaucracy feel about the Occupation and the peace settlement.

[5] *Nippon Times,* December 14, 1947.

5. "DEMOCRATIZATION": ECONOMIC

Rural Land Reform

THE EMANCIPATION OF THE PEASANT MUST be the first and most important step in any program for the economic and spiritual emancipation of the Japanese people. Nearly half of the Japanese people live in farm households. Their importance lies not only in their numbers, but in the fact that they represent what is most backward in Japanese society. Much more than any other class, they show the spirit and the habits of feudalism. No democracy can be built on a foundation of agricultural serfdom.

It is true that at the surrender the farmers found themselves in a peculiarly favorable position. Their homes had not been destroyed and the countryside was undamaged. They had always been able to keep enough of the food they grew to feed themselves, and after the surrender the Government was unable or unwilling to enforce rice deliveries. So the farmers ate their fill and still managed to sell a proportion of their produce on the black market at fabulous prices. It was a curious reversal of the traditional situation. But it had all the marks of being temporary, since every ton of food imported weakened the farmer's bargaining position, and it was to be expected that in any restoration of Japan's foreign trade, food imports would play a prominent part. Moreover, the shortages of fertilizers, implements and consumer goods emphasized the artificial and precarious nature of this wave of comparative prosperity. Yet this period of high food prices did enable many owner-farmers to reduce or pay off immense burdens of debt, and it did give the more successful tenant farmers their first opportunity to buy land for themselves, if any could be made available at something like "normal" prewar values. It was a situation which in no way reduced the need for rural reform, but rather presented a favorable opportunity for the launching of a comprehensive program.

It was against this background that SCAP issued a directive on December 9, 1945, ordering the Japanese Government "to exterminate those pernicious ills which have long blighted the agrarian structure of a land where almost half the total population is engaged in husbandry." The directive went on to state that one of the "more malevolent" of those ills was that "more than three-fourths of the farmers in Japan are either partially or totally tenants, paying rentals amounting to half or more of their annual crops."

SCAP, therefore, ordered the Japanese Government to submit on or before March 15, 1946, a program of rural land reform which would do four things: (1) It was to provide for the transfer of the land owned by absentee owners to local residents who would themselves work the land. A great deal of agricultural land had fallen into the hands of businessmen, money lenders and others as a result of farmers' bankruptcy. SCAP wanted to restore the ownership of farms to farmers. (2) It was to provide means by which the tenants could buy land from non-operating owners at equitable rates. (3) It was to provide a method by which tenants could pay by small annual installments commensurate with their incomes. (4) It was to provide methods for prohibiting tenant buyers from being forced back into a tenancy status.

It should be kept in mind that there were four groups directly involved in this program. Absentee owners were those who lived outside the district and played no part in cultivation. "Non-operating" owners were those who lived in the district, but were "non-operating" to the extent that they left the cultivation of part or all of their land to tenants. Owner-tenants were those who worked as tenants for a landlord, in addition to working their own small parcels of land. Lastly, there were the "pure" or landless tenants.

In obedience to the SCAP directive, the Japanese Government duly submitted its reform program. Its proposals were submitted by SCAP for the advice of the Allied Council. I expressed the view that these proposals were very unsatisfactory and would fail to fulfill the aims of the SCAP directive for the following reasons:

(a) The average limit of five *cho* of tenant-cultivated land allowed per landowner was too high and would mean that 70 per cent or more of tenant land would not be available for purchase by tenants.

(b) The provision whereby "farm lands which, though being possessed by non-operators at present, are expected to be operated by the owner in the near future" would be excluded from transfer, would allow landlords a convenient means of defeating the reform.

(c) The proposed machinery of transfer of tenant land was cumbersome and against the interests of tenants. Direct negotiation between landlord and tenant favored the landlord, while the Local Rural Land Commission seemed to be weighted heavily in favor of the landlords' interests. The composition of Prefectural Rural Land Commissions was described in vague terms, and there was no evidence that the tenants' interests would be safeguarded at this level either.

(d) The expectation of the Japanese Government that 70 per cent of the purchase funds would be provided by the Government and 30 per cent by the tenants might mean that tenants who could afford to provide 30 per cent of the purchase price would be given preference over tenants who, though capable farmers, were unable to make this deposit.

(e) No provision was made for periodical reappraisement of the obligations of buyers to protect them against insolvency through falling land values.

(f) The subsidies of 220 yen per *tan* of paddy fields and 130 yen per *tan* of upland fields seemed to raise the total purchase price of lands too high. These prices would be nearly 100 per cent above prewar levels.

(g) Outright purchase would require heavy credit advances, which were undesirable in existing conditions of inflation, unbalanced budgets and monetary instability.

(h) A period of five years for the acquisition of the lands seemed to be unnecessarily long.

(i) No adequate provision was made for the checking of excessive rents or for written tenancy contracts specifying rent payable and length of tenure.[1]

I went on to submit to the Allied Council a ten-point program for rural land reform. The program was as follows:

1. *The maximum average area of tenant-cultivated land which any non-operating landowner may own should be reduced to one cho* (2.45 acres).

The maximum area of tenant-cultivated land which may be owned by any non-operating landowner determines principally the area of land which shall be subject to purchase by tenants. To illustrate this point, the following figures are estimates of the *maximum* amount of land which would be available for transfer with different areas of tenant land owned by non-operating landowners. They are rough estimates, since the data available will not permit very accu-

[1] Minutes of Allied Council for Japan, Sixth Meeting.

rate calculations. In practice the area actually realized
would almost certainly be less than these estimates.

Average maximum land owned by non-operating landowners (*cho*)	Estimated area of land available for transfer from non-operating landowners (000 *cho*)	Land available for transfer from absentee landowners (000 *cho*)	Total area available for transfer (000 *cho*)	Percentage of total tenant land
5	770	130	900	32
3	1100	130	1230	44
1	1800	130	1930	69
0.5	1900	130	2030	73

A maximum of one *cho* of tenant land for non-operating
landowners would probably make nearly 70 per cent of all
tenant land available for sale. The Japanese Government's
plan would free only 30 per cent or less. I suggest that one
cho would, on the average, provide a living for a Japanese
family. I feel it would be precipitous to advocate the abolition of tenancy, and so long as tenants remain it is important that they should have the right to work on an area
large enough to maintain a family.

2. *The maximum area which any landowner may own
should be three cho, on the average, for the Islands of
Honshu, Kyushu and Shikoku and 12 cho for Hokkaido.*

Only about 3 per cent of farms in Japan are three *cho*
and over, so that restriction of ownership to this area
would not cause fragmentation of the unit of cultivation
to the detriment of efficiency. On the other hand, the relatively small number of landowners (about 7½ per cent of
the total) who own three *cho* and over possess together
nearly 50 per cent of all cultivated land. Stipulation of a
maximum area of three *cho* would probably assure the
transference of approximately 1,000,000 *cho* and prevent
(in addition to legislative prohibition to be proposed later)
owners of large estates from expelling their tenants and

nominally working their estates themselves to avoid compulsory transfer.

3. *Tenants should be limited to the purchase of family maintenance units of land.*

The size of the family maintenance unit would vary from district to district, but probably would not exceed one *cho* on the average. Restriction of purchases to such units would enable the maximum number of tenants to purchase land. The number of pure tenants in Japan is approximately 1,400,000, and a transference of 65 per cent of tenant lands would provide sufficient land to absorb all of these at an average holding of one *cho* per family, and still leave approximately 400,000 *cho* for distribution among part-tenants.

4. *A Land Acquisition Board should be established to administer the land transfer program. It should be under the chairmanship of the Minister for Agriculture and Forestry, and include equal representation of landowners and tenants. Prefectural and local Land Commissioners, representing equally the interests of landowners and tenants, should be appointed to administer the program at prefectural and local levels.*

Under the above proposal the local commissions would determine, subject to the ultimate approval of the Land Acquisition Board, the land to be made available for transfer in each locality and would receive application for land from tenants. There would be no direct negotiations between landlords and tenants.

5. *The Land Acquisition Board should purchase land for resale to tenants. The purchase price should be paid in Government bonds, to be redeemed periodically over a period of 24 years, as repayments are made by tenants,*

but with provisions for earlier redemption if circumstances are favorable.

Purchase of land by the Government for resale to tenants through the Local Land Commissions would provide the best means of ensuring that the tenant received land under fair conditions and at the official price. Payment to landowners over a number of years would prevent an undue expansion of credit, which would be undesirable while monetary instability continues. It might be convenient at a later date to redeem all bonds before maturity.

6. *Tenants purchasing land should be protected against the consequences of any future fall in land values by periodical reappraisements of their commitments.*

Falling land values, subsequent to purchase, have frequently caused the failure of land settlement and purchase schemes. In the absence of provision for the adjustment of debts, tenant purchasers are likely to be forced into insolvency.

7. *The provisions of the program should be applied to the land situation, as at December 8, 1945, and all subsequent sales of land and substitution of nominal owner operation for tenant cultivation should not be recognized.*

A provision of this nature is necessary to prevent landlords from evading the reform by "dummy" sales, and nominally reducing their tenant land before the program is put into effect.

8. *The time in which the transfer is to take place should be reduced from five years to three years.*

It should be possible to carry through the acquisition of the land from landowners within three years.

9. *Consolidation of holdings should be carried on, as far as possible, at the same time as the transfer of land from landlords to tenants.*

Many farms in Japan are composed of small scattered pieces of land. Such fragmentation of areas is a major barrier to more efficient working of farms. With the transfer of a large amount of land through Government bodies, an excellent opportunity for consolidation of holdings is provided. Where necessary, tenants should be encouraged to purchase consolidated areas.

10. *Provision should be made for rent ceiling and written tenancy contracts guaranteeing security of tenure to tenants and rights in any improvements they make.*

It is envisaged that 30 per cent or more of existing tenant lands will remain as such, and it is, therefore, important that conditions of tenancy should be improved.

This program was warmly supported by the Chinese member, who moved some minor amendments which were useful and acceptable, particularly an amendment reducing the time limit for transfer from three to two years. The Russian member also expressed his support for my program, though he went on to make certain supplementary proposals, some of which were inconsistent with mine. General Derevyanko proposed, for example, that compensation for land acquired should be paid on a decreasing scale, so that a landlord with a large area of land would receive the full rate of payment for the first three *cho* of alienated land, half rates for the fourth, fifth and sixth *cho,* and after that nothing at all. This last feature of the Russian member's plan was strongly opposed by the American member on the ground that it involved confiscation. He claimed it essential that SCAP should not countenance any abrogation of the rights of private property.[2]

In October 1946 the Diet passed two Government bills which included most of the substance and much of the detail of the ten-point program I had submitted to the Allied Council, though only, I believe, under persistent pressure from GHQ. This legislation provides compulsory means to enable about two million tenants, or three-quarters of all farmers, to acquire the land they work. It also seeks to improve conditions of tenancy for the remaining quarter.

Absentee landlords must sell all their land; non-operating landlords living in the local community must sell all land in excess of one *cho*, except in Hokkaido, where they may keep four *cho*. (Farming in Hokkaido is largely pastoral, and land values are only about a quarter, on the average, of what they are in the other three islands.) Farmers who work their own land are limited to the average ownership of three *cho* (12 *cho* in Hokkaido), plus the one *cho* allowed non-operating landlords. This means that the average farmer cannot own more than ten acres: 7½ worked by himself and family, and 2½, which he may lease to tenants.

Land is to be bought at a fixed price, and tenants may buy by installments over 30 years, at 3.2 per cent interest. The annual installments, plus taxes and other ownership obligations, are not to exceed one-third of the value of the crop of the purchased land.

Considered as reform legislation, the Land Reform Acts are generally very satisfactory. There may be some loopholes, such as the provision that an owner-operator may be allowed to have more than three *cho* if he can show that a reduction of the area worked by himself and family would

[2] Verbatim Minutes of Allied Council of Japan, Sixth, Seventh and Eighth Meetings.

be likely to reduce the productiveness of the land. The real test of the reforms, however, will be in the way they are administered by the Local Land Commissions, set up to supervise the transfers. There are some 10,000 of these commissions, made up of elected representatives of tenants, owner-operators and landlords, in the proportion 5 : 2 : 3. There are two stages in the process of transferring the land to the tenants. First, the "surplus" land is bought by the Government, acting through the local commissions, and then this land, after efforts at consolidating small strips, is resold to the tenants. Considerable progress has been made with the first stage, and GHQ officials anticipated that during the first quarter of 1948 resales to tenants would be possible on a big scale, and that the whole program of transfer would be completed by the end of 1948.

It is too soon to measure the success of the program. There has been plenty of evidence of the landlord's resistance. From the date of the surrender, landlords, anticipating reform measures, tried to dispossess tenants and distribute the land they worked among relatives and friends. From August 15, 1945, to June 10, 1946, there were 23,809 disputes arising out of landlords' demands for the return of tenant farms. In the Local Land Commissions at the end of 1946 there was evidence of improper pressure by landlords in a number of areas. In October 1947 a group of landlords on Tochigi Prefecture contested the constitutionality of the Land Reform Acts. Yet in some districts the commissions appear to be working with enthusiasm and efficiency in their effort to meet the needs of eager buyers.

The difficulties and delays in carrying out the program may sometimes be due not to the obduracy of the owners, but the inertia of the tenants. A proportion of tenants may feel that the legislated reforms in the tenancy system reduce the relative advantages of ownership. The new laws lay down that rents are henceforward to be paid in cash, not in kind, and in accordance with written contracts, instead of the verbal contracts which previously gave the landlords too great a sense of security. Moreover, the new rent ceilings, fixed by law, reduce the old rates by about half; rent is limited to 25 per cent of the value of the crop on paddy fields (wet cultivation) and 15 per cent of its value on upland fields (dry cultivation).[3]

It would be foolish to hope for too much from these reform measures, even if they are carried out according to plan. By enabling a tenant to become an owner-farmer you improve his condition by increasing his rights, particularly his right to a larger share of what he produces. But you do not necessarily increase the volume or value of his products. It is often said that farming is very efficient in Japan. This is true in the sense that the Japanese are expert in getting the maximum product from a given area. But the meticulous exploitation of every cultivable square yard is only carried on by the reckless expenditure of human labor. The basic problem of Japanese agriculture is economic—there is so little land and so much labor. At present more than two-thirds of the farms of Japan are of less than two and a half acres in area, and more than one-third of less than one and one-quarter acres. The average farm household is made up of about three adult farm workers, plus old people and children. The only permanent way to relieve the poverty and overcrowding of Japanese farms is to

[3] The Diet passed legislation in November 1947 to dissolve the wartime Agricultural Control Associations and enable farmers—whether owners or tenants—to form their own Cooperative Associations along democratic lines. This legislation was described by Lt.-Col. H. G. Schenck, Chief of the Natural Resources Section, GHQ, as of "far-reaching significance to the farmers of Japan" and "the second great step toward agrarian reform." Col. Schenck declared that the Agricultural Control Associations, being dissolved, had been "a vicious monopoly, exercising dictatorial control over every sphere of the agricultural economy." The new law would "restore to farmers the power to determine the destinies of their economic efforts through associations voluntarily organized and completely farmer-controlled." *Nippon Times*, November 9, 1947.

reduce the number of farmers. An increasing number must be absorbed in secondary and tertiary industries. This would make possible a consolidation of farm holdings, an increase in their size, and the introduction of more modern and mechanized agriculture. This would, in turn, imply the development of Japan's foreign trade and considerable food imports. It is only along these lines that Japanese farmers can hope to achieve the material basis for civilized living.

The Dissolution of the Zaibatsu

The term Zaibatsu, meaning literally "money group," is sometimes restricted to the four great business organizations—Mitsui, Mitsubishi, Sumitomo and Yasuda—but usually it is extended to include other leading families and combines, sometimes called the "lesser Zaibatsu." [4] In this chapter I use the term in this inclusive sense.

Before the surrender there was a good deal of difference of opinion among Western experts on Japan about what should be done with the Zaibatsu. There was an impressive body of opinion in Britain which opposed any plan to break up the Zaibatsu organizations. It was urged that the extreme concentration of economic power which these concerns represented was an integral feature of Japan's peculiar economic development, and that it would not be possible to destroy the Zaibatsu organization and leadership without dislocating the whole economy. It was claimed that the Zaibatsu represented the "moderate" forces, and that they had shown themselves often to be in strong opposition to the militarists. They stood for economic expansion, not for territorial aggression. Moreover, if Japan's p⸱⸱ ⸱⸱⸱

[4] Following its investigation of the "Big Four," SCAP called for⸱⸱⸱ tion on the assets of ten "lesser Zaibatsu" families—Rikawa, Asa⸱⸱ kawa, Kawasaki, Matsushita, Nakajima, Nomura, Okochi, ⸱⸱⸱ Shibusawa.

economy were to be restored, she could not dispense with the managerial ability of the Zaibatsu leaders.

Nevertheless, in 1945, the opposing school of thought got its view officially accepted. The Initial Post-Surrender Policy instructed General MacArthur "to favor a program for the dissolution of the large industrial and banking combinations, which had exercised control of a great part of Japan's trade and industry."

There were several reasons for this 1945 decision to dissolve the Zaibatsu. It was felt that during the war years the Zaibatsu and the militarists had been rivals rather than enemies. They had differed not so much, if at all, in their national objectives; their differences had mainly been on strategy and tactics. The Zaibatsu could, consequently, not be cleared of war responsibility. It was felt that the continued concentration of economic authority in a few hands was an essential feature of a totalitarian and expansionist policy. To tolerate its perpetuation would be to leave intact the industrial basis of Japanese militarism. Moreover, the continued concentration of wealth and power seemed inconsistent with the principles of democracy and social justice. This motive was reinforced by the traditional American aversion to trusts and monopolies. The aim was not to destroy or weaken the institution of private property, but to protect and enlarge it by ensuring that its ownership should be more widely and equitably distributed.

I shall not attempt to recount in any technical detail the vicissitudes of SCAP's dissolution program. I shall limit myself to describing the main lines of policy, to describing the difficulties in its formulation and supervision, and pointing to the problem still to be solved if, as now seems questionable, the Allies still want the program to be completed.

The Zaibatsu exercised their power mainly through holding companies, which held securities in subsidiaries in nearly all branches of industry and commerce. The first task, therefore, was to dissolve these holding companies. This was a project of baffling complexity. The first essential was full information about the ramifications of the Zaibatsu organization. GHQ did not possess this information, and, even if it had, it did not possess the trained staff capable of mastering it. SCAP, therefore, approached the task with understandable caution. It was suggested that the Zaibatsu themselves, in consultation with the Japanese Government, should work out a scheme for their own destruction and submit it to SCAP for approval. This procedure was followed. The first schemes put forward did not satisfy GHQ, which put pressure on the Zaibatsu to submit something more radical. In response, the Yasuda Holding Company formulated a plan on behalf of the "Big Four." SCAP approved this plan, and in an important directive of November 6, 1945, instructed the Japanese Government to supervise its operation. The Government was to set up a Holding Company Liquidation Commission. This Commission was to take over the securities held by those holding companies designated for dissolution, beginning with Mitsui, Mitsubishi, Yasuda and Sumitomo. These holding companies were then to be dissolved. The securities were to be sold to the public under conditions intended to prevent individuals or families from obtaining controlling blocks. In liquidating the Zaibatsu assets, the Commission was to safeguard the interest of small shareholders, and the employees of the companies were to be given preference in the sale of the shares. The Zaibatsu owners of the securities were to be paid compensation in Government bonds, non-maturing and non-negotiable for at least ten years, to the selling value of the securities, less the costs of dissolution.

There was a good deal of delay in getting this program started. SCAP rejected as inadequate the first draft of the Imperial Ordinance, No. 233, creating the Liquidation

Commission. After revision, it was finally approved by SCAP in a directive of July 23, 1946. The Liquidation Commission held its inaugural meeting on August 27, 1946.

There are certain features of this program, and of the machinery for carrying it out, which raise doubt whether its declared objectives can be achieved.

The first need, as I have already mentioned, is that Allied supervisors should possess comprehensive and accurate information, not only on the anfractuosities of Zaibatsu organization, but on the financial and commercial situation of perhaps thousands of companies. The Liquidation Commission, for example, must seek to determine the "fair value" of Zaibatsu-owned shares in the holding companies. To do this, it must be able to appraise the assets, liabilities and earnings of the subsidiaries. In September 1947 the subsidiaries of the holding companies already marked for dissolution numbered more than 1,200. Independent investigation of the affairs of all these companies is out of the question. Hence the Liquidation Commission and SCAP officers must mainly rely on reports from the companies themselves, which must have great temptation, as well as great opportunity, to sidetrack inquiries.

It is important, moreover, that the program for dissolution was formulated by the best brains the Zaibatsu could muster, men of great industrial and political experience. These Zaibatsu leaders were accustomed to criticism from the militarists on the one hand and from radicals on the other. They had become expert in meeting it and in defending their position against rivals and revolutionaries. They would have been well aware of the anti-trust feeling in the United States, and, as defeat drew near, it would be surprising if they did not work out plans for meeting Allied efforts to overthrow them.

It is perhaps equally important that the responsibility for controlling the firms and families whose assets have been frozen rests with the Japanese Government. SCAP officers "hope" that the Government is doing this faithfully and efficiently. The Japanese Governments since the surrender have relied for their support on the most conservative forces in Japanese society. The Government's record in attempting to carry out effective controls in other sections of the economy does not encourage confidence in its eagerness or competence to control the Zaibatsu. On the technical side, Japanese official auditing and accounting is notoriously loose.

The character and outlook of the members of the Liquidation Commission is a crucial factor. I do not pretend to any firsthand knowledge of this. It is interesting, though, that Susayama, the chairman, was employed by Yasuda from 1926 to 1931, and that he was later president of the Industrial Bank of Japan, a "national policy" concern now dissolved.[5] Moda, the liaison officer with GHQ, was formerly head of the Mitsui interests in the United States. I was sometimes told, without supporting evidence, that the Liquidation Commission was purely an Occupation-period front for the Zaibatsu, whose interests it was carefully protecting. On the other side, the GHQ officers directly concerned claimed that the Commission was doing an honest and courageous job. Only the future can provide conclusive evidence either way.

SCAP recognized that the strong family ties among the Zaibatsu might provide unofficial chains of control after the official chains had been broken. In an attempt to meet this danger, the Japanese Government was ordered to exclude from policy-making positions in holding companies and their subsidiaries "blood relatives to the third degree"

[5] The Japanese Government at first proposed Mauji Iijuma as chairman. He was not acceptable to SCAP. This was not surprising, in view of his published statement: "It is a great mistake to say that the Zaibatsu must be destroyed." Iijuma was later purged for having, by writings and in other ways, shown himself an active supporter of military aggression. *Summation of Non-military Activities,* July, 1946.

The significant thing was that the Japanese Government should have considered Iijuma a suitable chairman for the Liquidation Commission.

of those officials who had been purged. The intention of this regulation is clear, but it is doubtful whether it will be effective. The executives in Zaibatsu concerns may remain under the personal influence or domination of the Zaibatsu families. This is all the more likely if the young men feel that their elders are only in temporary eclipse. I had personal knowledge while in Japan of some "purged" presidents who continued to direct their companies from their homes, where their former subordinates would respectfully gather daily to make their reports and get instructions.

Such considerations illustrate the difficulties in the way of destroying the Zaibatsu power. But perhaps the greatest obstacle lies not in the resistance of the Zaibatsu, but in the general economic conditions in Japan. It is one thing for the Liquidation Commission to take over Zaibatsu holdings; it is another thing to find some useful way to dispose of them. It must be remembered that the positive aim of the program is to disperse ownership. The difficulty is to find suitable people who can buy the Zaibatsu securities. Inflation increases inequalities of wealth in favor of property owners and businessmen at the expense of wage and salary earners. Wage and salary earners have been forced to use their savings, where they existed, to meet their current needs. It is true that large incomes are being made in commerce, and on the black market, but it is hardly useful or desirable to take special steps to transfer economic power from an old to a new Zaibatsu. If it is not possible to distribute these securities widely among the "little men," the program will fail in its positive purpose. I know of nothing pointing to a solution of this major problem.[6]

[6] The Zaibatsu holdings might be made available to foreign investors. Mr. Edward C. Welsh, Chief of SCAP's Anti-Cartel and Trust Division, has pointed out that foreign investments would produce firmer prices for Zaibatsu stock and bring technological and other advantages to the Japanese economy. *Nippon Times*, October 5, 1947.

There are some indications that the United States Government will not press for the completion of the Zaibatsu program. On December 27, 1948, Mr. Robert Lovett, Under-Secretary of State, told a news conference that the Government was restudying the whole Zaibatsu picture, with a view to revising its views on future ownership and control, in the light of the fact that Japanese wartime control of these concerns had already been broken, and, in that respect, the Occupation aim had been achieved.

On January 6, 1948, Mr. K. C. Royall, U.S. Under-Secretary of the Army, developed this line. He pointed out that in 1945 the main American interest was to prevent any possible future Japanese aggression. The well-being of Japan, or her strength as a nation, was a secondary consideration. But, since then, Mr. Royall pointed out, new conditions have arisen in world politics. Hence the need to re-examine America's attitude towards Japan. These changes have produced "an inevitable area of conflict between the original concept of broad demilitarization and the new purpose of building a self-supporting nation." Mr. Royall went on to say that:

at some stage extreme deconcentration of industry, while further impairing the ability to make war, may, at the same time, destroy manufacturing efficiency of Japanese industry —may, therefore, postpone the day when Japan can become self-supporting.

Another border-line situation between demilitarization and economic recovery is presented in the case of personnel. The men who were the most active in building up and running Japan's war machine—militarily and industrially—were often the ablest and most successful leaders of that country, and their services would in many instances contribute to the economic recovery of Japan.

It is noteworthy that Mr. Royall spoke on the assumption that the earlier program for land reform and the dissolution of the Zaibatsu were completed, or in process of completion. "Land reform," he said, "would be completed by the end of 1948"; the power of the Zaibatsu "has now been virtually abolished." [7]

Mr. Royall's speech helps explain why SCAP did not intervene to prevent the Diet from watering down the provisions of the Economic Power Decentralization Bill in December 1947. This Bill, as originally drafted, was to have been complementary to the measures for dissolving the Zaibatsu.

The change in the U.S. attitude is, no doubt, largely due to a clearer perception of the real difficulties in the way of carrying out the original program. It appears also to reflect an anxiety, in the light of the international situation, not to destroy too impetuously the "stabilizing" influences in Japan's economy. There has lately been some criticism from Allied business circles that SCAP has been too severe and too radical in pushing measures for the reform of Japanese economic institutions.

Conclusion

I believe that the two most significant features of the situation at the end of 1947 were, first, the steadily returning confidence of the wealthy and powerful Japanese, whose interests SCAP's economic reforms appeared to threaten, and, second, a marked drop in the reformist impetus of GHQ.

The returning confidence of the conservative group began to find expression about the time of the announcement of the Truman doctrine. It was well expressed in a leading article in the *Oriental Economist* of March 29, 1947:

[7] The full text of Mr. Royall's speech was printed in *Nippon Times*, January 17, 1948.

In Greece and Turkey, Leftist and Rightist influences are being pitted against each other, with the former having an apparent edge over the latter. The situation in Japan is different. It is true that Leftist influence has begun to manifest itself through a phenomenal development of the labor movement, and its advance may become further accentuated if Japan's economic conditions worsen. For all that, the Leftist influence in Japan at present is still small and insignificant, compared with the overwhelming superiority of the Rightist influence. Such Rightist influence has not shown itself on the surface, although its dormant power is considered enough to overwhelm the Leftist influence once the weight of the Occupation forces is removed. The deep-rooted ideas of imperialism and militaristic patriotism, cultivated for years since the Meiji Restoration, and strengthened, during the ten-odd years following the Manchuria Incident, are not easily wiped away. Those adhering to such ideas are believed to be far larger in number than those upholding Leftist ideas and ideologies.

The loss of drive in GHQ's reform program has not been clear-cut and consistent, but the trend from 1945–48 is unmistakable. The program SCAP outlined in 1945 and early in 1946 would, if completed, produce fundamental changes in Japan's economic organization, and a great shift in the balance of economic powers. Indeed, if only the two measures discussed in this chapter—land reform and the dissolution of the Zaibatsu—were to be carried out thoroughly, they would amount to a social-economic revolution. There were officials in GHQ who planned and worked for this sort of revolution, and these Americans had the sincere support of a small group of Japanese radicals. But the senior officers in SCAP did not always share the reformist enthusiasms of their subordinates. General MacArthur's purpose in directing reform measures seems to spring mainly from the desire to eliminate those features of Japan's economy that are inconsistent with the philosophy of American individualism. He tends to equate what is un-American and what is undemocratic. Land reform was a blow at feudalism; the Zaibatsu program a blow at monopoly: both un-American concepts. But further than that General MacArthur seems reluctant to go. It is true that he has from time to time directed the Japanese Government to enforce certain economic controls, but he is usually careful to express the view that controls are in themselves evil, and only necessary as temporary and exceptional measures. This attitude came out clearly in his message to the Japanese people on New Year's Day, 1948:

> So long as your needs continue to be greater than your productive capacity, controls upon your internal economy will be essential, lest the weaker segments of your population perish. Such controls must, however, only be temporary, and subject to ultimate removal in favor of free enterprise.
>
> Economically, Allied policy has required the breaking open of that system which in the past has permitted the major part of the commerce and industry and natural resources of your country to be owned and controlled by a minority of feudal families and exploited for their exclusive benefit. The world has probably never seen a counterpart to so abnormal an economic system.
>
> It permitted exploitation of the many for the sole benefit of the few. The integration of these few with government was complete and their influence upon governmental policies inordinate, and set the course which ultimately led to war and destruction. It was, indeed, so complete a monopoly as to be, in effect, a form of socialism in private hands. Only through its dissolution could the way be cleared for the emergence of an economy conducive to the well-being of all the people— an economy embodying the principle of private capitalism, based upon free competitive enterprise; an economy which long experience has demonstrated alone provides the maximum incentive to the development of those fundamental requirements to human progress: individual initiative and individual energy.

General MacArthur here gave dogmatic expression to the widespread American view that individualism in economics is inseparable from democracy in politics. This view inevitably breeds reluctance to sponsor any measures which smack of a controlled economy or of socialism. In expressing it, General MacArthur officially aligned himself against the declared policy of the Japanese Social Democratic Party, and of the Prime Minister, Mr. Katayama.

I am not suggesting that controls are necessarily reforms, nor that "socialism" is intrinsically superior to "individualism." It remains true that in several Allied countries, including the United Kingdom, Australia and New Zealand, there are freely-elected Governments which believe that a controlled economy is consistent with democracy, and may, in certain economic circumstances, be necessary for democracy to survive. It is, therefore, interesting that General MacArthur, in his capacity as Supreme Commander for the Allied Powers, should warn the people of Japan that a regime of "private capitalism, based upon free competitive enterprise," is indispensable to their well-being.

The Short-Term Problem of Stabilizing Wage-Price Relationships

In the preceding paragraphs I have confined myself to a discussion of fundamental long-term economic reforms. Yet during the Occupation Japan's primary need has been for urgent short-term measures. General MacArthur consulted the Allied Council about these measures in April 1947, when he asked for its views on the stabilization of wage-price relationships. I expressed the view that the actual problem was mainly political, not economic; not to discover the sort of controls needed, but to find a Japanese government with the will and authority to impose them. Since, however, the Supreme Commander appeared to wish for fairly detailed recommendations in economic and administrative terms, I submitted the following analysis and recommendations.

ALLIED COUNCIL FOR JAPAN, TOKYO

Office of the Member representing jointly the United
Kingdom, Australia, New Zealand and India

STABILIZATION OF WAGE-PRICE RELATIONSHIPS

Summary of Conclusions and Recommendations

(i) The destruction and wastage of war and the dislocations
of defeat present the Japanese Government with a series of
major economic problems.

(ii) Japan today is faced with a twofold task. First, to restore
capital equipment for the production of peacetime goods, and,
second, to ensure that the goods produced are justly distributed. Efficiency and social justice must be the keynotes of economic policy.

(iii) Inflation must be stopped. It has produced inefficiency,
since available resources have been wasted in non-essential
uses. It has caused injustice by throwing the main burden of
sacrifice on wage and salary earners, while other sections of
the community have profited.

(iv) While the immediate cause of inflation is the unbalanced budget, a more fundamental cause is the failure to
make price control effective by strict control over the distribution of raw materials and consumer goods.

(v) The control of raw materials must be enforced to make
price control effective and to ensure that materials are reserved
for essential uses. It should be based on a permit system.
Permits should be necessary for both the purchase and transport of controlled materials. Records for Government inspection of movements of controlled materials should be kept by
suppliers, merchants, carriers and users.

(vi) Rationing of essential consumer goods is necessary to
ensure just distribution and should be controlled by a coupon
system.

(vii) Prices should be fixed to restrict profits to a minimum.
Control of prices to prevent profiteering is more important
than fixing a particular level of money wages, since, in the
present circumstances of Japan's economy, increases in wages
simply raise costs and prices and do not increase real wages.

(viii) Provided profiteering is eliminated by price control,
wages should be pegged as an additional safeguard against

excessive increases in costs and prices. These pegged rates should, however, be periodically reviewed and raised as production efficiency increases.

(ix) Every effort must be made to ensure that Government revenue keeps pace with expenditure. Taxes should be based on current income. Returns of business and professional incomes should be made at intervals of less than one year, if possible each quarter, so that taxes may be adjusted to current earnings.

(x) Government expenditure should be pruned to eliminate all but the most essential items. Accounts submitted by Government contractors should be carefully audited to prevent excessive charges.

The Nature of the Problem

1. This problem is an integral part of the question of over-all economic policy for Japan in its present stage and I propose to deal with it in that setting, leading up to specific recommendations.

2. The basic problem facing Japan today is to find just and efficient means of restoring her capital equipment in peacetime industries, and in such forms for direct use of her people as housing, hospitals and schools. Restoration of peacetime industries is essential to lay a basis for increased production. Without increased production there is no possibility of any permanent increase in living standards in Japan. But restoration of physical capital is the necessary first step.

3. Reconstruction involves sacrifices because production in Japan is at present at such a low level that only the barest essential needs of consumers can be met, if any margin is to be left for the building up of capital assets. Production is so low that, even if no margin were left for reconstruction, living standards in Japan would be much lower than the people have been accustomed to. But even this level could only be maintained temporarily, since it would

have to be attained at the expense of a further wastage of capital assets, and would result in reduced production later on. Such a trend has actually taken place in Japan since the surrender. Production recovered fairly rapidly, particularly in consumer goods, until the middle of 1946, then became stagnant, and finally appears to have fallen in recent months. Valuable stocks of raw material were wasted in non-essential production instead of being reserved for essential reconstruction. Such dissipation of resources must be stopped if extreme hardship is to be avoided. The inevitable restriction of living standards can be minimized if only essential goods are produced.

4. Because of the sacrifices involved, the means adopted must be just, so that the burden does not fall mainly on a limited section of the population. To date, the restriction of consumption, made inevitable by the wastage of the war and such reconstruction as has already been carried out, has been accomplished by inflation. This is the most unjust means, since the burden falls mainly on wage and salary earners, whose incomes lag behind prices and whose savings depreciate in value. On the other hand, some sections of the population have benefited from a situation in which all should have borne the sacrifices involved. Inflation profiteers not only make large gains, but find it relatively easy to preserve them against taxation, since taxes on business income and property are based on income and valuation at least one year before the tax is paid. By this time the currency has depreciated and payment is a relatively slight matter. Tax evasion is also relatively easy with this kind of income. The tendency, therefore, is to shift the burden on to a limited section of the population and make the distribution of wealth more uneven.

5. The means adopted must also be efficient, so that resources may be devoted to the most essential purposes and the period of restricted living standards made as short as

possible. So far, the absence of effective controls over the
distribution of resources, and the consequent inflation, have
resulted in a severe lowering of living standards for some
sections of the population, but have not caused the resources accumulated in other hands to be devoted to essential reconstruction. Instead, scarce raw materials have been
wasted in non-essential production and building.

6. Therefore, if justice and efficiency in reconstruction,
and a more equal distribution of wealth and economic opportunity in Japan are to be achieved, the present inflationary trend must be halted.

Basic Factors in the Inflation

7. The principal immediate cause of the present inflation has been the unbalanced budget and the finance of
the deficit by bonds and treasury bills taken up by the
Bank of Japan. So long as this continues, in the situation of
scarcity such as prevails in Japan today, there is no possibility of achieving stability of prices and wages. The budget
cannot be balanced, however, by mere arithmetic. There
is an intimate and mutually dependent relationship between the budget deficit, prices and wages. The budget
largely reflects other factors which produce inflationary
pressures. The basic factors are mainly:

(a) A shortage of commodities, leading to
(b) Scarcity prices and profiteering;
(c) Rising wage rates, in an attempt to keep up with
     prices;
(d) Higher costs and higher prices because of higher
     wage rates;
(e) Increased Government expenditure because of higher
     prices and wages;
(f) Failure of revenue to keep up with Government ex-
     penditure because of lag in tax assessments and tax
     evasion;

(g) A budget deficit, financed by the central bank, because of the unwillingness of the public to take up Government loans while currency is depreciating;

(h) Increase in currency and money incomes throughout the community.

All of these mutually dependent factors form the "vicious cycle."

8. The nature of the solution, as I see it, can best be illustrated by dealing with each of these factors and associated topics in turn.

Shortage of Commodities

9. The shortage of commodities can only be overcome when Japanese industry is restored. This is the main purpose of the policy being outlined here.

Scarcity Prices and Profiteering

10. Scarcity prices arise because the supply of essential commodities is much below the demand produced by customary standards of living. Scarcity prices enable large profits to be made by certain classes of manufacturers, farmers, merchants and speculators, because prices received are much above cost of production or buying prices. The aim in this case should be to restrict prices to levels which cover, on the average, cost of production, plus a minimum profit. Suppliers and speculators should not be permitted to make exorbitant profits at the expense of the rest of the community. This involves fixing official prices and enforcing controls over the use of raw materials and the rationing of consumer goods. Controls and rationing must be effective to restrict the amount of raw materials and finished goods which manufacturers and consumers may purchase. Otherwise competitive bidding arises, prices break through

the ceiling, and the fair distribution of available supplies, which is possible through rationing, is destroyed.

Control and Rationing

11. The following I consider to be the essential principles of an effective system for the control of raw materials and the rationing of consumer goods:

(a) Materials should be sold only against a permit or allocation certificate, issued by the controlling authority, and stating, at least, the quantity authorized and the purpose for which the materials are to be used.

(b) Manufacturers should keep an order-book, showing persons or corporations to whom materials have been sold, the quantities sold in each case, and the numbers of the respective permits or allocation certificates. Such books should be inspected regularly by officials of the controlling authority.

(c) Materials subject to control should not be transported by rail, sea or road unless the allocation certificate is produced. The carrier should keep a record, for inspection, of the names of consignees and the numbers of the appropriate allocation certificates.

(d) Merchants should not be permitted to buy controlled raw materials for stock, but only for specific orders covered by allocation certificates.

(e) Rationing of consumer goods should be based on a coupon system, the value of coupons being based on the ratio between essential requirements and the supply available.

12. The above principles are not intended to constitute a complete plan for the control and rationing of raw materials and consumer goods. There are obviously other principles and rules which can only be formulated by those closely in touch with actual administration. I do feel, however, that the principles I have listed should be a part of any scheme for effective economic control in Japan today.

13. Strict enforcement of such controls can prevent one of the major causes of instability—scarcity prices—and eliminate the major injustices and wastages of the situation which has existed since the surrender. It is the major step to be taken if economic stability and a fair sharing of sacrifices are to be achieved.

Wage Rates

14. Wage rates occupy a particularly important position in the Japanese economy today. Since the price level in Japan is not influenced by world prices, it is determined solely by local factors, and of these the basic factor is wage rates. A change in wage rates influences the price of practically all goods and services. So long as wages increase prices increase also, provided, perhaps, there is no increase in the efficiency of production at the same time through other factors. Unless there is an increase in production, scarcity, or black-market, prices will increase as wages increase, because workers have more money to spend with only the same amount of goods to buy, and "official" prices will increase also, because increased wage rates will mean increased production costs. If "official" prices are not increased, more goods will probably go through illegal channels, at black-market prices. Real wages cannot be increased, in these circumstances, simply by raising money wages, because wages and prices are so closely linked.

15. The maximum real wages, in the present situation, can be obtained by eliminating scarcity prices by the means outlined in the preceding paragraphs. The excess profit which the seller at present obtains from scarcity prices is thereby transferred to the consumer. Because of the close link between wages and prices, no useful purpose is likely to be served by attempts to determine a money wage which will secure a certain desired minimum standard of living.

Such estimates can only be made on the basis of existing prices, and if, for example, it is decided that money wages should be raised to obtain a higher real wage, the result will be not a higher real wage, but higher prices and the same real wage. Unless there is an increase in production and a lowering of unit costs, no increase in money wages in Japan today is likely to result in higher real wages. There may, of course, be room for adjustment of wages in some trades, relative to others, but not a general rise.

16. The essential measure, therefore, is to eliminate scarcity prices and profiteering by controls and rationing. By this means wage and salary earners may obtain the maximum possible share of consumer goods.

17. Elimination of scarcity prices will not by itself, however, prevent a rising price level, except insofar as it reduces the pressure for wage increases. If wage increases are still substantial, prices will continue to rise, though the rise will be controlled, and it will be difficult to avoid budget deficits. Wage earners will not necessarily suffer, so long as price control is effective, but those on incomes which rise more slowly, such as salaried workers, will. In order to secure complete stability of prices, therefore, it would be necessary to peg wages, after controlled prices have been fixed and made effective. After wages have been pegged, or "frozen," they should be reviewed periodically, say, every six months, and allowed to rise in accordance with any increases in productive efficiency. As production increases, efficiency should rise, and, in these circumstances, increases in wage rates need not necessarily result in higher costs and prices. The essential condition is that controlled prices, closely related to costs of production, should be effective.

18. Wage rates, however, should only be pegged after price control has been made effective and the wage earner can obtain his needs at official prices. Otherwise it would

be unjust to control the incomes of one class, while another was allowed to make excessive profits.

19. As it was pointed out in the Partial Staff Study on this question, the wage structure in Japan is extremely complex. A revision of the structure to standardize at least the relationships between basic pay and supplementary allowances would be necessary before an effective system of wage regulation could be applied. Regulation of the basic wage only should be necessary and the wage system so designed that other payments would be adjusted automatically to any movements in the basic wage.

Government Revenue

20. Budget deficits are difficult to avoid when prices are rising, because revenue tends to lag behind expenditure. In these circumstances taxes should be levied as much as possible on current earnings and deducted at the source. This is relatively easy to do with wages and salaries, but the problem is complicated with business and professional incomes. However, it is essential in Japan today that progressive income tax should be effectively levied on business and professional incomes. This is necessary to prevent large budget deficits, and to prevent the injustice of one class being taxed heavily and another class escaping its due share. Until prices are stabilized, therefore, extreme efforts should be made to tax business and professional incomes on the basis of current earnings. To make this possible, tax returns for these types of incomes should be made more frequently than annually. Quarterly might be taken as the minimum period.

Government Expenditure

21. Government expenditure should be reduced to the minimum level consistent with the proper exercise of the

Government's functions. All items should be scrutinized to eliminate all but the most essential expenditure. In particular, accounts submitted by contractors for Government work should be thoroughly checked to eliminate inflated charges. The principal determinant of Government expenditure, however, will be the extent to which other controls, outlined above, have been made effective. This, and the effectiveness of tax collection, will determine whether the budget can be balanced and finance by bonds and treasury bills avoided.

s/ W. MACMAHON BALL.

April 14, 1947

~~~~~~

DEMOCRACY, IN ITS MODERN, WESTERN FORM, is built on a belief in the individual. The rights of the individual are its starting-point; the self-realization of the individual is its goal. The insistence that the individual must be always the center of political gravity is a comparatively recent development in the history of the West. In Britain the idea made its way steadily from the seventeenth to the nineteenth centuries; in France and in the United States it achieved explosive expression in the last quarter of the eighteenth century. The French and the Americans then put the idea on paper in a way the British had apparently never thought of doing. In the Virginian Declaration of Rights of June 12, 1776, the American Declaration of Independence of July 4, 1776, and in the French Declaration of the Rights of Man and of Citizens of 1889, we have the basic texts of this modern Western faith.

This democracy is not only a body of ideas: it is also the expression of these ideas in distinctive laws and institutions. The primary idea is that the individual has inalienable rights—the right to liberty, the right to equality, and the right to pursue happiness. But protection of these rights depends on the adoption of a certain method of government and of a certain body of basic laws. The general right to equality, for example, involves the political right to an equal and universal franchise, and the civil right to equality before the courts. Since all men are equal in their rights, political power must no longer depend on birth or wealth or age or sex: it must rest equally with all the people. In practice this will mean representative government, controlled by the will of the majority. Yet democracy is much more than majority rule. It is rule by a majority under conditions to which the minority consent. Both majority and minority must enjoy the same political and civil rights. Otherwise the rule of the majority might be the worst tyranny of all.

These ideas and institutions that we call democracy have become accepted in countries like Britain, France and the United States as a result of certain internal changes which brought about a redistribution of economic and political power. Democracy was the spontaneous and indigenous expression of a process of social development. It was organic to a particular stage of national growth. Nevertheless, the converts to democracy, like most converts, generally believed that their new faith was not only the way to salvation for Englishmen, or Frenchmen, or Americans, at a particular stage of their history, but the true faith of all mankind. It was easy to overlook here an important distinction. It is one thing to believe that political progress is always and everywhere marked by a growth of respect for the individual, and increased provisions for his development; it is another thing to believe that the particular laws or institutions which further individual development in Britain in the nineteenth century, or America in the twentieth century, will necessarily serve the same purpose in all places at all times. For, if laws and institutions are to be good, they must be related not only to their final purpose, but to prevailing circumstances. They are means to an end, not ends in themselves.

No one with these ideas in mind could believe it an easy

thing for its conquerors to bring democracy to Japan. It would not be easy to win assent to the idea of equality in a nation saturated with inequalities. There were the unequal rights of the sexes, learned from infancy. In Japan a mother will call out to her small daughter, who has barely learned to walk, to keep behind her brother as they go along the road. There were the unequal rights of age. There is no word for brother or sister in Japanese: only words for elder brother or younger brother, elder sister or younger sister. There were the inequalities of birth, with the Emperor descended, "in a line unbroken from ages eternal," at the sacred pinnacle. Even the inequalities of wealth—still a prominent feature of Western democracies—tended in Japan to have a stable and inevitable character, owing to the tradition of feudalism in the countryside, and to the marriage of the Zaibatsu with the nobility. The Imperial family was a major Zaibatsu concern. Throughout the national life, in the capital, in every prefecture, and village and household, authority belonged to an established hierarchy, and, at least with the Emperor and the head of the household, this hierarchy was sanctified by religion.

Such was the problem set for the Allies. In the circumstances, it was not surprising that there was some uncertainty and perhaps some inconsistency in the formulation of our objectives. In the Potsdam Declaration it was provided, in paragraph 10:

The Japanese Government shall remove all obstacles to the revival and strengthening of democratic tendencies among the Japanese people. Freedom of speech, of religion and of thought, as well as respect for the fundamental human rights, shall be established.

And in paragraph 12:

The Occupying forces of the Allies shall withdraw from Japan as soon as there has been established, in accordance with the freely-expressed will of the Japanese people, a peace-fully-inclined and responsible Government.

The Initial Post-Surrender Policy elaborated this.[1]

It would seem that at Potsdam and in Washington it was recognized that, if democratic reforms were to be democratic in fact, and not only in form, they would have to represent the "freely-expressed will of the Japanese people." These reforms were to be "permitted," "encouraged," "favored," and the use of these words would suggest that the Allied authorities were to foster, but not to force, the reforms. Yet certain rights "shall" be established, certain laws "shall" be abrogated and repealed, the legal system "shall" be reformed.

The Allies faced the eternal dilemma. We wanted good laws and institutions to be the free choice of the Japanese people, but we also wanted to make sure that, in any case, they were given good laws and institutions. If Japan, at the surrender, had been a nation in which a politically-conscious and freedom-loving majority was enslaved by a ruling minority, our problem would have been compara-tively simple. Once we had overthrown the "militarists," demobilized the army and cleansed the police force, the oppressed masses could have claimed their inheritance. But the situation was not like that. The enslavement, as we re-garded it, of the Japanese people was not the product of police coercion. The police only dealt with a tiny minority of "dangerous thinkers." It was the product of long years

[1] Part III, Political.—"Laws, decrees and regulations which establish discriminations on ground of race, nationality, creed or political opinion shall be abrogated; those which conflict with the objectives and policies outlined in this document shall be repealed, suspended or amended as required; and agencies charged specifically with their enforcement shall be abolished or appropriately modified. Persons unjustly confined by Japanese authority on political grounds shall be released. The judicial, legal and police systems shall be reformed as soon as practicable . . . and, thereafter, shall be progressively influenced, to protect individual liberties and civil rights."

of conditioning by teachers, parents and rulers. Hence the Allies were faced not only with the opposition of the minority, whose privileges were threatened, but with the political inertia of the majority, the product of subservience and superstition. What, then, were we to do? Were we to wait, in hope and patience, until education opened the eyes of the people and made them demand their democratic rights? That might mean a very long wait. Or were we to insist firmly, despite official opposition and popular inertia, on a number of revolutionary changes in laws and institutions to make them consistent with those of the Western democracies? [2]

We decided on this second course. There were, perhaps, two main reasons. Laws and institutions are not only the external expression of ideas; there is constant interaction between them. Men make institutions, and the institutions tend to remake men. If the Japanese people were given democratic institutions which represented their real interests, they might come to learn their value. Perhaps the best way to get them to care for democratic rights was to give them to them, so that they could the more quickly come to appreciate them. More important, it was felt that these reforms would provide the indispensable conditions for the growth of a spontaneous liberal movement in Japan. It was recognized that the liberal forces in Japanese politics were not powerful, and if they were to increase their influence they would need full freedom to organize and to propagate their beliefs. They could only do this under a new constitution and a new body of laws.

The new Constitution is the basic feature of the reform program. This document has been very widely explained and discussed in recent periodicals, and the text is printed

[2] For an interesting analysis of the different problems that faced the Allied Occupation in Germany, see W. Friedmann's *The Allied Military Government of Germany*, Chapter VII.

as an appendix to this study. I shall not, therefore, attempt to discuss its details. It gives the Japanese people the kind of representative institutions and the kind of civil rights that have been established in Western democracies. It transfers sovereignty from the Emperor to the people. It strips the Emperor of all political authority by providing that he can only act on the advice of the Cabinet. It makes the Cabinet fully responsible to Parliament. Parliament is directly elected by the people on the basis of equal and universal adult franchise. The judiciary is made independent of the executive, and the Supreme Court has power to "determine the constitutionality of any law, order, regulation or official act." The Constitution includes, in Chapter III, a Bill of Rights:

All of the people shall be respected as individuals. Their right to life, liberty and the pursuit of happiness shall, to the extent that it does not interfere with the public welfare, be the supreme consideration in legislation and in other Government affairs. (Article 13.)

All the people are equal under the law, and there shall be no discrimination in political, economic or social relations because of race, creed, sex, social status or family origin. (Article 14.)

Specific articles protect freedom of thought, freedom of religion, freedom of assembly and association, and academic freedom.

The Meiji Constitution also purported to protect individual rights, but only "within the limits of the law." This meant that it was possible to abrogate these rights at any time by ordinary legislation or Imperial Decree. The new Constitution provides that these rights can only be limited by considerations of public welfare. It would presumably rest with the Supreme Court to decide whether legislation restricting these rights was justified by such consideration.

It would be unreal to analyze the text of the new Constitution too narrowly. It may exhibit some technical defects, but there can be no doubt that, taken as a whole, it gives the Japanese people the apparatus of government and the civil and political rights that mark the Western democracy. The circumstances in which the Constitution was adopted, and the way the Japanese feel about it, is much more important than its verbal content.

The Allied peoples now generally know what the Japanese people knew from the beginning: that the Constitution is essentially an American product. General MacArthur's first efforts to persuade Japan's political leaders to make a radical constitutional revision were unsuccessful. In the last quarter of 1945 Prince Konoye, "at the command of the Emperor," set up a committee under Toji Matsumoto to recommend revisions. The work of this committee failed to satisfy SCAP, mainly because it so strongly resisted any serious reduction in the Emperor's powers. General MacArthur, consequently, decided that the real work had to be done in his headquarters, if it were to be done at all. The draft which the Japanese Government published in March 1947 was a Japanese translation of the document written in English in GHQ. It bore in every line, in its ideas and wording, the marks of its origin. The ideas had been expressed in almost the same words in 1776, though, in order to leave a niche for the Emperor in an American type of political system, it was necessary to include the British idea of a constitutional monarch.

I have already referred to the Japanese reaction to this alien gift.[3] The ordinary people were quite disinterested. The political leaders, compelled by circumstance to father this unwanted child, did not succeed in concealing their real feelings. It was the responsibility of Mr. Yoshida, then Prime Minister, and Mr. Kanamori, the Minister of State, in charge of constitutional revision, to ensure that the Gov-

[3] See Chapter II.

ernment draft, already publicly applauded by General MacArthur, should be passed by the Diet without substantial amendment. It was a heavy and distasteful responsibility. Mr. Yoshida repeatedly reminded the Diet that the new Constitution was required by Japan's acceptance of the Potsdam Declaration, and by the "present international exigencies," which deprived the Japanese Government of its freedom in these questions. He argued that the change from the Meiji Constitution was not really so great as might appear on the surface. Mr. Kanamori put emphasis on this issue of historical continuity. He repeatedly insisted that the "national policy" was in no way changed by the new Constitution, though later, under pressure, he wrapped this thesis in ambiguity. The official translation of Mr. Kanamori's final commentary on the Government draft is a good example of this ambiguity and evasiveness, from which I quote the following paragraphs:

Popular sovereignty should be considered a change in recognition of the people.—Inadvertently speaking, the idea of popular sovereignty is not an entirely new one. The fundamental will of the nation was heretofore decided upon along this line, as seen in history. Sovereignty should be considered the very source of national will. However, in the past we failed to realize this fact, because of too much emphasis on mysterious myths regarding the origin of our country. Now this veil has been lifted and actualities have been made clear. It should be considered, therefore, that popular sovereignty is no more than a change in the recognition of the people.

Position of Emperor in system in which veil of mysticism has been lifted.—Heretofore, the Emperor was considered as having the ability to function as the very source of national will, and, in consequence, certain mysterious characteristics were attached to his position. However, the fact that the Emperor has such a mysterious character is impossible. The source of national will should lie within the entire populace. Therefore, the new Constitution stipulates that the position of the Emperor is based on the general will of the Japanese people.

Thus a drastic change has been made in the people's recognition of the position of the Emperor. The change in itself is not essential, but its effects are important. A definite change in such spiritual matters is virtually an essential one. However, a calm examination of the matter should show that no essential change has been made, except for the clarification, along national lines, of the heretofore vague conception of the position of the Emperor. It is from this point of view that I maintain that the Emperor is a symbol of Japan, instead of the source of our national will.

Symbolic position of Emperor in accord with his intrinsic character.—The position of the Emperor as a national symbol should be interpreted to mean that the Emperor has a legal position through which any one of the people can conceive of Japan as a nation in thinking of him. In addition, it is stipulated in the new Constitution that the Emperor is the symbol of national unity. The reason the words "national unity" are introduced in it should be to correct the past evil that individuals, who ultimately form a nation, were all too rarely recognized because of too much importance attached to the nation as a whole. The nation being clearly stipulated as a gathering of individuals, I do not believe that the Emperor's position as a symbol of the nation is without foundation, because fundamentally he has an intrinsic character as a national symbol.

The idea that Japan, as a body of the Japanese people, may be conceived more clearly in thinking of the Emperor, should be based on the fact that he constitutes the center of national adoration. True, emblems and the national flag are also symbols. However, the difference in significance between the symbol, essential to the Emperor's position, and such artificially-attached ones, should be clearly realized.

I have quoted this statement at some length because it is such a superb expression of the Government's equivocation. Yet it seems to me that the least equivocal parts of the statement are those in which Kanamori insists that no essential change has been made either in the national character or in the position of the Emperor.

In these circumstances it is the more important that so

much of the Constitution is rather a declaration of principles than a statement of legally-enforceable rights. "All people shall have the right and the obligation to work. '. . . Children shall not be exploited" (Article 27). It is also important that a constitution which guarantees the eternal enjoyment of so many rights can itself be amended with exceptional ease. Amendment only requires a two-thirds vote of both Houses of the Diet and confirmation by simple majority at a referendum. This feature of the Constitution would seem to stultify a major purpose of constitutional reform, to protect the rights of those liberal and radical groups still in a minority in Japan. In principle, the present Diet could pass amendments against all resistance of the Social Democrats, and, assuming no major change in electoral feeling, should have no difficulty in getting its amendments confirmed by a simple majority of the people.

The new Constitution is inconsistent with a great body of Japanese law, particularly with many of the provisions of the Civil and Criminal Codes. During the last year there has been a spate of implementing legislation, but the full program of revision necessary to bring other laws into line with the Constitution may take some years. Meanwhile, some parts of the Constitution will remain ineffective.

If the new body of laws are to give a larger measure of freedom to the Japanese people, much will depend on how they are administered by local authorities. It is not very useful for the Diet in Tokyo, under SCAP direction, to remake the Civil and Criminal Codes unless this legislative reform at the center produces a new spirit and kind of behavior among the policemen and municipal clerks in the towns of Hokkaido and Kyusha. SCAP has fully recognized the need for the reform of local government, reform "at the grass roots." There have been two main lines of reform, provision for the direct popular election of local legislators and executives, and a comprehensive program of decentralization. The first local election under the new system took place in April 1947. The results were disappointing, since, in most cases, the people elected the old guard of bureaucrats who had previously held office by appointment of the National Government. Hence the first result of the electoral reform of local government was to give conservatives and bureaucrats an authority and prestige they had never had before. They could now claim that their power rested on the free consent of the local people, not on the favor of the Home Ministry. The second line of reform, decentralization, hoped to correct the evils that flowed so heavily in the past from "Tokyo control." Until the Occupation, all high officials in local government, down to the policeman and school teacher in the smallest village, were appointed by the Home Ministry. This extreme centralization was an effective technique for drilling the nation for war. It produced uniformity and discipline, and ensured that the patterns drawn in Tokyo would be firmly stamped on every farm and village in Japan. SCAP recognized, rightly and wisely, that if the Japanese were to learn to govern themselves, they could learn best in the local community, where problems were comparatively simple and where people were in intimate daily contact with their local officials. The devolution of powers from national to local bodies would not only increase the ordinary people's sense of responsibility and give them experience in the ways of democracy; it would forestall the return of national regimentation in the interests of militarism.

There was great weight behind SCAP's reasoning. The ultimate objective was right. Yet the decentralization program tended to clash with other aims. During the Occupation reforms have necessarily been initiated at the center in Tokyo, and it is hard to see how they can be effectively carried out throughout the islands without central direction and authority. It may, in principle, be a good thing to foster a particularist and self-dependent spirit in the prefectures, but these distinctive tendencies may mean major deviations from Occupation policy. It is good to have a variety in secondary issues, but on the primary issues we cannot afford local dissent. SCAP is pitifully short of man power; it is easier to exercise authority at one central point than at an immense number of local centers. In my own view, some form of Allied control of Japan will be necessary for many years. We can be sure there will be a great shortage of man power for this. In these circumstances, I feel that some of the present measures of decentralization are probably premature, however necessary to the achievement of our final aims. It is necessary to remember that the towns and villages are the strongholds of feudalism and superstition in Japan. To weaken the opportunities for education and control from the center may merely enable backward rural communities to live on, undisturbed by the stream of ideas that SCAP has brought to Tokyo.

In this discussion of political reform, I do not want to suggest that the new legal structure has made no change in political habits. I believe that the legal provision of new political and civil rights is supremely important. But its importance lies in what it makes possible for the future, rather than in what has been achieved until now. The hope of progress is that liberal and progressive Japanese will use their new freedom to produce a real change in the economic and social structure. In the last analysis these changes can only be made by the Japanese themselves. They now possess the legal right to make them. But it is doubtful whether the legal right is enough unless Allied economic and political policy creates the extralegal conditions favorable to fundamental change.

Trade Unions

It is perhaps possible to get an idea of how much and how little the possession of legal rights can help to produce economic and social results by briefly considering the situation of the Japanese trade unions.

The Initial Post-Surrender Policy laid down that "encouragement should be given and favor shown to the development of organization in labor . . . on a democratic basis." Trade unions had never been deeply rooted in Japan. A few unions showed bursts of activity in the twenties and early thirties, but the idea of union organization was alien to the great majority of Japanese workers. From the middle thirties unions were ruthlessly suppressed in preparation for war. During the war labor was organized by the Government in two labor fronts or industrial armies.

Under pressure from SCAP, these wartime organizations were dissolved on September 30, 1945. On October 4 the directive which ordered the removal of all restraints on political and civil liberties opened the way for the formation of trade unions. The Labor Union Law, passed on December 21, 1945, gave specific rights to the unions—the right to organize, to bargain and to strike. This Law was a great advance on any prewar labor legislation in Japan.

(Nevertheless, when the Diet passed the Labor Relations Adjustment Law nine months later, on September 20, 1946, it put restrictions on the right of government workers to strike, and public utility workers, very broadly defined, were prohibited from striking for thirty days after appealing for mediation.)

With these new legal opportunities, and under eager encouragement from GHQ officials, trade unions had a mushroom growth. A year after the surrender more than 18,000 unions, representing four million members, had been registered. The local unions are mostly organized in national industrial unions, which are in turn grouped in three federations—the Congress of Industrial Organizations, the General Federation of Labor Unions and a new and small All-Japan Council of Trade Unions.

It is sometimes claimed that this huge and rapid growth of union organization is evidence of the speed with which Japan has been "democratized." I think it would be premature to make this inference. It is much easier to count the number of trade unions than to assess their achievements. They have been faced with two major and related issues during the Occupation: First, to what extent should union action be restricted by the needs of the Occupation forces, and, second, should "political" strikes be permitted, and not only those directed towards the improvement of economic conditions in a particular industry.

It is clear that any strike which affected public utilities and seriously inconvenienced a large section of the Japanese people would automatically inconvenience Allied forces and perhaps impede them in their work. I remember well the inconvenience I felt personally when a strike in the electrical industry meant that my Tokyo house was blacked out at intervals for some weeks, since we drew light and power from a Japanese main. Sometimes the consequences were much more serious than this, for it was not always practicable for the strikers to give Allied people immunity from actions that were aimed against their own employers or their own Government. It would make a military occupation a little ridiculous if the occupiers were to be deprived, from time to time, of lighting, heating, communications and transport. That was the first check on union militance, and it was very hard to remove in the circumstances.

The more serious restriction on union activities was that GHQ and the Japanese Government took the line that the right to strike did not include the "political" strike, since this did not properly fall within the trade union field. The Far Eastern Commission has agreed that Japanese unions "should be allowed to take part in political activities and to support political parties." [4] Yet in the preceding paragraph of the same policy decision the Far Eastern Commission provides that strikes may be prohibited "only when the Occupation authorities consider that such stoppages would directly prejudice the objectives or needs of the Occupation." This leaves wide discretion to General MacArthur and brings us back to the questions discussed in Chapter II. The Japanese Government is SCAP's main instrument for controlling Japan. Strikes, which undermine the authority of the Government, automatically impair SCAP's authority. It is not surprising that General MacArthur should discountenance or prohibit this type of strike.

On the other side, it must be recognized that if strikes which seek to influence government policy are labeled "political" and, therefore, banned, it will hardly be possible for industrial unions to use the strike weapon effectively. It is impossible to separate politics and economics in this way. In most countries today, certainly in Japan, the unionist's economic conditions are mainly determined by political policy. It is the Government, not his employer, that has the last word on his standard of living. The critical problem for Japanese unionists has been to try to make wage increases keep pace with price increases. Nominal wage increases are useless. But it is Government policy, and not his employer's policy, that mainly determines the price level. In June 1947 the official prices for foodstuffs in Japan were more than three times higher than in June 1946. Black-market prices were up to twenty times higher than official prices. Families spent about three-quarters of their income on food, and during some months about three-quarters of this expenditure was on the black market. In this race of prices and wages, the wages failed to keep

---

[4] Far Eastern Commission policy decision, December 6, 1946. *Principles for Japanese Trade Unions*, pars. 5, 6.

the prices in sight. Here was the real source of industrial unrest. It was a situation which could only be dealt with by political action on a national scale. Only the "political" strike could put pressure on the Government, and the Government action alone could achieve the desired economic ends.

Trade union militance reached its highest point at the end of January 1947, in the plan for the February 1 "general" strike. On January 28 about 400,000 Tokyo workers took part in a mass demonstration to demand the immediate overthrow of the Yoshida Government. It was estimated that about 2,600,000 workers in government and public services would strike. A number of national trade unions outside the public services declared that they would strike in sympathy, so that on the morning of January 31 it seemed that something like four million workers would be involved.

The government workers demanded something like a threefold increase in wages, in a desperate pursuit of prices. It was hard to see how the Government could possibly have agreed to these demands, and it was certain that, even had it done so, the strikers would have won only an illusory relief, while inflation continued.

The "general" strike was killed at 2:30 p.m., Tokyo time, on January 31, when General MacArthur issued the following statement:

Under the authority vested in me as Supreme Commander for the Allied Powers, I have informed the labor leaders, whose unions have federated for the purpose of conducting a general strike, that I will not permit the use of so deadly a social weapon in the present impoverished and emaciated condition of Japan, and have accordingly directed them to desist from the furtherance of such action.

It is with greatest reluctance that I have deemed it necessary to intervene to this extent in the issues now pending. I have done so only to forestall the fatal impact upon an already gravely threatened public welfare. Japanese society today operates under the limitations of war defeat and Allied Occupation. Its cities are laid waste, its industries are almost at a standstill, and the great masses of its people are on little more than a starvation diet.

A general strike, crippling transportation and communications, would prevent the movement of food to feed the people and of coal to sustain essential utilities, and would stop such industry as is still functioning. The paralysis which inevitably would result might reduce large masses of the Japanese people to the point of actual starvation, and would produce dreadful consequences upon every Japanese home, regardless of social strata or direct interest in the basic issue. Even now, to prevent actual starvation in Japan, the people of the United States are releasing to them quantities of their own scarce food resources.

The persons involved in the threatened general strike are but a small minority of the Japanese people. Yet this minority might well plunge the great masses into a disaster not unlike that produced in the immediate past by the minority which led Japan into the destruction of war. This, in turn, would impose upon the Allied Powers the unhappy decision of whether to leave the Japanese people to the fate thus recklessly imposed by a minority, or to cover the consequences by pouring into Japan, at the expense of their own meager resources, infinitely greater quantities of food and other supplies to sustain life than otherwise would be required. In the circumstances, I could hardly request the Allied peoples to assume this additional burden.

While I have taken this measure as one of dire emergency, I do not intend to restrict the freedom of action heretofore given labor in the achievement of legitimate objectives. Nor do I intend in any way to compromise or influence the basic social issues involved. These are matters of evolution which time and circumstances may well orient without disaster as Japan gradually emerges from its present distress.

It will be noticed in General MacArthur's statement that he gave his instructions direct to union leaders, not through the Japanese Government; that the emphasis was on the needs of the Japanese people, not on the needs of the Occupation; that, in General MacArthur's view, the movement behind the strike came from a small and unrepresentative minority, and that Allied assistance to Japan could hardly be expected unless Japanese trade unions refrained from planning this kind of strike.

In the following months a number of trade unionists told me that the officers of GHQ and of the Military Government teams privately advised them that certain projected "local" strikes would fall under General MacArthur's prohibition of the "general" strike. I was not able to check these reports. However, for whatever reasons, after February 1, 1947, there was a very marked reduction in the number of strikes or projected strikes.

Trade union activity has presented General MacArthur with a major problem of "democratization." Every strike dislocates industry and holds up the production of those goods and services Japan needs so urgently. They may thereby put heavier burdens on the American taxpayer. Moreover, a successful strike raises the prestige of the "militant" unionists. At least some of these leaders are Communists. It is, therefore, understandable that SCAP should seek to discourage the use of the strike weapon. Yet we need to remember that the strike has traditionally been the unionists' most effective weapon. In the circumstances, it is unlikely that trade unions in Japan will display vigor and aggressiveness, despite the immense increase in their nominal membership.

The Purge

The Potsdam Declaration laid down, in paragraph 6, that "there must be eliminated for all time the authority and influence of those who have deceived and misled the people of Japan into embarking on world conquest." The United States Government greatly elaborated and extended this general program. It directed General Mac-Arthur to "prohibit the retention in, or selection for, positions of important responsibility or influence in industry, finance, commerce or agriculture of all persons who have been active exponents of militant nationalism or aggression, and of any who do not direct future Japanese economic effort solely towards peaceful ends." In the absence of evidence to the contrary, he was directed to "assume that any persons who have held positions of high responsibility since 1937 in industry, finance, commerce and agriculture, have been active exponents of militant nationalism and aggression."

This was a very comprehensive program, and SCAP has been carrying it out, or rather directing the Japanese Government to carry it out, since the first weeks of the Occupation. In October 1945 steps were taken to purge the police force and the teaching profession. On January 4, 1946, SCAP issued the since-famous "Purge Directive," which was to make a clean sweep of all militant and ultra-nationalist organizations and exclude from public office all people who, either from the positions they held or the views they had expressed, were active and influential in the practice or preaching of militarism or ultra-nationalism.[5] The term "public office" applied to all public servants of the Chokunin rank or its equivalent. The Chokunin is the second highest rank in the public service. The directive had immediate and spectacular consequences for the elec-

[5] Removal from office was automatic for all persons who:

1. Have held important posts in ultra-nationalistic, terroristic or secret patriotic societies; in the Imperial Rule Assistance Association or the Political Association of Great Japan, or any of their affiliates;

2. Have held important posts in financial and development organizations involved in Japanese overseas exploitation;

3. Have held important offices in occupied territories;

4. Have been members of the top military organizations;

5. Have ever been commissioned officers in the regular army or navy, or in the special volunteer reserve;

6. Have been connected in any capacity, civilian or military, with any

tion of April 1946. Only about fifty Diet members were eligible as candidates. The Progressive Party found that about 200 of its 272 Diet members would be barred from running again. Altogether it is estimated that the purge directive excluded about 200,000 persons from public office.

Exactly twelve months later, on January 4, 1947, the Japanese Government, under SCAP direction, launched the "purge extension." The new scope of the purge was laid down in Imperial Ordinances, Nos. 1, 2 and 3, and in the Cabinet and Home Ministry Ordinance, No. 1, of 1947. The idea was to extend the purge to all local government executives and legislators, and to all persons in responsible positions in business and publishing. It also embraced the chief officeholders of political parties. On paper this made the purge policy extremely drastic and comprehensive. It meant, for example, that all who had held senior executive positions between July 7, 1937, and September 2, 1945, in the biggest businesses were to be automatically dismissed.

It was not surprising that this vast extension should have aroused dismay and resentment among Japan's leaders, and that this was reflected in some criticism in the United States.[6]

---

military or naval police, or with any secret intelligence organizations;

7. Have held important positions in the Ministry of War or Ministry of Navy.

And the following were to be excluded from office:

1. Any person who has denounced or contributed to the seizure of opponents of the militaristic regime;

2. Any person who has instigated or perpetuated an act of violence against opponents of the militaristic regime;

3. Any person who has played an active and predominant governmental part in the Japanese program of aggression, or who by speech, writing or action has shown himself to be an active exponent of militant nationalism and aggression.

[6] Particularly in an article in *Newsweek,* January 27, 1947. On January 31 General MacArthur replied to this criticism. See *Summation of Non-Military Activities,* January 1947, pp. 35-36.

Yet the new ambitious program does not seem to have been carried out according to plan, and there are many indications, including the statement by Mr. Royall (quoted on pp. 129-30) that the United States Government feels that GHQ was rather too enthusiastic about purging, forgetful that conditions and viewpoints had changed since the purge policy had been first formulated in 1945. A mere reading of the provisions of the purge directive or ordinances would, therefore, give a misleading impression of the actual course of events.

What results would it be reasonable to expect from the purge, and what results have, in fact, been achieved? [7]

The responsibility for carrying out the purge rests with the Japanese Government. The huge task of screening hundreds of thousands of people was beyond GHQ's resources. In earlier chapters I have tried to show that the Japanese Government has relied for its support on the most conservative forces in Japan. I have argued that its policy has been the silent sabotage of the Allied objectives of 1945. I think, therefore, that it would be naive to expect the Government to carry out the purge in good faith. It is hard to see how it could possibly have done so when so many Cabinet Members, at least up to the middle of 1947, themselves fell under the purge, as a consequence of belated scrutinies of their past records.

If SCAP's forced reliance on the Japanese Government has been the main practical difficulty, there were other difficulties rooted deeper in Japan's character and history. A purge assumes that it is possible to separate the sheep from the goats; the "moderates" and "liberals" from the "undesirables," the innocent followers from the wicked leaders. No such dichotomy is possible in Japan. The

[7] In the five months following the "purge extension" the Central Screening Committee examined the records of 20,648 persons, including those in business and publishing. Of these, 341 were removed from office and 217 excluded from office; i.e., less than 2½ per cent.

nation is exceptionally homogeneous. Indoctrination in the ways of nationalism and war has permeated every stratum of society. You cannot change the outlook of a group—of a party, or a school, or a business—by dismissing its leaders. The new leaders will carry on the old tradition, though with great circumspection under the exigencies of the Occupation. I am aware that this generalization needs qualification. There were real liberals and revolutionaries in Japan, mostly in jail. But they were too few and inexperienced in executive responsibility to assume leadership. In any case, it is doubtful whether SCAP would have encouraged their ambitions, since their past experiences had driven so many of them to the "extreme Left." The root problem of the purge is that it cannot be consistent without overreaching itself. You cannot purge a whole nation.

I have said that you do not change the outlook of a group by dismissing its leaders. But, in practice, when you purge the leaders, you do not destroy their personal leadership. You merely deprive them of titular authority. It is impossible, in a country like Japan, where most important decisions are made at "unofficial" meetings and in family councils, to deprive leaders of their power by removing them from office. There may be dangers in creating an embittered group of able men from whom you have stripped privilege but not power.

Perhaps the most important question today is not whether the purge has succeeded, but whether the United States now wishes it to succeed. The plain fact is that American aims in Japan today are different from what they were at the surrender. The ideas behind the purge, certainly those behind the "purge extension," are an overlap from 1945. This comes out most clearly in connection with the economic purge. Since the middle thirties the privately-owned industries of Japan have all been organized for war. For various historical reasons, the control of these industries has been highly centralized. All senior executives were, in a sense, involved in "monopolistic" or "militarist" enterprises. If, in accordance with the purge extension, they are to be removed from all positions of influence, this will deprive Japan of the managerial skill that would seem indispensable if she is to become the "workshop of East Asia" and a safe field for American loans and credits. There are many signs that Americans realize this,[8] and Japanese leaders have been quick to exploit this situation. In December 1947 the Japanese Government was able to announce that the purge was "virtually complete."

[8] Cf. statement by Mr. Royall, pp. 129-30.

7. MAJOR DEVELOPMENTS IN 1948

~~~~~~

DURING 1948 AMERICAN POLICY TOWARDS
Japan, and events in Japan, have surprised some observers.
Yet the most recent developments were clearly foreshadowed
during 1947. In 1947 the United States authorities were
reticent and tentative about amending or reversing the
Allied policies of 1945; during 1948 the new American
policy has been crystallized, publicized and developed.

America now aims to help Japan regain her prewar
position as the workshop of East Asia. She seeks to do this
in four main ways. First, she wants to permit Japan to
retain industrial plants which the Allies had previously
intended to remove as reparations. Second, she wants to
give Japan direct financial help to restore her secondary
industries, to re-equip her plants, to secure overseas raw
materials and overseas markets. Third, America wants to
restore to the large Japanese business groups many of the
freedoms of which SCAP had earlier intended to deprive
them. And, fourth, she wants to contract some of the new
freedoms which SCAP had previously given to Japanese
trade unions.

It was Mr. Kenneth Royall, Secretary of the Department
of the Army, who on January 6, 1948, first gave a clear
indication of the new trend of American policy.[1] In Chap-

[1] See above, p. 129.

ter 5 I have already discussed the main features of his statement. Subsequent events were clearly foreshadowed when he said, "We are not averse to modifying programs in the interests of our broad objectives. A bill recently submitted to the Japanese Diet setting up procedure for deconcentration of excessive economic power was changed before the final enactment—changed with a view of giving added weight to the economic needs of Japan."

The report, commonly called the Strike Report, made for the United States Department of the Army by Overseas Consultants Incorporated, confirmed the new trend of influential American opinion.[2] The report contains a good deal of technical detail, but its main theme is clear and simple. In assessing Japan's economic needs it takes 1953 as its "target" year. It is concerned to discover the means by which Japan might regain by 1953 the living standards she enjoyed in the years 1931–1937. It estimates that by 1953 Japan's population will have risen to 85,800,000 and that the non-farm population, that is, the proportion of the population that does not grow its own food, will be 60 per cent higher than in the early thirties. Japan has lost all her invisible income from foreign sources, the interest and dividends on foreign investments, returns from services abroad and from her overseas shipping services. The market for Japan's one important raw material export, raw silk, has been greatly reduced by the competition of nylon and improved rayon fabrics. Hence, the Strike Report continues, Japan's future exports must be almost wholly manufactured goods, and, in view of the reduction of her income from other sources, she must export a much greater volume of these in 1953 than in the 1930's, if she is to maintain her increased population at the former level. But she can do this only if she has the factories to do it. She

2 See the official summary issued by the Department of the Army, Washington, March 2, 1948.

consequently needs more and not less industrial capacity than she has at present. The Strike Report concludes: "Removal of productive facilities (except primary war facilities) which can be effectively used in Japan would hurt world production; would reduce the likelihood of her becoming self-supporting, and in any case increase the time required for accomplishing this objective; would be expensive to the American taxpayer, and, in our opinion, would not be in the best interests of the claimant nations."

The Strike Report was followed by an even more authoritative statement by Mr. W. H. Draper, Under-Secretary of the United States Department of the Army, to a press conference in Tokyo on March 26. Mr. Draper said that the United States would give Japan extensive financial aid to become self-supporting, and that the United States wanted to permit Japan as high an industrial level as possible without threatening peace. Mr. Draper took with him to Japan an advisory group of prominent American businessmen (including Mr. Paul Hoffman) under the chairmanship of Mr. Percy H. Johnston. Mr. Johnston's influential group urged in its report that the United States should, in its own interest, now assist in the industrial recovery of Japan. It repeated the Strike recommendation that any equipment which could help this recovery should be left in Japan. It emphasized the importance of encouraging Japan to increase its merchant shipping both by new building and by chartering available bottoms. Finally, the Johnston group warmly supported the program sponsored by the Army and the State Department. which would call for the provision of $220,000,000 over twelve months for aiding the recovery of Japan, Korea, and the Ryukyu Islands.[3]

[3] Press release issued by Mr. Johnston, April 6, 1948. For the text of the report of the Committee, issued in Washington by the Department of the Army on May 19, 1948, see Appendix II below, pp. 211-38. For an appraisal of the Strike and Johnston reports see Jerome B. Cohen's article, "Japan: Reform vs. Recovery," *Far Eastern Survey*, June 23, 1948.

Meanwhile General MacArthur has continued to re-shape Occupation methods. In particular he restated his attitude towards trade unions and towards the Zaibatsu. In a letter dated July 22, to Mr. Ashida, the Japanese Prime Minister, General MacArthur dealt with the "existing inadequacies" in the National Public Service Law.[4] He urged that the law be amended to prohibit strikes and, in effect, any collective bargaining by public servants or workers in government industries. He distinguished sharply between "employee relationships in government and labor relations in private industry." To allow government workers the right to collective bargaining, with the reserve power to strike, would be to subordinate the interests of the whole community to those of a section, to undermine popular sovereignty, and put the Government's authority at the mercy of a militant minority controlling a trade union. Hence government workers could not be given the same freedom as workers in private industry. At the same time General MacArthur emphasized that it was the responsibility of the Government to ensure that its workers were granted fair and proper conditions. They must continue to enjoy the right to express their views and grievances, individually or collectively, but must be deprived of the right to push their claims by the threat to cease work.

General MacArthur's letter produced the immediate resignations of the chief of his Labor Division, Mr. James E. Killen, and of the deputy-chief, Mr. Paul Stanchfield. In announcing his resignation Mr. Killen said, "I cannot adjust myself to the new SCAP policy which denies the right of collective bargaining to the legally constituted unions of government employers."[5] Commenting on this statement Mr. Blaine Hoover, the chief of SCAP's Civil

[4] The full text of the letter was published in the *Nippon Times*, July 24, 1948.

[5] *Stars and Stripes*, August 3, 1948.

Service Division, said that it was "complete nonsense." Mr. Hoover stated that General MacArthur had been forced to intervene to forestall "a paralyzing strike of Government workers announced for August 7, which in Japan's impoverished condition would have resulted in starvation and disaster to large sections of the Japanese people." General MacArthur's letter was designed "to bring the relationship of government and public servants in complete consonance with American policy and practice." [6]

Meanwhile, on July 31, the Japanese Cabinet issued an order to implement the principles set out in General MacArthur's letter. The order stated that the Government did not recognize the right of the workers to conduct collective bargaining on an equal basis; that the existing labor contracts would be considered invalidated and that consequently the labor-government consultative council would be dissolved. This order aroused bitter opposition from the trade unions and left-wing political leaders. But it was made clear that any violation would be treated as direct defiance of the Supreme Commander, so that, despite earlier threats, the unions made no serious resistance. There was, however, a good deal of "job desertion" by government workers. It was reported that during August, 1,963 government railway and communications workers deserted their jobs; that 400 of these had been arrested, and warrants issued for the arrest of 515 others. [7] On September 10 Mr. Charles L. Kades warned the trade unions that Article 61 of the Criminal Code provided that anyone who instigated another to commit a crime should himself be considered a principal, and this applied to the instigation of strikes among government workers.

The revision of the National Public Service Law has been the occasion of the most serious conflict yet to develop

[6] *Nippon Times*, August 5, 1948.
[7] *Nippon Times*, September 2, 1948.

between the trade unions and the Japanese Government. General MacArthur's insistence that essential public services should not be interrupted can be fully appreciated, for the reasons explained earlier.[8] Yet it may be noticed in passing that government workers in Japan are a much larger class than public servants in most capitalist countries, since they include workers in a number of public utilities like the railways; that government wages and salaries have generally lagged a good deal behind those paid in private industries; and that no satisfactory methods of conciliation and arbitration have yet been established. For all these reasons General MacArthur's stand, and the consequent actions of the Japanese Government, have been a serious set-back to a very large and important group of wage and salary earners. It may be that a number of the government workers' unions have come under the influence of a Communist minority, but in Japan, as in other Eastern countries, Communists appear to have won influence owing to the lack of unity among those with more moderate views. Often the Communists have seemed to be the only people with enough courage and determination to accept the responsibilities of leadership. And insofar as Communist leadership aims at tangible improvements in the worker's living standards, it has genuine mass support, whatever ulterior motives its leaders may cherish. It is unlikely that the enforcement of an amended public service law which weakens the bargaining power of the government workers will improve the quality of their work, unless positive steps are taken simultaneously to remove the causes of their strongest discontents.

The present SCAP tendency to contract rights earlier given to workers' organizations goes hand in hand with a tendency to permit big business to continue to enjoy freedoms which SCAP had previously planned to restrict. I

[8] See Chapter VI, pp. 159-60.

have referred to Mr. Royall's statement that the Economic Power Deconcentration Act of December 1947 had been amended after submission to the Diet in the effort to avoid the disruption of efficient business organizations. During 1948 SCAP showed increasing reluctance to interfere with the prewar organization of big business. It should be recorded that SCAP officials maintain that there has been no basic change, still less reversal, of the original Occupation policy on the deconcentration of industrial control. This may be legally correct, since the principles laid down in the Deconcentration Act were shaped in very general terms, which allowed great latitude of interpretation. What seems certain is that during 1948 SCAP, in applying the deconcentration principles, has reversed the earlier expectations of Japanese big business, and removed many of its fears. The sense of relief has been freely expressed in the Japanese press. At the beginning of July it was announced that 70 per cent of the 325 companies earlier designated as "excessive concentration" would, after examination, not be required to undergo any structural changes. The five great banks, Mitsubishi, Sumitomo, Teikoku, Sanwa and Yasuda, were reprieved early in August. Mr. Edward C. Welsh, chief of the SCAP Anti-Trust and Cartels Division, pointed out that some large concentrations had not been broken up since they had "the efficiency advantage of large-scale production or well-integrated operations." [9]

On September 11 the SCAP Deconcentration Review Board laid down four new basic principles which seemed to mark a further retreat from earlier objectives.[10] For example, the Board laid down that the mere possession of non-related lines of business did not bring a company within the scope of the deconcentration law; that the claim that a large company restricted competition must be based

[9] *Nippon Times,* July 1, 1948.
[10] *Nippon Times,* September 12, 1948.

on evidence of "concrete facts"; that the Liquidation Commission must no longer take the initiative in ordering a company to reorganize, but deal only with reorganization plans submitted by the company itself. The announcement of these basic principles obliged the Liquidation Commission to re-examine the position of a number of large companies previously ordered to reorganize.

It should be remembered that the plans for the deconcentration of business control were intended to complement the plans for the redistribution of ownership, which was to have been achieved by the liquidation of large holding companies. But difficulty is still being experienced in reselling the securities which the Liquidation Commission took over from the holding companies. It had been planned to sell them to the public in a way that would disperse ownership and prevent individuals or families from acquiring controlling blocks.[11] Altogether there are many reasons why the Zaibatsu should be now throwing off the deeper anxieties they felt during the early stages of the Occupation.

The most significant official indication of the new American attitude came on December 9 when the United States member of the Far Eastern Commission announced that his Government was formally abandoning its earlier proposals for industrial deconcentration in Japan, as embodied in the well-known, controversial plan known as FEC 230, submitted some nineteen months earlier but never officially ratified. In announcing the decision,[12] the American member maintained that the deconcentration plan had now become unnecessary mainly because of SCAP's success in carrying out a program of reorganization of industrial ownership and control and because of the Japanese Government's enactment of an anti-trust law. He emphasized

[11] See p. 125.
[12] For text see Appendix III below, pp. 239-43.

that this did not mean that the deconcentration program had been completed but that there was no longer any need for the development of a *policy* on the subject.

It is hardly possible to assess the significance of these changes in United States policy, nor to speculate on their likely results, without considering other salient features of the Japanese scene in 1948. To get a clear picture it is necessary to consider not only what is changed and what unchanged in American policy, but what is changed and what is unchanged in Japan.

On the third anniversary of the Japanese surrender in Tokyo Bay, General MacArthur made an encouraging statement he had made two years before.[13] He said, *inter alia,* "There need be no fear concerning the future pattern of Japanese life, for the Japanese people have fully demonstrated both their will and their capacity to absorb into their own culture sound ideas, well tested in the crucible of Western experience, in lieu of those concepts responsive to the myths and legends which have so handicapped their task. And today those practical weapons needed to repel the totalitarian advance—liberty, dignity and opportunity— now safely rest in every Japanese hand, and the nation has thereby become an asset upon which the free world can confidently count."

Some observers were doubtful, however, how far three years of occupation had produced fundamental change in the Japanese outlook. Mr. Russell Brines, chief of the Tokyo bureau of the Associated Press, wrote, "Headquarters has dropped its previous contention that democracy has arrived. Now the phrase is 'wait and see.' "

There is no doubt that important progress has been made in some fields. Perhaps the most notable success has been the carrying out of the land reform program. This program aroused strong opposition from the landowners,

[13] See pp. 10-12.

and in its early stages seemed to have poor prospect of success.[14] During 1948, however, very rapid progress was made. The Land Reform Laws had provided that the Japanese Government should buy from the landowners about 80 per cent of the fields cultivated by tenants, an area of about five million acres, and resell this land to the tenants. According to Mr. W. I. Ladejinsky, an American authority on Japan's rural economy, the Government had bought the whole of the land marked for transfer, and resold three-quarters of it to tenants, by the end of July 1948.[15] This is a remarkable achievement. It is due, in my view, chiefly to the exceptionally high quality of the experts in the SCAP Natural Resources Section responsible for formulating and enforcing the reform. It does not detract from the greatness of the achievement to point out that whether the reform measures bring permanent benefit to the farmers will depend on the future policy of the Japanese Government. A future conservative government, if freed from SCAP control, would be able, if it desired, to frustrate the purposes of the reform in a variety of ways.

Other features of the Japanese scene, as revealed in 1948, are less pleasant. It seems that the series of ambitious and comprehensive reforms which SCAP has imposed on the political and industrial structure have generally failed to gain Japanese support.

Despite the new Constitution and the electoral reforms, political life has been disrupted by a series of major "scandals." Perhaps the most spectacular was the Showa Denko case, which finally brought about the fall of the Ashida Cabinet in October, after nine months of uneasy and barren office. Investigations showed that the Government, through its Reconstruction Finance Bank, had granted the

[14] See pp. 112-23. Also Andrew J. Grad, "Land Reform in Japan," *Pacific Affairs*, June 1948, and William J. Gilmartin and W. I. Ladejinsky, "The Promise of Agrarian Reform in Japan," *Foreign Affairs*, January 1948.
[15] *Nippon Times*, July 29, 1948.

Showa Denko Company a loan of nearly 3,000 million yen. This was about two-thirds of the total sum the Government was authorized to lend the fertilizer industry, although the Showa Denko produces only about 15 percent of the national output. A number of leading politicians, public servants and businessmen, including leaders of the three parties who formed the Ashida Government coalition, were later charged with bribery and corruption, and on December 8 Dr. Ashida was jailed pending a trial. In the Arms Disposal case it was shown that the Japanese authorities were able to account for only 10 percent of the war stores handed back to them by SCAP for civilian disposal. In the Coal Mines case a number of coal owners were charged with spending large sums to bribe members of Parliament to oppose the Katayama Government's Bill for the public control of the coal mines.[16]

There is also evidence that state prosecutors and the courts have in some cases been influenced by political pressure, which includes the pressure of the bureaucracy. On July 6 Mr. Frank E. Hays, of the SCAP Government Section, warned that "an insidious effort to undermine the procurators who are loyal to the interests of the people by the bureaucratic clique which does not consider itself to be the servant of the people still continues and must be crushed." Mr. Hays went on to say that the purge had left untouched the legal and political bosses, "who administered one law for the rich and powerful and another for the poor and weak." [17] As I pointed out earlier, the Japanese bureaucracy has almost certainly succeeded better than any of the other old ruling groups in retaining its power.[18] The senior classes of the public service seem still to be dominated by a clique of graduates of Tokyo Imperial University.

In relations between capital and labor there seems also

[16] See pp. 77-8.   [17] *Nippon Times*, July 7, 1948.   [18] See p. 86.

to have been a general failure to act in accordance with either the letter or the spirit of the new "democratic" regulations. A Japanese Labor Ministry survey recorded that in the February-June period of 1948 there were 122,095 violations of the Labor Standards Law. There was considerable discussion in the Japanese press of the reasons for these defaults. The general press opinion seemed to be that they were due partly to ignorance and partly to an inability of both wage-earners and employers to free themselves from ingrained feudal sentiments. Employers seemed to feel no obligation to shoulder new responsibilities where they could evade them, and workers were generally subservient and submissive even when they realized that their employers were breaking the new regulations.

To sum up, Japanese domestic developments during 1948 provide, in my view, further evidence that earlier claims that a social and spiritual revolution had occurred in Japan were inconsistent with the available facts. There has been no appreciable change in the basic social and mental habits of the Japanese people.

The policy of the Soviet Union and of the Japanese Communist Party has, however, changed significantly in the last quarter of the year. General Derevyanko, my former colleague on the Allied Council, returned to Tokyo on September 1. General Derevyanko had been the official head of the Soviet Mission in Japan since the surrender, but he had been away a good deal. At the end of 1945 he was recalled to Moscow because, according to Mr. Stalin's report to Mr. Byrnes, General MacArthur had been treating him like a "piece of furniture" and refusing to let him share in framing Occupation policy. Derevyanko was recalled again in August 1947 and it was generally believed in Tokyo that he would not return. Since his return home he has been active in the struggle between Russia and America for the loyalty of the Japanese people. The Soviet

Mission has strongly protested against the SCAP restrictions on the rights of trade unionists, and ardently supported radical trade union leadership. The Japanese Communist Party simultaneously issued a call for an early peace treaty with Japan, a reversal of its previous policy. It protested against the American intention to develop Japan as a military base, and asked for an immediate withdrawal of Occupation forces. It urged a peace settlement which would give Japan "full independence without any obligations impairing her sovereignty," and asked for the return of adjacent islands "which could be considered nationally and historically as belonging to Japan." On September 25 the Soviet representative on the Far Eastern Commission, Ambassador Panyushkin, announced Russia's desire for an early peace treaty. He urged, moreover, that no limits should be set to the expansion of Japan's peace-time industry, nor of Japanese exports, since this would help the physical well-being of the Japanese people. There should, however, be careful control to prevent the development of war industries, and this control should be enforced "by those powers most interested in prevention of Japanese aggression." [19]

I can only speculate on the reasons for this change in Soviet policy, but I think it is possible to speculate with some confidence. Until lately the Soviet had hoped to increase her influence in Japan despite the American Occupation, and, partly indeed, because of the Occupation. The early Occupation policy was to give full freedom to all political organizations and trade unions. Leftist leaders, including the most active Communists, were freed from prison or allowed to return to Japan from exile. The Communists hoped to use their new freedom to organize

[19] This Soviet proposal was rejected on December 9 by the Far Eastern Commission by a vote of ten to one, mainly on the ground that the plan was either superfluous because of present policies of the Commission or because it raised issues which could only be decided in a peace treaty.

a social revolution along party lines. The very slow rate of economic recovery; the inflation, which embittered the wage and salary earners; the earlier SCAP resolve to weaken the hold of big business on Japan's economy; all these factors seemed to make an atmosphere that, as Lenin would have said, was "friendly to revolution." But the picture rapidly changed. The United States showed increasing determination to hold fast to her controlling position in Japan. She had resolved that Japan should be rebuilt, on the basis of private capitalism, as the workshop of East Asia. Meanwhile the American Army has been building large modern airfields in Japan, capable of taking the heaviest types of long-range bombers, and has been arming Occupation aircraft. American economic aid had enabled conservative Japanese governments to postpone or avert the worst political and economic consequences of their own sabotage and inefficiency. Faced with these developments the Soviet Union apparently began to fear that it was fast losing position in its struggle to control Japan. It seems therefore to have radically revised its tactics.

Meanwhile the old guard in Japan is jubilant at receiving American backing for suppressing its own radicals and militants. It hopes for great things from being taken into American partnership in the fight against Communism and Russia. The militant radical groups are becoming increasingly sullen and resentful, though they still shrink from overt defiance of the Occupation. And the ordinary people of Japan, who have learnt in the desolate wastes of their ruined cities what to expect from war, carry on with dumb fatalism, wondering whether it will now be long before some new terror enflames their skies.

8. THE FUTURE OF JAPAN

IN THIS LAST CHAPTER I SHALL TRY TO SUM-
marize my argument and show its main implications for
future Allied policy in Japan.

My argument rests on two basic propositions. First, since
1945 there has been a far-reaching change in the attitude
of the United States towards Japan. The hated enemy has
become the coveted ally. Second, during the same period
there has been no fundamental change in Japan's social
structure or in the political outlook of her leaders.

In 1945 America wanted to demilitarize and democratize
Japan. Demilitarization meant not merely the elimination
of armaments and armed forces, but the attempt to educate the Japanese to renounce war as an instrument of
national policy. Democratization was not to be restricted
to law and politics, but to involve revolutionary changes
in Japan's social and economic structure. Japan was to be
"permitted to maintain such industries as will sustain her
economy and permit the exaction of just reparations in
kind, but not those that would enable her to re-arm for
war." [1]

But that was in 1945. Since then, as I have tried to
show, much has happened to bring solace to Japan's rulers.
The United States has tried to persuade the other Allies

[1] Potsdam Declaration.

that reparation claims should be reduced to the minimum, if not abandoned. The Allies, in response to American persuasion, have greatly raised the levels of permitted production in secondary war-industries, such as steel, aluminum, magnesium and shipbuilding. Washington has quietly put the brake on the "democratization" program, particularly on the purge and the dissolution of the Zaibatsu. On the positive side, American policy aims at establishing Japan as the "workshop of East Asia." American loans and credits are being provided for the restoration of Japanese industry and foreign trade.[2] There is no secret about the reasons for America's changed outlook. There is the simple and understandable wish to make Japan self-supporting and not a permanent burden on the American taxpayer. But the root motive is political. It is fear of Russia and Communism. America desires a strong and prosperous Japan as a backing against the extension of Russian influence in the Far East and the growth of Japanese Communism.

American policy in Japan is a regional expansion of her world policy. This policy crystallized in the first half of 1947. It was authoritatively formulated in the Truman Doctrine on March 12 and the Marshall Plan on June 5.

It was partly because the United Kingdom was so rapidly reducing her foreign commitments that America felt

[2] The change in United States policy in Japan runs parallel to its change in Germany; e.g., in the Allied agreement of March 28, 1946, Germany was to be permitted a level of production about 55 per cent of her 1938 output. In the Anglo-American agreement of August 28, 1947, Germany is to be allowed to produce 80 per cent of her 1938 output, or the equivalent of her 1936 output. The United States recognizes that in Japan, as in Germany, economic recovery is not possible without the restoration of industrial production. According to Professor Edward D. Mason, "the shift in American opinion away from economic disarmament and toward a substantial measure of economic rehabilitation in Germany is the result of a growing conviction that economic disarmament is both ineffective and unnecessary." *American Policy Toward Germany*, Foreign Policy Report, November 1, 1947, Foreign Policy Association, New York.

obliged to assume many new responsibilities abroad. It was not until February 24, 1947, that the British Ambassador told the United States Government that Britain would be unable to go on giving economic help to Greece and Turkey after March 31, or to maintain British forces in Greece much after that. The United States felt the immediate need to sustain the interests Britain had been supporting in the Eastern Mediterranean against Soviet encroachment. This led to the appeal to Congress for "emergency aid" to Greece and Turkey, and the formulation of the Truman Doctrine.

In the Far East the transfer of responsibility from British to American hands was more gradual and aroused less public attention, but the same process was taking place. The strength of the British Commonwealth Occupation Force was steadily reduced, and an Occupation, which had from the beginning been predominantly American, tended to become exclusively American. There is a tendency in some quarters in the British Commonwealth to present the extension of American influence in Europe and the East as an American effort to "push out" the British. This is not only unjust and ungenerous, but inconsistent with the historical record. It was only when the British withdrew that the Americans moved in. Naturally, some American circles feel satisfaction in the consequent extension of American power and prestige. If non-Americans keep the circumstances in mind, and also remember their long impatience with America's past isolationist policy, they would be chary of criticizing too quickly the present foreign policy of the United States. The United States Government, with less experience than Britain in the conduct of foreign relations, with a shortage of experienced officers, and with a public opinion still capricious on world questions, is resolved to add to her foreign burdens those that Britain has laid down.

In these circumstances, British observers should try to avoid "sniping" at the efforts of the United States. It is still important, I believe, that we should not endorse them uncritically. It seems to me that the soundness of America's policy today depends in great part on the emphasis that is put upon its different aspects. American policy is sometimes expressed in a negative and military form, sometimes in a positive and social-economic form. The program of aid for Turkey was exclusively for military expenditure, and it was quite clear that Turkey's defenses were being strengthened only against Russia. The aid for Greece was partly military—defense against Communist threats from across the frontiers and from Greek "guerillas," and partly economic, to promote the welfare of the Greek people. The projected aid for Japan is, at least ostensibly, purely economic and positive, since Japan is disarmed. In announcing his proposals of aid for Europe, Mr. Marshall tried to avoid the negative and military, and emphasize the positive and economic aspects. "Our policy," he said, "is not directed against any country or doctrine, but against hunger, desperation and chaos." It aimed at "the revival of a working economy in the world, so as to permit the emergence of political and social conditions in which free institutions can exist." [3]

The basic drive behind American policy, whether in Europe, the Middle East or the Far East, is resistance to Russia and Communism. Yet a great deal, perhaps everything, depends on the strategy of this resistance. If the emphasis is consistently placed on the welfare and freedom of the ordinary people of the countries "threatened" by Communism, and if every precaution is taken to ensure that this objective will in practice be realized, American

[3] For an excellent summary of American aid programs, see *American Policy Toward Greece,* by Winifred Hadsell. Foreign Policy Report, September 1, 1947, Foreign Policy Association, New York.

policy will win the widest acceptance in countries outside the Soviet orbit, and have the best prospects of success.

Insofar as America's plans to restore Japan's economic strength give good promise of raising the living standards and enlarging the freedom of the Japanese people, they should be fully supported. Yet there are great dangers that, in the present situation, American aid will not only fail in its positive purpose, but have dangerous consequences. American aid to Japan—with whatever supplementary contributions other Allies are prepared to make—will be given through the Japanese Government. I have reiterated that the Japanese Government represents the most conservative forces in Japan, that its pre-surrender outlook is unchanged, despite its gesture of cooperation with SCAP authority. It is hardly possible for a Japanese Government of different character to emerge in the near future. It is my thesis that since the surrender the Japanese Government, in response to the pressure groups that control it, has sabotaged economic recovery in the effort to frustrate the Allied aims of 1945, and that it has done this with frivolous indifference to the sufferings it has brought to the mass of the Japanese people. I can see no grounds for the belief that such a Government will want to use American aid to construct a welfare economy and enlarge the liberties of the working people. It seems nearly certain that it will try to use its new resources to consolidate the power and privilege of the ruling groups.

There is another immediate danger, perhaps less easy to recognize. It is the difficulty of reconciling the American faith in individualism with a sound program for Japan's economic reconstruction. It is possible for the United States, because of its immense wealth, to resist the kind of controls in economic life which other countries have adopted, and still maintain an endurable or, by comparison with some other countries, a comfortable standard of living for its poorest classes. Other countries cannot afford the wastes, or tolerate the inequalities, which such a full measure of individualism invariably involves. Outside the United States it is widely accepted that a considerable measure of political control in the economic field is necessary or desirable. The degree and kind of control can only be decided in terms of changing situations. It is not an ideological battle between "individualists" and "socialists," in which the belligerents hurl nineteenth-century epithets at each other. It is a practical problem of administration whether, in a particular country at a particular time, there should be public control of, say, the coal industry, and, if so, what particular technique of control will produce the best balance of economic welfare and personal freedom. The Prime Minister of the United Kingdom (Mr. Atlee) has recently described current British policy, not as diluted individualism, or diluted socialism, but as a positive effort to synthesize security and freedom. Such an approach avoids the rigidity of both "socialism" and "individualism." To those who hold this view, Russian policy smacks of the "extreme Left" and American policy of the "extreme Right."

I have already referred to General MacArthur's insistence that Japan must establish democracy through private capitalism, under a regime of free competitive enterprise. If that continues to be Allied policy in Japan, it must, in my view, mean depression and want for the Japanese masses, though perhaps with great wealth for the few. It will perpetuate the sort of social and economic conditions that favor the spread of Communism. It is perhaps not surprising that Communists in Japan are at present so restrained in their activities. They are confident that time is on their side.

I believe there is another great danger, though less immediate, in the present American policy towards Japan.

It is that in helping Japan rebuild her industrial strength and restore her foreign trade, the United States will enable Japan to establish an industrial and economic supremacy in East Asia which her leaders will once again exploit for political purposes. Economic penetration is the first step; political domination the second.

Japanese industrial technique will be vastly improved by the lessons learned from the Americans during the Occupation. And not only in industry, transport and science, but in medicine, hygiene and public health, the Japanese are avidly absorbing American know-how. We can expect that she will establish a long lead over other Asiatic countries in all these fields. Moreover, Japan's future trade opportunities seem likely to depend increasingly on the development of heavy and medium industries; that is, in secondary war industries. Silk exports will continue to diminish, owing to the competition of nylon and rayon. The exports of textiles will almost certainly become of less relative importance in Japan's trade, since other Asiatic countries are eager and able to manufacture these goods. It is, therefore, in the heavy and medium industries that Japan's best prospects lie. These should assure her a dominating position in the economy of East Asia.

It may be argued that there are no dangers in such a prospect since Japan's leaders have learned to renounce war, and will, in any case, be without the means to wage it. I can see no reason why Japan will be less likely in the 1950's than in the 1930's to want to use war as an instrument of national policy. Imperialism and militarism may well be the inevitable expression of the sort of economic and social system that still stands in Japan. It is true that at present Japan is disarmed. But we should remember that disarmament has meant the destruction of the weapons with which Japan fought the last war. It is not easy to be sure which weapons will be most useful if there is another war. It will, therefore, be harder to continue to prevent rearmament, and this difficulty will be increased if Japan develops a great variety of manufacturing industries.

It may be true that, so long as the United States maintains her present strategic interests in the Far East, she can easily forestall any hint of future Japanese aggression. Yet the maintenance of American military and political control in this area is likely to remain a considerable call on American resources, with trivial commercial compensation. We cannot be sure that America will be prepared to maintain these commitments indefinitely. An economic depression in the United States might make Congress want to reduce commitments abroad. Lastly, what happens in Japan will depend in a hundred ways on what happens in China.

In face of these manifold uncertainties, I believe it is rash and dangerous to assume that Japan cannot in the foreseeable future again become a danger to her neighbors.

For all these reasons, I think the first task for the peacemakers is to establish firm safeguards against the renewal of Japan's military power. I have referred to the proposal that Japan should be permitted a small army, perhaps 100,000, for "police duties." This proposal should be firmly rejected. While a small, lightly-equipped army might not in itself be a danger to any of Japan's neighbors, the prohibition of every sort of military formation is psychologically important. The army of 100,000 men permitted Germany after World War I became a rallying point for the revival of German militarism. We should not forget that experience.

If the earlier plans for Japan's economic disarmament are to be radically changed in the interests of her industrial development, it is the more important that there should be thorough and continuous Allied supervision of

Japan's imports, with the purpose of ensuring that the import of raw materials, which might be used for war, are no greater than necessary for the current output of civilian products. This determination of the quantity and quality of imports needed for Japan's peacetime industry is a highly technical task and full of difficulties. What is important to recognize is that the greater the quantity and variety of imports permitted, the greater the need for Allied controls. It should go without saying that all arms manufacture should be prohibited.

There is one other condition which the Allies should resolve to enforce. While any real reform in Japan's social and economic life must come from the Japanese themselves, this is only possible if the Japanese reformers continue to enjoy the political and civil rights granted them under the Occupation. I recognize that it would be impracticable, indeed impossible, to ensure that these rights should be faithfully honored by every bureaucrat and policeman in Japan. There are powerful forces which will seek to abridge or destroy them. Yet it should be possible for the Allied control authority to ensure, at the minimum, that all political parties shall remain free to pursue their aims with freedom of speech and assembly, and that radical leaders shall not be imprisoned for dangerous thoughts.

If the Allies resolve to do these two things—to prevent any form of rearmament and to sustain the "bill of rights" —it will be a great deal, and it is probably all that can be effectively done.

There is some temptation for those who feel strongly about the need for social and economic changes to urge that the Allies should force the Japanese to make these changes. This temptation should be resisted. The extent to which the Allies will be able to use physical force in Japan after the Treaty will be very limited, and the terms of the Treaty should be consistent with these limitations.

It is undesirable to extract undertakings from Japan as part of the peace settlement, unless we have the will and the resources to ensure that they will be carried out. That would mean a devaluation of the whole settlement. In practice the military enforcement of the Treaty will depend on air power, based on Okinawa; sea power, deployed in the Far East; and, possibly, on a token occupation force inside Japan. It would be unreal to expect American warships to blockade the ports, or American aircraft to bomb the cities of Japan, because the Japanese Government had defaulted in some program of domestic reform. Moreover, with every month that passes there will be an increasing Allied reluctance to revert to "bayonet control." In any case, reforms are unlikely to succeed in their purpose if imposed by outside physical force.

There is a big difference between physical coercion and economic inducement. Japan's economy is specially dependent on the outside world. She cannot restore her industries or regain her foreign trade without considerable outside aid by loans or credits, and her subsequent failure or success will depend on access to foreign markets and raw materials. Since the surrender, all of Japan's foreign trade has been carried out under the supervision of SCAP, to ensure that it would only be of a kind that would promote the objectives of the Occupation. The recent tendency is to encourage a return to "normal" foreign trading and finance, that is, to restore these activities to private firms working under the usual commercial incentives. The kind and quantity of financial aid tends to be determined by purely business considerations, without regard for its social and political implications. This is likely to result in a great strengthening of the position of the old or the new Zaibatsu and retard economic reforms. I have pointed out in an earlier chapter how food imports from the United States in 1946 enabled the Yoshida Government to avoid, or postpone, the political penalties of its failures. When the Occupation is over, the same sort of process is likely to take place on a much greater scale.

I think there is only one way to avoid this and that is for the Allies to insist that economic and financial aid will be always contingent on the Japanese Government's domestic policy. The flow of external aid should be closely geared to the rate of internal reform. I am arguing, if you will, for the use of economic sanctions. And the aim of these sanctions should be not only negative, to prevent the establishment of war industries, but positive, to press for fulfillment of the economic and social reforms initiated under the Occupation. If this plan were to be adopted, it would mean that all of Japan's foreign trade and finance would be controlled by agreement of the Allied Governments. Private concerns would only be permitted to operate in accordance with the terms decided by the Allied authority.

To carry out these controls it will be necessary to set up an Allied control body in Japan.

It is probably undesirable to decide in advance the precise period for which control will be necessary, since that will depend on the progress of domestic reforms, and particular controls should be relaxed or lifted when the Japanese give evidence that they are no longer needed. It seems probable, nevertheless, that strong controls will be necessary for at least a generation, or, say, twenty-five years. It is hard to believe that the re-education of the Japanese and the consolidation of new leadership could be achieved in a shorter period.

The first essential, if the Allied control body is to succeed, is that it should have the unqualified right to inspect and investigate anything happening in Japan. It would normally work through a group of expert committees, each concerned with a particular section of Japanese activity. Each committee would keep the control body continuously informed about what is happening in its own domain.

It has been suggested that the Allied body should be made up of the diplomatic representatives in Japan of the Allied Powers. This idea should be firmly rejected. It is a diplomatic tradition that embassies and legations should spend a great part of their time and energy in conscientiously entertaining one another, and, after the Treaty, Allied diplomats in Japan will almost certainly resume cordial official relations with the members of the Japanese Government. In these circumstances, it would be unreasonable to expect the diplomats to display the vigilance and firmness necessary for the success of the Allied body. The people responsible for controlling Japanese authorities should be free from the inhibitions of protocol.

The administration of the control machinery should be wholly American, if the United States is ready to undertake that responsibility. For some time at least America will be preponderant in Japan, and there would be insoluble problems of discipline and loyalty in the effort to give non-Americans executive positions in a predominantly American administration, particularly if the non-Americans should be Russians. The policy of the American administration should be controlled by an Allied body. There is much debate whether this commission should represent the four Powers, with its decisions subject to veto, or eleven Powers, with decisions taken by a two-thirds majority. The Soviet Union wants the first, the United States the second. The British Commonwealth countries involved, and other Allies, support the United States view.

There is, on principle, a very strong claim that all the nations who played an active part in the Pacific war should have a share in the postwar control of Japan. But the important issue is not whether there should be a four- or an eleven-Power Council, but whether the Great Powers should have the right of veto.

The strong Anglo-Saxon opposition to the veto in international councils is, at bottom, opposition to Russia's right to veto. A good deal of nonsense has been written about the veto. It is pointed out that it is inconsistent with democratic principles and so forth. Such criticism overlooks the basic fact that the condition of democracy in any country is that all groups should feel a fundamental identity of interests. When the groups in a community are united on primary issues they can agree to settle their secondary differences by a majority vote. But this basis of agreement does not exist, or, at least, it is not recognized, between Russia and the Western nations. It is, therefore, useless to concentrate attention on the veto as though it were a thing in itself intrinsically evil. The evil thing is the disunity between Russia and the Western world. In urging Russia to surrender the veto, the Western Powers are asking her to agree that the decisions of a majority of nations should be treated as the decisions of all the nations; that the Western Powers, by majority agreement, express the conscience of the world. I think the Western Powers are hardly likely to succeed in this.

I am not here concerned with the distribution of moral responsibility for this clash between Russia and the West. I am aware of the stubborn and provocative, the almost paranoiac, character of Russia's recent diplomacy. The Soviet Union's suppression of freedom of thought wherever its influence extends is the negation of all that is best in Western civilization. At the same time, I doubt whether Western civilization, and all that is good in it, can survive a third world war. That means that the first task of Western statesmanship today is to learn how to live in peace with Russia.

The situation in Japan is one part of that world-wide problem. It is, therefore, supremely important that the West should work with Russia in making the peace settlement and in the subsequent control of Japan. Russia's diplomatic intransigence may make the United States and the British Commonwealth despair of cooperation, and go ahead without her. In that event, it is particularly important for us to remember that we do not eliminate Russia's influence in Japan by dispensing with the presence of a Russian representative in Allied councils there. In race, in culture, in economic interest, Japan is part of East Asia. In Manchuria, China and Korea there are millions of people living in misery, now stirred, however dimly, with the resolve to win for themselves a better life. It is these deeper social forces that will decide the future of the Far East and of Japan, not the number of Allied troops, whether American, British or Russian, that are stationed there. In a word, if we want Japan as our ally, the way to succeed is not by subsidizing reactionary governments, or resuming trade relations with a disguised Zaibatsu, but by giving firm friendship and effective help to the Japanese people. At present the Japanese masses lack political consciousness and experienced leaders; they are still sunk in the past. But when they are without food or clothing or shelter, they want radical change. Those who help them achieve this change will be their friends; those who resist the change will be their enemies.

THE CONSTITUTION OF JAPAN[1]

We, the Japanese people, acting through our duly elected representatives in the National Diet, determined that we shall secure for ourselves and our posterity the fruits of peaceful cooperation with all nations and the blessings of liberty throughout this land, and resolved that never again shall we be visited with the horrors of war through the action of government, do proclaim that sovereign power resides with the people and do firmly establish this Constitution. Government is a sacred trust of the people, the authority for which is derived from the people, the powers of which are exercised by the representatives of the people, and the benefits of which are enjoyed by the people. This is a universal principle of mankind upon which this Constitution is founded. We reject and revoke all constitutions, laws, ordinances, and rescripts in conflict herewith.

We, the Japanese people, desire peace for all time and are deeply conscious of the high ideals controlling human relationship, and we have determined to preserve our security and existence, trusting in the justice and faith of the peace-loving peoples of the world. We desire to occupy an honored place in an international society striving for the

---

[1] Text from Publication 2836, Far Eastern Series 22, U. S. Dept. of State, Wash., D. C., 1947. The Constitution of Japan was promulgated on November 3, 1946, and became effective on May 3, 1947.

preservation of peace, and the banishment of tyranny and slavery, oppression and intolerance for all time from the earth. We recognize that all peoples of the world have the right to live in peace, free from fear and want.

We believe that no nation is responsible to itself alone, but that laws of political morality are universal; and that obedience to such laws is incumbent upon all nations who would sustain their own sovereignty and justify their sovereign relationship with other nations.

We, the Japanese people, pledge our national honor to accomplish these high ideals and purposes with all our resources.

Chapter I. The Emperor

Article 1. The Emperor shall be the symbol of the State and of the unity of the people, deriving his position from the will of the people with whom resides sovereign power.

Article 2. The Imperial Throne shall be dynastic and succeeded to in accordance with the Imperial House Law passed by the Diet.

Article 3. The advice and approval of the Cabinet shall be required for all acts of the Emperor in matters of state, and the Cabinet shall be responsible therefor.

Article 4. The Emperor shall perform only such acts in matters of state as are provided for in this Constitution and he shall not have powers related to government.

The Emperor may delegate the performance of his acts in matters of state as may be provided by law.

Article 5. When, in accordance with the Imperial House Law, a Regency is established, the Regent shall perform his acts in matters of state in the Emperor's name. In this case, paragraph one of the preceding article will be applicable.

Article 6. The Emperor shall appoint the Prime Minister as designated by the Diet.

The Emperor shall appoint the Chief Judge of the Supreme Court as designated by the Cabinet.

Article 7. The Emperor, with the advice and approval of the Cabinet, shall perform the following acts in matters of state on behalf of the people:

Promulgation of amendments of the constitution, laws, cabinet orders and treaties.

Convocation of the Diet.

Dissolution of the House of Representatives.

Proclamation of general election of members of the Diet.

Attestation of the appointment and dismissal of Ministers of State and other officials as provided for by law, and of full powers and credentials of Ambassadors and Ministers.

Attestation of general and special amnesty, commutation of punishment, reprieve, and restoration of rights.

Awarding of honors.

Attestation of instruments of ratification and other diplomatic documents as provided for by law.

Receiving foreign ambassadors and ministers.

Performance of ceremonial functions.

Article 8. No property can be given to, or received by, the Imperial House, nor can any gifts be made therefrom, without the authorization of the Diet.

CHAPTER II. RENUNCIATION OF WAR

Article 9. Aspiring sincerely to an international peace based on justice and order, the Japanese people forever renounce war as a sovereign right of the nation and the threat or use of force as means of settling international disputes.

In order to accomplish the aim of the preceding paragraph, land, sea, and air forces, as well as other war potential, will never be maintained. The right of belligerency of the state will not be recognized.

CHAPTER III. RIGHTS AND DUTIES OF THE PEOPLE

Article 10. The conditions necessary for being a Japanese national shall be determined by law.

Article 11. The people shall not be prevented from enjoying any of the fundamental human rights. These fundamental human rights guaranteed to the people by this Constitution shall be conferred upon the people of this and future generations as eternal and inviolate rights.

Article 12. The freedoms and rights guaranteed to the people by this Constitution shall be maintained by the constant endeavor of the people, who shall refrain from any abuse of these freedoms and rights and shall always be responsible for utilizing them for the public welfare.

Article 13. All of the people shall be respected as individuals. Their right to life, liberty, and the pursuit of happiness shall, to the extent that it does not interfere with the public welfare, be the supreme consideration in legislation and in other governmental affairs.

Article 14. All of the people are equal under the law and there shall be no discrimination in political, economic or social relations, because of race, creed, sex, social status or family origin.

Peers and peerage shall not be recognized.

No privilege shall accompany any award of honor, decoration or any distinction, nor shall any such award be valid beyond the lifetime of the individual who now holds or hereafter may receive it.

Article 15. The people have the inalienable right to choose their public officials and to dismiss them.

All public officials are servants of the whole community and not of any group thereof.

Universal adult suffrage is guaranteed with regard to the election of public officials.

In all elections, secrecy of the ballot shall not be violated. A voter shall not be answerable, publicly or privately, for the choice he has made.

Article 16. Every person shall have the right of peaceful petition for the redress of damage, for the removal of public officials, for the enactment, repeal or amendment of laws, ordinances or regulations and for other matters; nor shall any person be in any way discriminated against for sponsoring such a petition.

Article 17. Every person may sue for redress as provided by law from the State or a public entity, in case he has suffered damage through illegal act of any public official.

Article 18. No person shall be held in bondage of any kind. Involuntary servitude, except as punishment for crime, is prohibited.

Article 19. Freedom of thought and conscience shall not be violated.

Article 20. Freedom of religion is guaranteed to all. No religious organization shall receive any privileges from the State, nor exercise any political authority.

No person shall be compelled to take part in any religious act, celebration, rite or practice.

The State and its organs shall refrain from religious education or any other religious activity.

Article 21. Freedom of assembly and association as well as
speech, press and all other forms of expression are guaranteed.

No censorship shall be maintained, nor shall the secrecy of
any means of communication be violated.

Article 22. Every person shall have freedom to choose and
change his residence and to choose his occupation to the extent
that it does not interfere with the public welfare.

Freedom of all persons to move to a foreign country and to
divest themselves of their nationality shall be inviolate.

Article 23. Academic freedom is guaranteed.

Article 24. Marriage shall be based only on the mutual
consent of both sexes and it shall be maintained through
mutual cooperation with the equal rights of husband and
wife as a basis.

With regard to choice of spouse, property rights, inheritance,
choice of domicile, divorce and other matters pertaining to
marriage and the family, laws shall be enacted from the standpoint of individual dignity and the essential equality of the
sexes.

Article 25. All people shall have the right to maintain the
minimum standards of wholesome and cultured living.

In all spheres of life, the State shall use its endeavors for the
promotion and extension of social welfare and security, and of
public health.

Article 26. All people shall have the right to receive an
equal education correspondent to their ability, as provided by
law.

All people shall be obligated to have all boys and girls under
their protection receive ordinary education as provided for
by law. Such compulsory education shall be free.

Article 27. All people shall have the right and the obligation to work.

Standards for wages, hours, rest and other working conditions shall be fixed by law.

Children shall not be exploited.

Article 28. The right of workers to organize and to bargain
and act collectively is guaranteed.

Article 29. The right to own or to hold property is inviolable.

Property rights shall be defined by law, in conformity with the public welfare.

Private property may be taken for public use upon just compensation therefor.

Article 30. The people shall be liable to taxation as provided by law.

Article 31. No person shall be deprived of life or liberty, nor shall any other criminal penalty be imposed, except according to procedure established by law.

Article 32. No person shall be denied the right of access to the courts.

Article 33. No person shall be apprehended except upon warrant issued by a competent judicial officer which specifies the offense with which the person is charged, unless he is apprehended, the offense being committed.

Article 34. No person shall be arrested or detained without being at once informed of the charges against him or without the immediate privilege of counsel; nor shall he be detained without adequate cause; and upon demand of any person such cause must be immediately shown in open court in his presence and the presence of his counsel.

Article 35. The right of all persons to be secure in their homes, papers and effects against entries, searches and seizures shall not be impaired except upon warrant issued for adequate cause and particularly describing the place to be searched and things to be seized, or except as provided by Article 33.

Each search or seizure shall be made upon separate warrant issued by a competent judicial officer.

Article 36. The infliction of torture by any public officer and cruel punishments are absolutely forbidden.

Article 37. In all criminal cases the accused shall enjoy the right to a speedy and public trial by an impartial tribunal.

He shall be permitted full opportunity to examine all witnesses, and he shall have the right of compulsory process for obtaining witnesses on his behalf at public expense.

At all times the accused shall have the assistance of competent counsel who shall, if the accused is unable to secure the same by his own efforts, be assigned to his use by the State.

Article 38. No person shall be compelled to testify against himself.

Confession made under compulsion, torture or threat, or

after prolonged arrest or detention shall not be admitted in evidence.

No person shall be convicted or punished in cases where the only proof against him is his own confession.

Article 39. No person shall be held criminally liable for an act which was lawful at the time it was committed, or of which he has been acquitted, nor shall he be placed in double jeopardy.

Article 40. Any person, in case he is acquitted after he has been arrested or detained, may sue the State for redress as provided by law.

CHAPTER IV. THE DIET

Article 41. The Diet shall be the highest organ of state power, and shall be the sole law-making organ of the State.

Article 42. The Diet shall consist of two Houses, namely the House of Representatives and the House of Councillors.

Article 43. Both Houses shall consist of elected members, representative of all the people.

The number of the members of each House shall be fixed by law.

Article 44. The qualifications of members of both Houses and their electors shall be fixed by law. However, there shall be no discrimination because of race, creed, sex, social status, family origin, education, property or income.

Article 45. The term of office of members of the House of Representatives shall be four years. However, the term shall be terminated before the full term is up in case the House of Representatives is dissolved.

Article 46. The term of office of members of the House of Councillors shall be six years, and election for half the members shall take place every three years.

Article 47. Electoral districts, method of voting and other matters pertaining to the method of election of members of both Houses shall be fixed by law.

Article 48. No person shall be permitted to be a member of both Houses simultaneously.

Article 49. Members of both Houses shall receive appropriate annual payment from the national treasury in accordance with law.

Article 50. Except in cases provided by law, members of both Houses shall be exempt from apprehension while the

Diet is in session, and any members apprehended before the opening of the session shall be freed during the term of the session upon demand of the House.

Article 51. Members of both Houses shall not be held liable outside the House for speeches, debates or votes cast inside the House.

Article 52. An ordinary session of the Diet shall be convoked once per year.

Article 53. The Cabinet may determine to convoke extraordinary sessions of the Diet. When a quarter or more of the total members of either House makes the demand, the Cabinet must determine on such convocation.

Article 54. When the House of Representatives is dissolved, there must be a general election of members of the House of Representatives within forty (40) days from the date of dissolution, and the Diet must be convoked within thirty (30) days from the date of the election.

When the House of Representatives is dissolved, the House of Councillors is closed at the same time. However, the Cabinet may in time of national emergency convoke the House of Councillors in emergency session.

Measures taken at such session as mentioned in the proviso of the preceding paragraph shall be provisional and shall become null and void unless agreed to by the House of Representatives within a period of ten (10) days after the opening of the next session of the Diet.

Article 55. Each House shall judge disputes related to qualifications of its members. However, in order to deny a seat to any member, it is necessary to pass a resolution by a majority of two-thirds or more of the members present.

Article 56. Business cannot be transacted in either House unless one-third or more of total membership is present.

All matters shall be decided, in each House, by a majority of those present, except as elsewhere provided in the Constitution, and in case of a tie, the presiding officer shall decide the issue.

Article 57. Deliberation in each House shall be public. However, a secret meeting may be held where a majority of two-thirds or more of those members present passes a resolution therefor.

Each House shall keep a record of proceedings. This record shall be published and given general circulation, excepting such parts of proceedings of secret session as may be deemed to require secrecy.

Upon demand of one-fifth or more of the members present, votes of the members on any matter shall be recorded in the minutes.

Article 58. Each House shall select its own president and other officials.

Each House shall establish its rules pertaining to meetings, proceedings and internal discipline, and may punish members for disorderly conduct. However, in order to expel a member, a majority of two-thirds or more of those members present must pass a resolution thereon.

Article 59. A bill becomes a law on passage by both Houses, except as otherwise provided by the Constitution.

A bill which is passed by the House of Representatives, and upon which the House of Councillors makes a decision different from that of the House of Representatives, becomes a law when passed a second time by the House of Representatives by a majority of two-thirds or more of the members present.

The provision of the preceding paragraph does not preclude the House of Representatives from calling for the meeting of a joint committee of both Houses, provided for by law.

Failure by the House of Councillors to take final action within sixty (60) days after receipt of a bill passed by the House of Representatives, time in recess excepted, may be determined by the House of Representatives to constitute a rejection of the said bill by the House of Councillors.

Article 60. The budget must first be submitted to the House of Representatives.

Upon consideration of the budget, when the House of Councillors makes a decision different from' that of the House of Representatives, and when no agreement can be reached even through a joint committee of both Houses, provided for by law, or in the case of failure by the House of Councillors to take final action within thirty (30) days, the period of recess excluded, after the receipt of the budget passed by the House of Representatives, the decision of the House of Representatives shall be the decision of the Diet.

Article 61. The second paragraph of the preceding article applies also to the Diet approval required for the conclusion of treaties.

Article 62. Each House may conduct investigations in relation to government, and may demand the presence and testimony of witnesses, and the production of records.

Article 63. The Prime Minister and other Ministers of State may, at any time, appear in either House for the purpose of speaking on bills, regardless of whether they are members of the House or not. They must appear when their presence is required in order to give answers or explanations.

Article 64. The Diet shall set up an impeachment court from among the members of both Houses for the purpose of trying those judges against whom removal proceedings have been instituted.

Matters relating to impeachment shall be provided by law.

Chapter V.   The Cabinet

Article 65. Executive power shall be vested in the Cabinet.

Article 66. The Cabinet shall consist of the Prime Minister, who shall be its head, and other Ministers of State, as provided for by law.

The Prime Minister and other Ministers of State must be civilians.

The Cabinet, in the exercise of executive power, shall be collectively responsible to the Diet.

Article 67. The Prime Minister shall be designated from among the members of the Diet by a resolution of the Diet. This designation shall precede all other business.

If the House of Representatives and the House of Councillors disagree and if no agreement can be reached even through a joint committee of both Houses, provided for by law, or the House of Councillors fails to make designation within ten (10) days, exclusive of the period of recess, after the House of Representatives has made designation, the decision of the House of Representatives shall be the decision of the Diet.

Article 68. The Prime Minister shall appoint the Ministers of State. However, a majority of their number must be chosen from among the members of the Diet.

The Prime Minister may remove the Ministers of State as he chooses.

Article 69. If the House of Representatives passes a non-confidence resolution, or rejects a confidence resolution, the Cabinet shall resign en masse, unless the House of Representatives is dissolved within ten (10) days.

Article 70. When there is a vacancy in the post of Prime Minister, or upon the first convocation of the Diet after a general election of members of the House of Representatives, the Cabinet shall resign en masse.

Article 71. In the cases mentioned in the two preceding articles, the Cabinet shall continue its functions until the time when a new Prime Minister is appointed.

Article 72. The Prime Minister, representing the Cabinet, submits bills, reports on general national affairs and foreign relations to the Diet and exercises control and supervision over various administrative branches.

Article 73. The Cabinet, in addition to other general administrative functions, shall perform the following functions:

> Administer the law faithfully; conduct affairs of state.
>
> Manage foreign affairs.
>
> Conclude treaties. However, it shall obtain prior or, depending on circumstances, subsequent approval of the Diet.
>
> Administer the civil service, in accordance with standards established by law.
>
> Prepare the budget, and present it to the Diet.
>
> Enact cabinet orders in order to execute the provisions of this Constitution and of the law. However, it cannot include penal provisions in such cabinet orders unless authorized by such law.
>
> Decide on general amnesty, special amnesty, commutation of punishment, reprieve, and restoration of rights.

Article 74. All laws and cabinet orders shall be signed by the competent Minister of State and countersigned by the Prime Minister.

Article 75. The Ministers of State, during their tenure of office, shall not be subject to legal action without the consent of the Prime Minister. However, the right to take that action is not impaired hereby.

CHAPTER VI. JUDICIARY

Article 76. The whole judicial power is vested in a Supreme Court and in such inferior courts as are established by law.

No extraordinary tribunal shall be established, nor shall any organ or agency of the Executive be given final judicial power.

All judges shall be independent in the exercise of their

conscience and shall be bound only by this Constitution and the laws.

Article 77. The Supreme Court is vested with the rule-making power under which it determines the rules of procedure and of practice, and of matters relating to attorneys, the internal discipline of the courts and the administration of judicial affairs.

Public procurators shall be subject to the rule-making power of the Supreme Court.

The Supreme Court may delegate the power to make rules for inferior courts to such courts.

Article 78. Judges shall not be removed except by public impeachment unless judicially declared mentally or physically incompetent to perform official duties. No disciplinary action against judges shall be administered by any executive organ or agency.

Article 79. The Supreme Court shall consist of a Chief Judge and such number of judges as may be determined by law; all such judges excepting the Chief Judge shall be appointed by the Cabinet.

The appointment of the judges of the Supreme Court shall be reviewed by the people at the first general election of members of the House of Representatives following their appointment, and shall be reviewed again at the first general election of members of the House of Representatives after a lapse of ten (10) years, and in the same manner thereafter.

In cases mentioned in the foregoing paragraph, when the majority of the voters favors the dismissal of a judge, he shall be dismissed.

Matters pertaining to review shall be prescribed by law.

The judges of the Supreme Court shall be retired upon the attainment of the age as fixed by law.

All such judges shall receive, at regular stated intervals, adequate compensation which shall not be decreased during their terms of office.

Article 80. The judges of the inferior courts shall be appointed by the Cabinet from a list of persons nominated by the Supreme Court. All such judges shall hold office for a term of ten (10) years with privilege of reappointment, provided that they shall be retired upon the attainment of the age as fixed by law.

The judges of the inferior courts shall receive, at regular

stated intervals, adequate compensation which shall not be decreased during their terms of office.

Article 81. The Supreme Court is the court of last resort with power to determine the constitutionality of any law, order, regulation or official act.

Article 82. Trials shall be conducted and judgment declared publicly.

Where a court unanimously determines publicity to be dangerous to public order or morals, a trial may be conducted privately, but trials of political offenses, offenses involving the press or cases wherein the rights of people as guaranteed in Chapter III of this Constitution are in question shall always be conducted publicly.

CHAPTER VII. FINANCE

Article 83. The power to administer national finances shall be exercised as the Diet shall determine.

Article 84. No new taxes shall be imposed or existing ones modified except by law or under such conditions as law may prescribe.

Article 85. No money shall be expended, nor shall the State obligate itself, except as authorized by the Diet.

Article 86. The Cabinet shall prepare and submit to the Diet for its consideration and decision a budget for each fiscal year.

Article 87. In order to provide for unforeseen deficiencies in the budget, a reserve fund may be authorized by the Diet to be expended upon the responsibility of the Cabinet.

The Cabinet must get subsequent approval of the Diet for all payments from the reserve fund.

Article 88. All property of the Imperial Household shall belong to the State. All expenses of the Imperial Household shall be appropriated by the Diet in the budget.

Article 89. No public money or other property shall be expended or appropriated for the use, benefit or maintenance of any religious institution or association, or for any charitable, educational or benevolent enterprises not under the control of public authority.

Article 90. Final accounts of the expenditures and revenues of the State shall be audited annually by a Board of Audit and submitted by the Cabinet to the Diet, together with the statement of audit, during the fiscal year immediately following the period covered.

The organization and competency of the Board of Audit shall be determined by law.

Article 91. At regular intervals and at least annually the Cabinet shall report to the Diet and the people on the state of national finances.

CHAPTER VIII. LOCAL SELF-GOVERNMENT

Article 92. Regulations concerning organization and operations of local public entities shall be fixed by law in accordance with the principle of local autonomy.

Article 93. The local public entities shall establish assemblies as their deliberative organs, in accordance with law.

The chief executive officers of all local public entities, the members of their assemblies, and such other local officials as may be determined by law shall be elected by direct popular vote within their several communities.

Article 94. Local public entities shall have the right to manage their property, affairs and administration and to enact their own regulations within law.

Article 95. A special law, applicable only to one local public entity, cannot be enacted by the Diet without the consent of the majority of the voters of the local public entity concerned, obtained in accordance with law.

CHAPTER IX. AMENDMENTS

Article 96. Amendments to this Constitution shall be initiated by the Diet, through a concurring vote of two-thirds or more of all the members of each House and shall thereupon be submitted to the people for ratification, which shall require the affirmative vote of a majority of all votes cast thereon, at a special referendum or at such election as the Diet shall specify.

Amendments when so ratified shall immediately be promulgated by the Emperor in the name of the people, as an integral part of this Constitution.

CHAPTER X. SUPREME LAW

Article 97. The fundamental human rights by this Constitution guaranteed to the people of Japan are fruits of the age-old struggle of man to be free; they have survived the many exacting tests for durability and are conferred upon this and future generations in trust, to be held for all time inviolate.

Article 98. This Constitution shall be the supreme law of the nation and no law, ordinance, imperial rescript or other act of government, or part thereof, contrary to the provisions hereof, shall have legal force or validity.

The treaties concluded by Japan and established laws of nations shall be faithfully observed.

Article 99. The Emperor or the Regent as well as Ministers of State, members of the Diet, judges, and all other public officials have the obligation to respect and uphold this Constitution.

Chapter XI. Supplementary Provisions

Article 100. This Constitution shall be enforced as from the day when the period of six months will have elapsed counting from the day of its promulgation.

The enactment of laws necessary for the enforcement of this Constitution, the election of members of the House of Councillors and the procedure for the convocation of the Diet and other preparatory procedures necessary for the enforcement of this Constitution may be executed before the day prescribed in the preceding paragraph.

Article 101. If the House of Councillors is not constituted before the effective date of this Constitution, the House of Representatives shall function as the Diet until such time as the House of Councillors shall be constituted.

Article 102. The term of office for half the members of the House of Councillors serving in the first term under this Constitution shall be three years. Members falling under this category shall be determined in accordance with law.

Article 103. The Ministers of State, members of the House of Representatives and judges in office on the effective date of this Constitution, and all other public officials who occupy positions corresponding to such positions as are recognized by this Constitution shall not forfeit their positions automatically on account of the enforcement of this Constitution unless otherwise specified by law. When, however, successors are elected or appointed under the provisions of this Constitution, they shall forfeit their positions as a matter of course.

REPORT OF THE JOHNSTON COMMITTEE [1]

~~~~~~

GENERAL ANALYSIS OF THE SITUATION IN JAPAN

Japan's prewar social and economic policy was developed to serve political and military purposes. Growth in population continued without regard to the limited resources of the four islands which are the homeland of Japan. A large part of Japanese working effort, capital and resources were absorbed in the maintenance of armed forces and the construction of arms plants. Part of the rest was used to develop railways, mines, factories and other sources of supply in the conquered lands—Formosa, Korea, Manchuria and North China. Industry was forced to conform to military needs and purposes and became subject to government orders.

Economic development within Japan and peacetime needs suffered; much of the effort, capital and resources that might have served to improve industry and agriculture within Japan proper were diverted. The stocks of gold, foreign exchange and raw materials were expended in the same effort. Japan supported her expanding population by getting food, raw materials and the product of controlled labor from the countries brought under its domination.

In short, Japan's economic life was shaped to fit its attempt to become the dominating center of Asia and of the whole

. [1] Released by the Department of the Army, Washington, May 19, 1948. The Report is prefaced by a Summary and concludes with a few paragraphs of notes on Korea, which are here omitted; otherwise it is reproduced verbatim.

Pacific world. The working lives and prospects of the Japanese people crowded on the home islands were put on the gaming table of expansion and war. This reckless gamble was lost.

Defeat left Japan a ruined nation. The conquered empire was lost; with it, the great investments which Japan had made. Within Japan proper, there was great destruction of houses, cities and factories. The merchant fleet, by means of which Japan carried on its trade, was also lost. Remaining inventories of raw materials, especially imported raw materials, such as oil, cotton, wool, coking coal, rubber and salt were small. Farm lands were neglected and supplies of fertilizer, seeds and tools insufficient. Food production within Japan was insufficient to supply even a minimum subsistence for the increased population; for, besides a rate of growth of about one million per year, some five or six million Japanese were returned from the lost territories. Coal production within Japan was completely inadequate for minimum needs of power, fuel and transport.

Finances of the government were in disorder. The financial situation of many banks and corporations was shattered because of the loss of assets abroad, war destruction, or depreciation of properties.

Such were the consequences of Japan's gamble in the use of force as a way of building a satisfactory economic life. Such is the situation which the Japanese people of today have inherited.

It is needless to emphasize the great measure of sober understanding, hard work, endurance and patient cooperation that will be necessary to correct it. In judging the Japanese effort to do so, it should be borne in mind that success or failure will not lie entirely within Japan's control. Peace and productive progress in the outside world, especially in the rest of Asia, will make Japan's task easier; a continuation of international dissension and world-wide shortages of goods will make Japan's task harder.

The American Government has accepted and is discharging broad responsibilities as the occupying power. It has sustained order without which the effort of recovery could not go on. It has encouraged the adoption of a new basis of government in which individual energies and abilities may find greater growth and opportunity. It has prevented starvation and disease, making more generous appropriations for such essentials as food, oil, fertilizers and seeds than any victor has ever before given any conquered enemy. It is aiding the Japanese people in their effort to adjust their economy to the circumstances that confront them. Congress is now being asked to consider a program for providing Japan an essential minimum of supplies, particularly raw materials, required to make progress toward self-support. This would be a new departure in American policy in Japan. It is based on a common sense approach: Some branches of Japanese industry could be making goods that other countries need if these industries had the raw materials; but Japan cannot pay for them now; we could finance them; Japanese industry could convert them into finished goods; by selling part of these goods abroad it could get the dollars to pay for the raw materials; the rest of the product could remain in Japan where it is badly needed.

This program should be carried forward by the American Government. The accepted responsibility has been to maintain order, to stimulate reform, to prevent disease and unrest. Now we should concentrate upon the ways of revival and provide certain minimum essentials without which Japan cannot become self-supporting.

The first economic need of Japan is increased production. The production of domestic industrial raw materials and fabricated goods now is less than 45 per cent of what it was during the years 1930–1934. Exchange of Japan's fabricated products for such raw materials as oil of the Dutch East Indies, iron ore of North China, sugar of Formosa, wool of Australia, rubber of the Malay States, rice of Indo-China, all have almost ceased for the time being. Domestic cereal production takes care of only 80 per cent of Japan's current need. Fishing, the other main source of food in Japan, is only half what it was; the Japanese fishing fleet is reduced and unable to fish in many waters hitherto open to it.

The Committee, therefore, looked into the present obstacles to production to discern the means by which they could be lessened. There are many deterrents and each affects the rest. But for the purpose of examination, they may be divided into two main groups. One of these may be called physical, the other institutional.

The three main deficiencies in the physical means available

to Japan are: (1) lack of essential raw materials, (2) the bad condition of many existing factories, (3) the poor state of transport. The deterrent effect of each of these upon production is evident, but it may be useful to illustrate each briefly.

1. Because of a shortage of coking coal even such parts of the Japanese steel industry as are in physical condition to operate, cannot do so fully. Cotton looms and spindles stood idle because of lack of raw cotton until the United States provided some. Without enough wood pulp, the rayon mills must remain largely without work; without enough hides, the shoe and leather industries cannot resume satisfactorily; without rubber, all branches of industry making vehicles suffer; without enough salt, operations of the chemical industries cannot provide the chemicals needed by other branches of manufacture; without enough oil, machines cannot be lubricated, ships cannot run, trucks cannot carry products from place to place.

The existing shortage of raw materials today is keeping Japan's production much below its potentialities. Despite all the other existing defects of the Japanese economic situation, a marked improvement will result if and when raw material supplies are more adequate. Processed and sold abroad, they could provide the financial means for successive steps forward; in contrast unless these raw materials are secured, trade will be very small and Japan cannot avoid a long period of suffering and dependency.

An increase in the production of all raw materials that can be produced within Japan (such as coal, copper, brick, cement and wood products) should be the first order of Japanese business. There should be, as far as possible, an adaptation of the Japanese economy and life to the use of local materials, since even if trade grows rapidly, available imports are almost sure to be less than the total needs of a fully employed Japan.

2. During the war, and since, equipment in many important industries, suffered war damage, fell into disrepair, or had vital parts broken or vital machinery removed. For example, the present initial output of aluminum is handicapped by the state of the lining of the furnaces; coal production is much lower than it would be if the machinery at the mines were in good shape. Next to the acquisition of raw materials, the repair and modernization of such plants and equipment offers the best and quickest contribution to recovery.

3. Production is suffering many delays and interruptions because of the poor state of the railways and railway equipment and lowered operating efficiency. Also contributing is the extra burden placed upon the railways by the dearth of coastwise shipping. Many branches of industry in the Tokyo region, for example, recently were forced to suspend operation because of the failure of charcoal shipments to arrive from other parts of Japan; much cut timber is lying in the forests of Hokkaido, waiting to be taken away; movement of badly needed iron pyrites to the fertilizer plants has been delayed.

These physical deficiencies can be overcome gradually as Japan makes fuller use of its natural resources, improves its methods of production and rebuilds trade with the outside world.

Despite all physical limitations, production could even now be at a higher level, were it not for other deterrent influences affecting adversely the desire to produce, work, plan and invest. These mount up to a lack of reasonable assurance of reward and incentive. The whole production effort is taking place in an atmosphere of uncertainty, which affects workers, managers and owners. It is causing production and effort to be reduced, fitful and unsteady. This uncertainty must be eliminated.

The Committee has studied its several causes attentively. Some are the direct and unavoidable consequences of the war and war settlements. Important enterprises in Japan suffered great losses through war damage, cessation of arms production or when their property outside Japan was lost. Their financial bases have been weakened or destroyed and their organization disrupted. The necessary financial reorganization of these enterprises should be carried out rapidly.

The threat of removal for reparations hangs over much of Japan's industry, especially heavy industry. Owners and directors who fear that their property may be taken from them will not exert themselves to bring that property back into production or to use it fully. It is, therefore, imperative that decision be reached promptly as to which excess Japanese plants and equipment are to be subject to removal as reparations and that the rest be given assurance that they will remain untouched.

Another element of uncertainty derives from the changes being effected in the control of Japanese industry. A very large part of Japanese industry before the war was dominated either by the government or by private monopolistic groups. Many of the principal enterprises established in conquered countries such as Formosa or Manchuria were creatures of the government. A great part of Japanese industry, trade, shipping, and banking were under the control of a few small family groups collectively known as the "Zaibatsu." These and other interests were linked together in many and close associations and groups to regulate production and control competition.

Japan has a well established social structure and code of economic rights and duties, especially as between workers and employers, quite different from that prevailing in the United States. Some important industries, for example, carry out stages of their production in thousands of small family workshops; the organized handling of their products was customary and in some ways useful. It was customary for some industries to continue employment and wage payments to all employees, whether there was work for them or not; and wages were graded according to the personal and family needs of the workers. These and other customary practices naturally led to limitations on the intensity of competition. Such customs and practices cannot and should not be violently disregarded or abruptly terminated and must be borne in mind when judging agreements among employers.

But the practices of combinations, monopoly and concentrated control in Japan went far beyond arrangements required to utilize the family workshops or maintain customary social protection. As already observed, a small number of family groups, through holding companies and controlled banks, owned and directed a large part of all Japanese industry, shipping and finance. In various basic fields such as steel and paper, one company controlled 80 per cent or over of all production, maintaining a suppressive monopoly. Such excess concentration of power and ownership had bad economic, political and social effects. They could, and sometimes did, dominate the government. They could be inefficient and still survive. They could and did repress the emergence of business ability. This concentration of control lent itself to easy domination over production for aggressive war.

For these reasons the Japanese Government, under the Allied policy, is seeking to diffuse the ownership and control of Japan's productive plants more widely and to develop greater competition. This policy should, after the adjustments have been made, bring greater and more effective production—if care is taken in carrying out the necessary measures of reorganization. But during the process of deconcentration, which is now going on, uncertainty is inevitable and may now be holding back production in some fields, since existing managements do not know how to plan.

The period of uncertainty caused by this economic reform should be made short and the area of uncertainty lessened as rapidly as possible. The possible disturbing effects should be allayed by care not to hurt production, and by limiting reorganization to the minimum necessary to insure reasonable competition. This we understand is the intention of the occupation authorities and is further assured by their establishment of an American review board to see that deconcentration plans do not adversely affect production and the broad program to achieve economic recovery. Care must also be taken that breaking up of the Zaibatsu monopolies does not lead to the growth of governmental monopolies.

Such are some of the elements of uncertainty bearing on the conduct of business enterprise. There is another of a general character—the serious inflation prevailing in Japan. Prices of essentials (food, clothing, housing, fuel and light) are about four times higher than they were at the beginning of 1946, despite official controls and subsidies. The increase in prices and the general level of costs of production would be much higher still if the American government had not, under the relief program, supplied large amounts of essential products such as food, fertilizer, seeds and oil. These have made it possible to prevent prices of food and other consumer goods and of goods used in production from rising so greatly as to destroy trust in the value of money. Paper money outstanding has increased many more times than the volume of goods; in 1939 it was less than four billion yen, at the end of the war it was about 55 billion yen, and in March 1948 it was about 220 billion yen.

This inflated price situation means that employees of factories and offices and farmers, whose money income has vastly increased but who cannot buy many of the things they want, live anxious lives. Their real return for work ceases to be related to effort and becomes subject to chance and sudden change. This discourages steady effort, diverts activities and products to the black market where shrewdness and selfishness count more than usefulness. It penalizes integrity and rewards chicanery. Similarly, the managers of business, large and small, often cannot tell whether they are making a profit or loss. Costs become uncertain and long-term contracts impossible. Business becomes dependent on the government or banks for working capital. Interest rates become so high that only those who know they can sell at an advanced price can borrow. Goods are hoarded. The costs of government are forced up, revenues lag, deficits grow, and the inflation and its demoralizing effects are extended.

It has become imperative that the course of extreme inflation within Japan be arrested. Moderate general price increases may sometimes stimulate production; and relative increases in particular prices may stimulate the production of goods particularly needed. But the price situation and trend in Japan is now retarding industrial production and causing widespread anxiety for the future.

The Japanese Government, encouraged and supported by the American occupation authorities is making strenuous efforts to curb the inflation and not without success in certain strategic elements of the problem. Collection of foodstuffs has been much better than before; the rationing system has become more effective; coal production has been substantially increased; tax collections have improved and the will to restrain public spending has strengthened. These are encouraging signs.

The Japanese people must adjust their supply of monetary means of payment to their supply of goods. This can only be done by ceasing to add to their supply of money and increasing their supply of goods. Neither can be done entirely by gentle means; each group, section and part of Japanese life will have to reconcile itself to getting along with little until there is more to share. There must be a government strong enough to stand out against those who will not do so voluntarily.

Basically, the inflation is the result of the scarcity of goods. But it has been cumulatively increased by meeting government deficits by additions to the volume of currency. Even under the present straitened circumstances the attainment of a balanced budget, or substantial progress toward that goal, should be possible. The vast outlay previously carried by the Japanese Government for military purposes is now saved although this is partially offset by necessary occupation costs. Nonetheless, the attainment of a budget balance will require the most stubborn will, great political courage on the part of the government, and great patience on the part of the Japanese people.

No matter how determined an effort may be made to limit the supply of money, it is certain to fail unless Japanese production grows. Reference has already been made to certain deterrents to this urgently needed increase in production. There are still others to which attention might well be directed.

The output of workers in various branches of industry and mining is lower than before the war. This is due in large part to defective tools, interruptions in the supply of raw materials, inadequate food, housing and clothing. Output will probably increase when and as these conditions are improved. But in some measure it appears to be caused by lessening of effort and hindering rules or terms of work. Such tendencies appear whenever, as now, there is fear of lack of work to go around.

It is essential that the Japanese workers should during this period of strain and scarcity labor hard and well, as they have in the past. Japan needs their product, both to supply the domestic market and to provide the means of trade. To rebuild the required volume of trade, Japanese industries will have to meet external competition, and find their way into foreign markets by offering goods on attractive terms. The alternatives are for the Japanese people to endure an even lower standard of living on their crowded islands, or to be permanently dependent on outside charity.

Resumption of Japanese trade will be affected by the attitudes and policies of other countries, their willingness to permit Japanese shipping to carry a reasonable tonnage, and recognition that discrimination against Japanese trade would not be in the long-range interests of world trade and prosperity. Again, if production and trade of other foreign countries increases, Japan's prospects will benefit; if they lag, Japan's task of regaining balance and stability will be the harder. Reciprocally, an improvement in Japan's production and trade will aid other countries if they make use of Japanese goods and services.

The return of tranquility and settled political conditions in those other Asiatic countries which are among Japan's natural customers would help greatly. An increase in total world supplies of raw materials would help Japan by encouraging other countries to enter into trade agreements with Japan and by reducing the prices of needed materials. So also Japan's exports sales would be aided if the present world-wide dollar shortage is alleviated. For this reason the European Recovery Program should benefit Japan as well as the countries directly helped.

In essence, it may be said that the three connected problems that Japan must solve are: (1) to increase production, (2) to end inflation, and (3) to develop trade. All will take time and all originated in a condition of disturbance and scarcity. The means of production are scarce. It is therefore necessary that they be put to the best use, that available supplies of tools, parts and raw materials be allocated to those who can make them yield most, and that food and consumers goods be fairly and honestly shared.

This justifies the controls now being exercised by the government over the supply and use of such goods. But it places upon the Japanese people and government the duty and burden of seeing that the controls are intelligently and honestly exercised.

Controls on prices are also necessary for the present to combat the inflation and to promote the general welfare. Again they call for moderation and patient acceptance by all. Constant pressure by wage-earners for higher money wages will either force constantly rising prices or require larger and larger government subsidies. Unjustified demands by producers of industrial goods for higher prices will intensify pressure for higher wages and increase social unrest. Cost-price relationships in industry must give producers some incentive but no excess gain. They cannot be expected to operate at a loss, as some are doing at present; but they cannot expect to rebuild their business or fortunes quickly in this time of scarcity.

The same comment applies to the farmers of Japan. Before the war and before the reforms encouraged by the occupying authorities they were an oppressed group within Japan. Making up about 45 per cent of the Japanese people, they received little more than 10 per cent of the national income. Now they are comparatively much better off; it is roughly estimated that they receive nearly 35 per cent of the reduced national income. It is of first importance that they (1) continue to increase food production, (2) deliver their products into regular channels, and (3) recognize that higher prices for the food they produce will only increase inflation.

Trade unions in Japan are being given a chance to prove that they can protect the interest of employees without frustrating production. Business under government control is being given a chance to prove that it can gradually reconstruct a self-supporting and socially satisfying situation on the ruins of war. Each is dependent on the other and both must accept governmental controls on their private desires as long as they are necessary. As scarcities diminish, these controls should be relaxed or removed. They are, it is to be hoped, only temporary aids on the road to the establishment of a free enterprise system.

Our Committee, in its studies of the Japanese economy, has assumed that peace will continue, that the cooperative relationship between the Japanese and the occupation authorities will be maintained, and that Far Eastern countries, along with other areas of the world, will gradually recover from the dislocation and shortages caused by the war. Discussion and specific recommendations dealing with the various subjects to which the Committee addressed itself follow.

RAW MATERIALS AND FOREIGN TRADE

To achieve economic recovery, Japan must secure a far greater volume of raw materials than at present. It can, by careful planning and effort increase the supply of a limited group of raw materials found within Japan: bituminous coal, copper, lumber and other building materials. But most of the products required by industry are not found within Japan. These are too numerous fully to list: textile fiber and wood-pulp for its cotton and rayon industries; iron ore, manganese and coking coal for her iron and steel industry; bauxite for the aluminum industry; rubber, tin, zinc, lead for the manufacture of vehicles, farm tools and machines; salt and other chemicals for her fertilizer plants; copra for soap-making; oil for the whole of her economy. To secure these Japan must begin to trade again with the rest of the world on a large scale. Hardly less important is Japan's need for certain essential parts and components for its industrial plants, which Japan will have to import until its own industries are repaired and reestablished.

The relatively meager revival of Japanese foreign trade has until now been largely dependent upon raw materials and supplies made available by the United States. Failure to press vigorously for restoration of foreign trade would prolong the expensive necessity of underwriting Japanese deficits.

SCAP has estimated that under favorable conditions and with reasonable aid from the United States, a balance between exports and imports should be attainable by 1953.

It has been estimated that Japan will require about $1,575,000,000 of exports each year (at current prices) to pay for essential imports of food and raw materials (and necessary invisible imports) to maintain a tolerable food ration and standard of living at home. A balance of payments could, of course, be maintained with lower exports and imports, but at the cost of a lowered and perhaps unbearable standard of living in Japan. An increase of at least eight to nine times 1947 exports is necessary to meet the goal set. Under favorable circumstances of world and Japanese trade the Committee considers that this goal may be attainable, although the realization of these estimates is obviously subject to many uncertainties both in Japanese and in world-wide economic and political conditions.

During 1947, imports into Japan were $526,130,000 and exports were $173,568,000. Approximately 25% of the imports were financed by foreign exchange created by the sale of Japanese exports, the balance being the value of relief supplies procured with United States appropriated funds. It will be seen, therefore, that the most strenuous efforts will have to be employed to reach the 1953 targets. The Committee makes the following comments and suggestions which, if successfully carried out, should assist materially toward this end. It recognizes fully that the occupation authorities have been striving to overcome many of the obstacles involved.

First, Japan's merchant fleet should be substantially enlarged. Out of 5.75 million gross tons of steel vessels over 1,000 gross tons before the war, there are now afloat in the hands of the Japanese 1.15 million gross tons of serviceable or repairable vessels. Since a large number of these vessels are necessarily engaged in domestic coastwise services, the reduction in vessels available for overseas foreign trade has been greater than the overall 80 per cent loss indicated by this tonnage comparison. Even if given every opportunity to increase merchant shipping, by building, purchasing and bareboat chartering, it will be many years before Japan's merchant tonnage can be reasonably adequate for its needs.

Prevailing costs of transporting goods to Japan are extremely high. For instance, salt, which sells at $3.00 f.o.b. Mediterranean port, costs $14.00 additional to land in Japan. Iron ore, at $7.00 f.o.b. Hainan, costs $9.25 additional to land in Japan. Coking coal, at $12.00 f.o.b. Canada, involves a freight charge of $14.00 to $16.00 to deliver in Japan. The Japanese have always been effective ship operators and builders. Their shipbuilding and ship operating costs have been low as compared with other countries. They have the know-how and the manpower. To the extent that they are able to employ domestic shipping and shipbuilding facilities, they will be enabled to reduce their substantial need for foreign exchange now required for shipping services.

Japan has valuable facilities for the construction of ships of all sizes. Present restrictions on building vessels of six thousand gross tons and more should be lifted to permit building for their own use and on contract for foreign buyers. There are indications that such orders would be available to them.

The argument has been made that Japan's shipping should be limited because of its war potential. However, Japan's army, navy and air force have been abolished so there should be little fear of future Japanese aggression from the mere existence of a merchant fleet. Also, it has been historically the American position, and generally recognized by maritime nations, that world trade and the long-range interests of all nations are best served when the high seas are open to all. Purely competitive considerations do not, in our opinion, justify a prohibition that would prevent the Japanese from developing the necessary merchant shipping to assist in balancing their foreign trade.

Second, the Committee recognizes that by reason of the economic upheaval stemming from war, Japan will, of necessity, be forced to seek export business throughout the world. Besides textiles, it is capable of producing modern machinery and metal products of diversified character. Chemicals, rubber products, pottery, toys and handicraft all are potential exports. Where its products are fairly competitive and it uses fair methods of marketing, they should be admitted to the world's markets.

It is important to the Japanese (and to the American tax-payer) that we use our influence to overcome the understand-able trade discriminations which are practiced against Japan, especially in markets in which they have heretofore enjoyed large trade. In the judgment of the Committee the countries involved are impairing their own well-being by refusing to trade with Japan and are retarding the reactivation of a poten-tially valuable economic asset for the benefit of all Asiatic countries. We, in the United States, have been called upon to overcome deep and justifiable resentment in our attitude toward Japan. Neighboring nations have much to gain by the adoption of a new and more receptive attitude. The reciprocal advantages ensuing are unmistakable.

Third, our financial assistance to both China and Japan can be most productively employed if active trade between them is resumed. However, China is not at present trading any important volume of goods with Japan. Many raw materials can be sold by China to good advantage in Japan; in turn, Japan has many commodities and facilities which China needs. United States trade policy is emphatically in accord with this philosophy. The European Recovery Plan is based upon it.

Fourth, it would be advantageous if Japan could obtain the foods it imports from nearby sources as in the past, rather than from the more expensive dollar areas as at present. Perhaps this cannot be arranged immediately, but, as these neighboring countries move toward more normal production, restoration of these trade patterns should be possible. This will be helpful to both the Far Eastern and American economies.

Fifth, the Committee recognizes that, in a scarcity economy requiring equitable allocations of available raw materials and other products, government must continue to play an impor-tant supervisory role over trade. However, the restrictions and red tape now required by the Japanese authorities are un-doubtedly hampering trade. Although the Committee has been informed that both the Japanese Government and the occupation authorities are taking steps to simplify and stream-line the methods of handling business transactions, it urges that this be done quickly and thoroughly. Direct business contracts between buyers and sellers should be encouraged. Liquidation of the Foreign Trade Kodans (government buying and selling monopolies) as soon as the acute need for raw material allocations ends, and limitation of the operations of Boeki Cho (government foreign trade agency) to the minimum, seem to be well advised.

It is also desirable to establish direct contact between Japanese businessmen and their potential customers by permitting the movement of Japanese nationals to foreign markets.

Sixth, all export possibilities must be stimulated. As has been already stated Japan historically has always been a processing nation which purchased raw materials abroad, manufactured them in Japan and sold a major portion of the finished products abroad to pay for its necessary imports of raw materials and food. This economic pattern has been even more true of Japan than of Great Britain or Western Germany, and must be revived on a large scale for Japan to live.

Prior to the war textile products constituted 60 per cent of Japan's exports. The remaining 40 per cent comprised mainly machinery, metal products, chemicals, rubber products, pottery, toys and handicraft articles.

The cotton textile industry represents a vital force in the creation of a healthier Japanese economy. There is a present demand for its products, but great difficulties have been experienced recently in making foreign sales in dollars because of the world-wide dollar scarcity. Under existing circumstances, attention should be given to three-way transactions, such as shipment of cotton from the United States to Japan, manufactured textiles from Japan to the Netherlands East Indies and tin from there to the United States in an amount sufficient to repay the cost of the raw cotton. Normally, the cotton industry is highly competitive; to operate successfully, Japan must be in a position to adjust its marketing practices to this reality.

The Commodity Credit Corporation contract for the manufacture and sale of cotton yarn and goods produced from raw cotton supplied by it has not yet been liquidated. All possibilities of sale must be vigorously pursued. The large potential United States market should not be excluded from this effort. The possible volume of Japanese cotton textiles that might be offered for sale in the United States would be only an insignificant percentage of United States production and constitutes no threat to American producers as long as present fair merchandising methods are pursued.

It is obvious that unless a sufficient portion of the textiles manufactured from American cotton to repay the cost of the raw cotton is sold for dollars or for some commodity or currency which can be converted into dollars, Japan will be unable to buy American cotton. Historically the Japanese used a large percentage of American cotton and it is of great interest to American cotton growers that this problem be solved realistically so that the large potential Japanese market not be lost.

We endorse the cotton credit now pending in the Congress; it should include only sufficient limitations requiring direct or indirect dollar sales of goods to assure repayment of the credit. Japan should be permitted to accept sterling for that portion of fabric and yarn sales not needed for dollar repayment, purchasing therewith necessary imports from sterling areas. Japan's textile manufacturers are at present unable to employ the hedging facilities of the cotton futures markets, and this disadvantage should be overcome as soon as possible.

The expanded use of the woolen and worsted facilities of Japan can produce substantial benefits and should be encouraged.

The rayon industry has been dependent in large measure upon domestic pulp supply. Arrangements have been recently completed for a substantial tonnage of Swedish pulp, with which it is hoped to improve the quality and quantity of rayon production. Inasmuch as Japan has no facilities to supply rayon yarn in cone form, it is limited to skein packaging. This fact, plus the fact of the comparatively inferior quality of the Japanese product, puts it at a disadvantage in world markets, more especially in countries equipped with high-speed processing facilities. While the export of rayon yarn is desirable, too much early hope should not be built up in this direction. The relatively low price of rayon staple fiber throughout the world and the fact that the Japanese product is not favored because of its poor quality do not encourage the belief that they can quickly develop large export demand. Therefore, in the judgment of the Committee, rayon yarn and staple fiber production should be planned with primary emphasis on spinning and weaving these rayon products in Japan. A large percentage of this fabric production should be readily salable in this form to foreign buyers.

Raw silk and silk products were one of Japan's chief prewar trade assets. Export sales of raw silk for 1935–39 ranged between 400,000 and 500,000 bales annually and those of silk fabrics ranged between 75 and 125 million yards annually. From the surrender to the end of December 1947 (over two years) only 44,210 bales and 12.5 million yards were sold. Since January 1, 1948, with more realistic pricing and sales policies, 20,000 bales and approximately 5.2 million yards were moved.

Before the war, and increasingly during the war and since, silk has lost favor. Growing nylon and rayon competition has been largely responsible for this decline.

The Japanese are using all their ingenuity to overcome some of the technical difficulties which the use of silk involves in competition with other fibers. It is likely that the situation is now at its worst and that gradual improvement both in raw silk and silk fabric sales will be experienced.

In addition to gradually increasing textile exports, it is planned to expand largely export sales of machinery and metal products, ceramics, minerals, chemicals, drugs, handicraft, toys, processed fish, and paper and wood products.

Fundamental to any successful export program is control of inflation, which is dealt with in another section of this report, and the supply of the necessary imported raw materials to get the program under way.

We find a difficult circle of circumstances in the Japanese productive economy. Insufficient necessary raw materials result in insufficient production; insufficient production results in insufficient exports; insufficient exports result in insufficient foreign exchange to pay for the necessary raw materials. Until this circle is broken Japan's economy will remain prostrate and dependent upon a food dole such as the United States is presently supplying. The best way to break the circle is by supplying sufficient dollar exchange to enable Japan to purchase the initial foreign raw materials.

REPARATIONS

Reparations policy toward Japan has been in the process of development since the surrender in August 1945. Reports of the Pauley Committee, the National Engineers Council, the Special Committee on Japanese Reparations (Strike Report), the Economic Analysis of the State Department, reparations studies of SCAP, studies made by the members of the Far Eastern Commission and finally the comprehensive report of Overseas Consultants, Inc., all of which have contributed to a better understanding and clarification of the problem.

These reports differ in many respects, yet all are in agreement on these two premises:

(1) Japan's industries must be so demilitarized as to prevent it ever again becoming a threat to the peace of the world.

(2) Japan should be left sufficient industrial capacity so that it will have an opportunity to develop an economy which will provide a tolerable standard of living.

In seeking to determine the amount and character of industrial plants required to meet the objective stated in (2) above, various estimates were offered. The earlier estimates differed so widely that the occupying authorities decided that there was need for an all-inclusive and detailed analysis of the Japanese plant and its potential. Consequently, in June 1947, Overseas Consultants, Inc., an organization of eleven distinguished industrial engineering and appraisal companies, was formed and engaged by the Secretary of War to make such an analysis.

Its report, presented on February 26, 1948, consisted of two major sections described as follows in a letter of transmittal:

"Section A presents designations of those plants and facilities which should be retained and those which should be made available for reparations under terms of State-War-Navy Coordinating Committee 236/43, together with estimates of the value of the facilities available for reparations. These designations were based upon a literal interpretation of original instructions, as amended, establishing the productive capacities in certain industries to be retained in Japan, outlined in State-War-Navy Coordinating Committee 236/43. In this section we express no opinions in regard to the adequacy of such retained capacities for achieving a self-sustaining civilian economy.

"In Section B, we make recommendations and name plants and productive capacities which, in our opinion, should be retained. These are the results of a study of economic conditions in Japan, made by our representatives, based upon data made available to us by the Economic and Scientific Section, (hereinafter referred to as ESS), the Natural Resources Section and other divisions of SCAP, and by various Japanese agencies, and upon our analysis of basic requirements of food, clothing and raw materials, the need for rehabilitation of industrial plants and utilities, and the restoration of areas damaged during the war."

The report of Overseas Consultants, Inc., in effect advised against the removal of productive facilities (except primary war facilities) which might effectively be used in Japan; this view was derived from the judgment that, only if Japan was permitted to retain all facilities that might contribute to its production and potential trade, could it by its own efforts maintain a satisfactory minimum standard of living.

The value to the recipients of the industrial reparations which would result from the new formula recommended by Overseas Consultants, Inc., would be disappointingly small in contrast to that which has been requested and expected by some of the Allied Powers. It must be remembered that much of the industrial plant within Japan was either destroyed or badly damaged by the war and that actual productive excess, except in a very few fields, is correspondingly small. In our opinion, even if the Allied Powers received all the reparations requested from the home islands of Japan, they would gain little because experience has shown that the costs involved in moving plants and equipment from a conquered nation and reestablishing them in a victorious nation are high and that the ultimate usefulness and value of such plants are small, being poorly adapted to needs of the new owners. World War I experience proved that reparations paid out of current production were illusory and most difficult to collect; World War II is proving that reparations paid in the form of plant equipment are also of dubious value.

Japan did have one form of assets of real value as reparations. These assets were investments throughout the world and particularly in Japanese territories and protectorates. They have a value of many billions of dollars. Both Soviet Russia and China have benefited from the billions in assets, undamaged by war, which Japan invested in Sakhalin, Manchuria, North China and Formosa.

The cost in lives and treasure to bring about the surrender of Japan was enormous. The United States bore a heavy share of that cost. Since victory was achieved, military government and relief costs have been borne almost entirely by the United States. Until the new Japan, shorn of its empire, can become self-supporting it will continue to be a burden. The loss of plants, equipment or machine tools needed to help Japan achieve a self-supporting basis would result in an increased necessity for the United States to make up the deficiency or lessen the chances of attaining economic solvency. Under such circumstances, reparations become a direct charge on the United States.

The United States is also paying a high price for delay in the settlement of the reparations question. As long as uncertainty prevails as to what is to be taken as reparations it is impossible to plan intelligently for the rehabilitation of Japan's industry. The Congress of the United States is considering an appropriation of some $144,000,000 for the economic revival of Japan, in addition to nearly $400,000,000 for general relief purposes for the fiscal year of 1948–1949. Accordingly, an early definitive and authoritative action on reparations problems is imperative; the success of the entire recovery program will be affected thereby.

During the past two and one-half years, the Far Eastern Commission has agreed to but few policies affecting certain phases of the reparations program. An "advanced delivery program" was adopted by the United States to provide foreign nations with some badly needed equipment. To this date this program has made available 19,032 machine tools and 3423 pieces of laboratory testing and measuring equipment.

The Committee has given careful consideration to studies

and recommendations made by the various groups heretofore, and, after carefully considering on-the-scene data, recommends that:

(1) External assets formerly owned by Japan be formally released to the countries holding jurisdiction over the territories in which these assets were located at the time of the Japanese surrender.

(2) There be made available as reparations from the home islands of Japan the machinery and industrial equipment in all government-owned arsenals except for (a) such equipment as is deemed necessary by SCAP for the Japanese economy or for occupation use, and (b) such non-armament facilities (fertilizer, fuel, oil storage, etc.) as were exempted from the interim reparation program by the FEC policy decision of 13 May 1946.

(3) There be made available for reparations certain other plants and equipment in amounts as listed by industries at the end of this section.

(4) These recommendations be made effective at the earliest possible moment by appropriate directives to SCAP, which directives should include (a) percentage shares of the total to be allotted to each FEC nation or a limiting date prior to which those nations should settle the division between them of the total available items, (b) a limiting date for the acceptance by each nation of the items allocated to it, and (c) a statement that these directives supersede all previous directives on the same subject.

(5) No industrial equipment in addition to that included in these recommendations be made available for reparations: *Provided, however,* that SCAP should be authorized to substitute for any item specified in those recommendations any other item of equivalent productive capacity.

If the above recommendations for a final reparations settlement are carried out, the amount of plant equipment and the number of machine tools available for reparations will be reduced below the level recommended by Overseas Consultants, Inc. Our major purpose in recommending this reduction is to retain for the rehabilitation of Japan's peacetime industry a substantial number of machine tools of modern design. Only by retaining such tools can the peace-time industry of Japan quickly be rehabilitated on an efficient basis. In view of the developments of the last two years and the continuing deficit economy, there is, in our opinion, a cumulative urgency for the rapid rehabilitation of Japan's industry.

Paramount to all other considerations is the need for prompt and final action. Further delay in the settlement of the reparation problem will not help the claimant nations and will hurt Japan greatly.

RECOMMENDED REMOVALS FOR REPARATIONS

Industry	Annual Capacity		Value 1939 Yen
Nitric Acid	Metric tons	82,000	8,000,000
Synthetic Rubber	Metric tons	750	10,000,000
Shipbuilding	Gross tons	152,300	50,000,000
Aluminum and Magnesium Fabricating	Metric tons	50,000	21,688,000
Magnesium Reduction	Metric tons	480	12,559,000
Sub total			102,247,000
Primary War Facilities			560,000,000
Total			662,247,000

NOTE: Only those primary war facilities in government owned arsenals should be made available for reparations. Those facilities within the government owned arsenals designated by the Supreme Commander for the Allied Powers, as essential for the rehabilitation of Japan's industrial economy, should be exempted.

THE POSITION AND PROSPECTS FOR FOREIGN INVESTMENT

The present situation in Japan as to capital needs is somewhat obscured by the uncertainty about reparations. However, assuming a reasonable and prompt settlement of that problem, Japan would retain sufficient industrial plant and machine tools for the production of a volume of most products needed to meet internal needs and provide a surplus for export. A very different situation prevails as to working capital. Most

Japanese concerns, both industrial and marketing, because of operating losses and inflation, are hampered by a dire lack of funds to purchase raw materials, to replenish inventories and for similar purposes. This is a problem chiefly of foreign currency needs which could best be met by equity investment. Unfortunately, almost no new foreign investment is permitted in Japan at the present time.

Foreign private commercial representatives have recently been authorized by SCAP to enter Japan to seek restitution of prewar holdings and to engage in export-import trade. They may now work out arrangements under which raw materials are shipped into Japan and finished products shipped out, the object being to provide an opportunity for profit both to its suppliers of raw materials and the Japanese economy. They may also send in management or technical personnel for discussion with Japanese firms in which investments might be made later, and supply these firms with a knowledge of modern management methods and technical know-how.

SCAP has been considering proposals which would permit foreign nationals to engage, on a non-discriminatory basis with Japanese nationals in foreign trade with the Boeki Cho (the Japanese Government foreign trade agency), and in those specific business activities in Japan which positively aid in Japanese economic rehabilitation or provide a source of foreign exchange for Japan or are otherwise in furtherance of occupation objectives.

Any acquisitions of business property from Japanese nationals should be permitted under adequate supervision and only if the Japanese Government certified that the acquisition was not made under conditions of fraud, duress or undue influence attributable in any way to the occupation. Conversion of yen return on investment into foreign currencies would, under existing circumstances, be permitted only under special SCAP license, but it is not proposed that such permission be granted for the time being.

Your Committee recommends that the Department of the Army and SCAP approve proposals of this type.

Various obstacles to foreign private investment remain which must be removed before any substantial flow of such investment can be anticipated. The absence of a peace treaty is one of the most difficult of these. Prior to the completion of a treaty—or thereupon—if the Japanese Government desires to attract large scale foreign private investment, its laws and policies should, in our judgment, provide:

(1) Protection of foreign investments from confiscation and discriminatory taxation.
(2) Reasonable freedom of export of dividends and profits.
(3) A tax structure which would permit the earning and payment of reasonable profits.
(4) Permission to foreign nationals to control enterprises proportionately to their investments.

While the United States Government is supplying with its funds the necessary food and other imports, it is obviously too early to consider granting permission to export foreign exchange.

As a practical matter, the first important inflow of foreign capital may well be for factoring purposes under which imported raw materials and inventories would be financed. Capital of this type has contributed most importantly to building up of new industries in the United States and elsewhere. If investment funds used for factoring earn a satisfactory return, that fact would serve to acquaint investors with the potentialities of the Japanese economy and encourage the making of funds available in increasing volume and later lead to investment and equity financing.

BUDGET AND FOREIGN EXCHANGE POLICY

The Japanese Government has failed to balance its budget since the fiscal year 1930–31. The more serious excess of expenditures over revenues began to appear in the fiscal year 1937–38 and reached a peak in the fiscal year 1945–46 when expenditures approximated six and one-half times revenues.

The unbalanced state of the Japanese budget is an integral part of the inflationary processes which dominate the economy today. The origin of the inflation goes back to wartime excesses and distortions. By the summer of 1945 prices had risen to about fifteen times prewar levels. The economic collapse of Japan immediately following the surrender powerfully stimulated this inflation. When the American forces arrived in

September 1945, the economy was highly disorganized. Production was almost at a standstill, the distribution process had broken down and governmental machinery, including the tax collection organization, was disrupted. The task of restoring order in all these fields devolved upon the occupation forces, but it was some little time before the necessary measures began to have some effect. Thus, inflationary pressure continued to grow in strength and by February 1948, prices were more than seven times the September, 1945, levels.

As a consequence of this immense rise in prices and the growth of government outlay (partly for extraordinary termination of the war purposes) the budget deficit has been great. It has been met by the issuance of currency, which has in turn carried the inflation forward.

SCAP has been fully aware of the desirability and necessity of achieving a balanced budget. Five principal factors have interfered with the achievement of this objective.

(1) The number of personnel employed in national and local government enterprises, at continuously mounting money wages, has approximately doubled since 1945. Reemployment of former employees released from the armed forces and employment of repatriates from the colonial possessions account for much of this increase.

(2) Increasing subsidies have been paid to agriculture and industry, directly and indirectly, for the purpose of holding down prices and the cost of living and assuring the masses of poor Japanese of minimum essentials. Similarly, the services of government enterprises, such as transportation and communications, are rendered at prices which fail to provide sufficient income to meet expenses. This also is a subsidy but in different form.

(3) Taxes have not been satisfactorily collected because of an inefficient and antagonistic tax collecting agency and failure of the authorities to force those who file income tax returns (as opposed to those wage-earners whose taxes are withheld) to report their full incomes.

(4) The usual lag exists in obtaining increased tax revenues to meet rising costs accompanying the inflationary spiral.

(5) Occupation costs have constituted a substantial percentage of total governmental expenditures.

The Committee recommends that:

(1) Efforts should be continued to establish a balanced budget at the earliest possible moment.

(2) The Japanese should be encouraged to take advantage of every opportunity rapidly to reduce governmental expenditures.

(3) The occupation authorities should continue their efforts to reduce occupation costs.

(4) Controlled prices should be adjusted, as expeditiously as possible, to costs of production. Many basic industries now operating with losses are being supported by subsidies and government loans. Continuation of such subsidies is justified only to the extent that they are essential during this period of scarcity to keep living costs from rising to a point which would cause further inflation.

While, normally controls hamper recovery and should be eliminated, the Committee recognizes that the existing scarcities make their continuation necessary for those few commodities basic to the existence of the great majority of the Japanese people. This applies particularly to the allocations of scarce raw materials and the rationing of food.

Cost of services rendered by most government enterprises should be established on a basis which will permit them to cover expenses.

So long as price controls are retained, wage controls are essential.

(5) Military teams should continue vigorously to insure that Japanese tax collecting forces maintain and augment collection of taxes. These efforts recently have shown marked success.

(6) Greater effort by the Japanese should be made to

reach the undisclosed income undoubtedly present among those groups who file their own tax returns and do not have their taxes withheld at the source. Substantial profits made in black market operations largely escape their fair share of tax burden.

The Committee recognizes that the present foreign exchange situation is unsatisfactory and that a definitive exchange rate is badly needed. Judgment as to the appropriate solution is difficult, not only because of its inherent nature, but also because of the advisability of relating American foreign exchange policy in Japan to American policy in general. It is understood that the United States Government and SCAP are at present considering the questions involved.

The Committee, therefore, limits itself to recommending generally that:

(1) Policy should be directed toward the establishment of a definitive exchange rate as soon as monetary and economic conditions become sufficiently stable, which in the Committee's opinion is not yet the case.

(2) Foreign trade, now carried on almost exclusively by the Japanese Government, should be returned to private channels as soon as feasible, recognizing that this cannot be fully accomplished until an effective commercial exchange rate has been established.

(3) The present rate of fifty yen to the dollar, known as the "military exchange rate," should be modified to reflect more nearly the relative purchasing power of the yen, and its use should be extended to buyers of yen for educational and missionary purposes, for private and personal remittances, for authorized yen expenditures of foreign enterprises doing business in Japan, and to new foreign capital which may desire to make authorized investments in Japan. It is recognized that such a modification in rate involves various important governmental financial policies and that the posi-

tion of the Washington authorities, including the Treasury Department, is not known to the Committee.

CONCLUDING COMMENTS

The Committee is confident that Japan's economic difficulties—great as they are at present—are manageable; that Japan can in due course find the ways and means to sustain its people by peaceful pursuits at levels equivalent to those which prevailed in the past; and that the Japanese people are capable of making an orderly transition to a more democratic kind of life and economy.

The task will be hard and the required effort and talent great; Japanese self-help is demanded to work out their own salvation. Continuation of support and guidance by the American occupying authorities is essential; willingness of other countries in the Pacific area to permit Japan to resume trading and shipping activities is hardly less so.

Our recommendations result mainly from our interest in seeing a revival of economic activity which can contribute to the revival of the Far Eastern area and provide the Japanese people with a tolerable livelihood, workmen in Japan and elsewhere with employment, business interests with fairly earned profits—while diminishing as rapidly as possible the burdens that have fallen upon the United States.

The program of the Department of the Army, approved by the Department of State, provides the key to increased production by making available the initial imported raw materials required to augment production quickly and to restore trade relations. It is indispensable to reviving the economy so that the burden on the American taxpayer for providing the bare essentials to prevent "disease and unrest" may be decreased at an early date and, eventually, eliminated.

We express our conviction that a recovering and hopeful Japan will be more inclined to be a good neighbor and to contribute its share to the general welfare of the world and to the maintenance of peace.

Accordingly, the Committee recommends prompt enactment by the Congress of pending bills carrying out this recovery program.

U. S. STATEMENT ON JAPANESE INDUSTRIAL DECONCENTRATION[1]

Some months ago, my Government suspended its participation in discussions in the Far Eastern Commission of a United States policy proposal which was then under active consideration in the Commission. This proposal, designated as FEC 230, presented an extremely detailed plan for the implementation of a general policy which already had been stated in existing directives to the Supreme Commander. That policy, which called for the dissolution of certain Japanese combines and a widening in the distribution of the income and ownership of Japanese industry, was then and continues to be, in the view of my Government, a fundamental objective of the Occupation.

The action of the United States in suspending consideration of its proposal, however, has led to certain questions among the members of this Commission and among the Japanese people. The purpose of this statement is to clarify the position of the United States with respect to FEC 230.

Since the very first weeks of the Occupation, the Supreme Commander has devoted a considerable part of the time and resources of his staff to the problem of reorganizing the financial and industrial institutions of Japan. This program which has been based upon the Post Surrender Directive issued December 6, 1945 and on the Far Eastern Commission's own

[1] Presented by General Frank McCoy, United States Member, to the Far Eastern Commission, Washington, December 9, 1948.

Basic Post-Surrender Policy for Japan, was designed to make possible the early development of democratic and peacefully-inclined economic institutions in Japan. To bring about that result, plans were immediately developed and put into effect to dissolve the control of Japanese finances and industry which rested in the hands of a few powerful Japanese families.

As a part of this program, the Supreme Commander directed the Japanese Government to adopt various laws and to create certain governmental bodies charged with the responsibility of undertaking a major reorganization of the ownership and control of Japanese industry. In the brief span of three years substantial progress has been made by these bodies. The assets of the fifty-six persons who comprised the heads of the ten major zaibatsu families and the assets of the eighty-three holding companies controlled by these persons have been acquired by the Government and are in process of being sold to the Japanese public. A much larger number of companies have been compelled to divest themselves of holdings in and control over smaller enterprises. Such control was exercised through inter-corporate stockholdings, interlocking directorates and similar devices. Contractual arrangements to which these Japanese enterprises were parties which had the effect of placing the control of production or trade in the hands of such enterprises have been declared void. The innumerable Control Associations through which Japanese enterprises exercised their collective authority are being liquidated. Action is being taken and is well-advanced toward reorganization of former savings banks, trust companies and governmental banking institutions, making possible the emergence of a significant number of new commercial banks, to compete with and supplement the few large banking combines which formerly dominated Japanese credit sources. Finally, some scores of Japanese companies whose present state may constitute a threat to competitive enterprise are being scrutinized, one by one. Where necessary, these combines will be subjected to such reorganization as may be required to remove the existing threat.

To insure that the dispersion of economic control which is developing from these measures will not likely be reversed in the years to come, substantial revisions have been effected in the basic economic legislation of Japan. To begin with, an Antitrust Law has been adopted and a Fair Trade Commission set up to enforce the Law. In general, the Law seeks to restrain the development of new combines, excessively large or powerful, by outlawing agreements which restrain production or trade, by placing limitations upon intercorporate stockholdings, interlocking directorates, and similar devices for the concentration of corporate control, and by setting up procedures and penalties for the enforcement of these provisions. Other legislation now requires Japanese corporations to make considerably more information available to their stockholders and the public than heretofore has been the case and generally requires the management of corporations to adhere to much higher standards of public responsibility in the managements of their enterprise.

Moreover, many existing laws which tended to centralize the control of Japanese industry within a small group have been abrogated outright. Others have been modified drastically. The Fair Trade Commission and other Government agencies are analyzing still other Japanese laws to eliminate provisions which confer special privilege or tend to restrain or eliminate competition. Various laws relating to the conduct of Japanese banking have been placed under particularly careful scrutiny. One of the principal objectives of the revision of Japanese banking laws is to create a climate in which the undesirable prewar concentration of Japanese credit in a few hands could not recur.

In all this, the Japanese Government has demonstrated a commendable ability to comprehend Allied objectives and has cooperatively fulfilled its obligations. The Japanese Fair Trade Commission has prosecuted a significant series of cases against Japanese businessmen who were violating one provision or another of the statutes which seek to prevent new concentrations of Japanese industry. The Japanese Holding Company Liquidation Commission has made a careful study of the structure of the larger Japanese combines and, in close cooperation with the Supreme Commander, is currently developing plans for such reorganization of these combines as may be needed.

As the occupation and the economic situation have developed, there has been a corresponding evolution in the deconcentration program. For example, it has proved possible and desirable to dissolve most of the wartime control associations.

As new sources of credit have been created through the conversion of other financial institutions to commercial banks, it has been possible to reconsider the need for the actual dissolution, once believed necessary, of Japan's biggest banks which under earlier circumstances had dominated the credit structures of Japan.

With the daily growth of indication that the Japanese propose to enforce their fair trade laws vigorously and effectively, it has been possible to reconsider the standards to be used in the dissolution of some of the combines still existing. These changes in emphasis have been responsive to changing circumstances and have represented relatively minor alterations in a program which basically remains unchanged. That program, adhering to the broad purposes of the directive of the Far Eastern Commission, seeks to achieve in Japan an economic climate conducive to the development of a democratic society. It seeks to prevent the resurgence of economic power in the hands of a few who recognize no responsibility to the Japanese people or the world at large.

When the United States suspended its participation in the discussion of FEC 230 in the Far Eastern Commission, that decision was based upon the growing realization that the guidance for the Supreme Commander and the Japanese envisaged therein had largely been overtaken by events. The major points of procedure set out in that document already had been implemented in Japan. Other details believed necessary to the accomplishing of the major objectives either had been faithfully adopted or had become unnecessary or inappropriate. Useful as the paper might have been at an earlier stage of the Occupation, that usefulness no longer appeared to exist.

That the paper has become outmoded in so brief a period is a singular tribute to SCAP and the Japanese Government. Procedures which it was thought would take years to carry out in many cases have been accomplished in a matter of months. Major technical obstacles have been overcome and the demonstrated determination of the Supreme Commander to carry the program through has elicited a gratifying degree of cooperation from the Japanese themselves. Accordingly, upon a careful re-survey of the deconcentration program now well advanced in Japan, the United States now believes that, as a practical matter, there is no need to lay down policies for the guidance of the Supreme Commander with respect to any remaining significant aspect of the program. Indeed, to do so in the outmoded terms in which FEC 230 is cast might well do more harm to the program than good. Hence, the United States has withdrawn its support of FEC 230 as a proposal upon which the Far Eastern Commission could act with benefit to the Occupation.

This does not mean that the deconcentration program has been completed. Considerable amounts of securities still remain in the hands of the Government and must be disposed of. Ingenuity and vigor must be brought to this task. Existing banking legislation will undoubtedly be elaborated and refined in consonance with the objectives of this program. Those remaining Japanese combines whose existence may constitute a threat to competitive enterprise will, where necessary, be reorganized as required to remove such threat. But these programs no longer call for the development of policy. They call largely for a practical application of judgment, energy and enterprise in implementing a program whose philosophy and objectives are clearly understood by the Supreme Commander and the Japanese Government, as they have already convincingly demonstrated.

INDEX

About W. Macmahon Ball

W. Macmahon Ball is an Australian who has ha
a distinguished academic and public servic
career. Soon after his return from Europe an
the United States in 1939, he was appointed Cor
troller of Overseas Broadcasting for the Con
monwealth Government. This work was asso
ciated with the Intelligence Branches of the Ser
vices and the Commonwealth Government Politi
cal Welfare Committee, of which he was a mem
ber. In 1945 Mr. Macmahon Ball returned to hi
post as Head of the Political Science Department
University of Melbourne, but later visited Sar
Francisco as Advisor to the Australian Delega
tion, United Nations Conference. He was also
sent on a special mission to the Netherlands Eas
Indies and Malaya, and was Australian Politica
Representative in Batavia. During 1946-47 he
was the British Commonwealth member representing jointly the United Kingdom, Australia,
New Zealand and India on the Allied Council
for Japan. From April to September, 1947, he
was concurrently Australian Minister in Japan.